Insurgent Labor
The Vermont AFL-CIO
2017–2023
David Van Deusen

Foreword by Kim Kelly
Introduction by Steve Early

Insurgent Labor: The Vermont AFL-CIO, 2017–2023
© 2024 David Van Deusen
This edition © 2024 PM Press

ISBN: 979-8-88744-036-1 (paperback)
ISBN: 979-8-88744-046-0 (ebook)
Library of Congress Control Number: 2023944236

Cover by John Yates / www.stealworks.com
Interior design by briandesign

10 9 8 7 6 5 4 3 2 1

PM Press
PO Box 23912
Oakland, CA 94623
www.pmpress.org

Printed in the USA.

Contents

Marching toward Migrant Justice picket line against Hannaford supermarket, May Day 2022, South Burlington, Vermont. Holding Vermont AFL-CIO banner are Andrew Sullivan, UE Local 255 (left), and Vermont AFL-CIO executive director Liz Medina (right).

Toward Working-Class Liberation

Kim Kelly

I heard stories about David van Deusen long before I ever met him. "Did you know that the head of the state fed in Vermont is an anarchist biker?" "I heard he used to live in a green anarchist commune in the woods." "Apparently he's an old Anti-Racist Action guy who used to fight Nazis!" Every time his name came up in conversation, it was accompanied by yet another fascinating tidbit. By the time I began reporting on the organized labor movement, I'd already met a handful of union leaders, but none of them were anywhere near as interesting as this mysterious New Englander seemed to be. How could someone with even half of his radical bona fides find his way onto a stuffy central labor council, let alone successfully organize under the auspices of the relentlessly cautious, often conservative AFL-CIO? I must have misheard; the sheer notion was simply too far-fetched.

His name continued to pop up, though, and we finally crossed paths in 2020 (virtually, at least—this was early in the COVID-19 pandemic, and even the most exciting conversations were all happening on Zoom). As I got to know David and learned more about the work he and his compatriots on the United! reform slate were doing, I was thrilled to realize: it had all been true. There *was* an antifascist, libertarian-socialist biker running the Vermont AFL-CIO, and what's more, he was doing a bang-up job of it. By the time we connected, he had already weathered several years of tumult at the labor council, but the revolutionary principles under which he's been organizing for the past two decades have remained firm—and so has his ironclad resolve. True working-class liberation will take a wide array of tactics and requires building power wherever possible. As he wrote in the prelude to his *Anarchist, Socialist, and Anti-Fascist Writings of David Van Deusen, 1995–2018* essay collection, "The best we can do is what we can: subversive art, clandestine operations, militant street actions, building of counter-institutions, union organizing, and even the occasional election should not be understood as mutually exclusive endeavors to an effective movement. Together they are a mosaic that gives depth to our noble if quixotic adventure into a future yet unwritten."

For David, a primary part of that glittering, hopeful mosaic has been the labor movement. This new collaboration with his coconspirators at PM Press tracks five years of growth, change, upheaval, and resistance within the Green Mountain State's largest labor federation. *Insurgent Labor: The Vermont AFL-CIO, 2017–2023*, is a comprehensive case study of David and the United! slate's successful experiment in increasing rank-and-file democracy within their state labor council. It offers strategic lessons and honest analysis of what worked and what didn't, and it charts the progress of the revolution in union leadership ushered in by the United! campaign. The progressive slate was unified around a working-class-left program that faced a number of stark challenges during the 2019 leadership elections but ultimately proved to be remarkably effective. As David had suspected when he first decided to run, rank-and-file union members across the state were ready for change.

Instead of rubber-stamping Democrats for office and spending valuable resources on lobbying, United! touted the need for more aggressive organizing, expanding social benefits for the working class, supporting the Green New Deal but insisting on a just transition that would protect union jobs, and loosening ties with the Democratic Party. Their Ten-Point Program for Union Power emphasized union democracy, working-class unity, striking when necessary, and connecting with organizations outside of labor who shared similar goals. To many rank-and-file union members, it doesn't sound all that radical—if anything, much of what United! advocated for seemed like plain common sense—but when compared to the stultifying liberalism that pervades so much of organized labor, particularly within union leadership, it was clear that something revolutionary was brewing up in Vermont.

I won't spoil the ending or give away too much about what happened next, since David goes into plenty of detail in the book you're holding in your hands, but I will say that I was personally deeply inspired by everything I heard about what he and his comrades were working on up north. As the United! campaign began to heat up, I was midway through my second term on my own union's council, and I found myself sighing with envy as I followed along from afar. By then, I had become even more knowledgeable about what kind of sausage was being made at various unions' internal leadership meetings, and it was enough to turn anyone vegan. For union members like myself who hope to continue the labor movement's proud history of revolutionary politics and working-class resistance, it can be awfully dispiriting to confront the harsh reality that, in many ways, we remain outliers—even in our own unions. That spirit of rebellion that drove us toward every step of progress we've made as a movement and as a class is missing in far too many union halls and Washington, DC, meeting rooms. I shudder to think of what the likes of "Big Bill" Haywood, Lucy Parsons, or Ben Fletcher would think of labor's photo ops at the White House and continuing support for the very police unions whose members brutalize the poor and working class with impunity.

Later on, I decided to try to do something about that and became part of a reform slate that ultimately swept our union's 2021 leadership election. I have to thank United! for giving me much-needed inspiration to continue pushing forward through all the friendly fire we dealt with on our end. (As you'll read, the Vermont AFL-CIO became experts in that particular area!) They showed us what was possible, and they followed up their stated principles with action. *Insurgent Labor* drills into the hows and whys of what made their campaign work, and it provides a fascinating blueprint for those who are interested in replicating their success. David is clear about the unavoidable fact that small, rural, fiercely independent Vermont is a unique environment for this kind of ambitious organizing project; it remains to be seen whether their program would work as well in Wisconsin or Florida, but it's only a matter of time until we find out.

I'm writing this at the end of 2023, one of the biggest years for labor in recent memory in terms of enthusiasm and rising militancy. There have been over four hundred strikes this past year, and countless gains for union members around the country. Workers in a number of new industries, from tech to media to banking to nonprofits to strip clubs to cafes, have risen up and organized. The United Auto Workers (with a directly elected reform president of their own, Shawn Fain, at the helm) just browbeat the Big Three automakers into acquiescing to huge new contract gains and announced plans to organize 150,000 nonunion auto plant workers across the country. Incarcerated workers in Alabama have filed a class action suit demanding the end of forced labor in the Yellowhammer State. There is so much labor news to keep up with that it feels almost impossible—and to be clear, that is a very good thing. The working class has been flexing its muscles, and Lord knows we're going to need them this year. There is a sure-to-be-nightmarish presidential election cycle looming in the near distance, and the Democrats have already shown their cruelty and weakness; meanwhile, the Republicans continue their push for full-blown fascism. There is no one coming to save us. There is only you, and me, and our fellow workers. Building working-class power has seldom felt so important.

So for my fellow travelers on the left who have shied away from labor because it has felt like there is no room for us amidst the bureaucracy and wishy-washy liberalism, take heart. As this book will show clearly, the working class in this country has *always* been radical, and there *is* a place for us within this movement. The labor left is having a moment too, as younger generations of workers begin to join the fray and work to reform labor's weak spots and rotten blemishes—or reimagine it entirely.

And for my union siblings who have despaired of making any real change within your own top-down or stiflingly conservative unions, take action. Use this book as your blueprint, and tweak its lessons as needed. No matter where you live, where you work, or who leads your union right now, there is something in here that you can use—and if you want your union to change, you're going to have to be the one who changes it. Yes, it might be uncomfortable, or it may even seem impossible, but we have concrete proof that it is possible to make a real, radical impact. You're just going to have to start going to even more meetings. (I know, I'm sorry!)

I am thankful that David has written this book and excited to see what happens when this new, fired-up, militant class of workers, labor organizers, and hellraisers gets their hands on it. That's enough out of me, though. Hurry up and turn the page. There is no time to waste—we've got a world to win!

Can Labor Councils Be Revived? Vermont Workers Say, "Yes, We Can!"

Steve Early

The AFL-CIO reform struggle described in this book will be dismissed by some readers as the product of Vermont exceptionalism. Is it really surprising that the home state of America's most successful socialist politician, on the national stage, or its most effective progressive third party, at the local level, has also spawned a feisty, left-leaning labor movement?

Well, as an observer of politics and labor in Vermont since the 1970s, I can report that the organizational upheaval chronicled in *Insurgent Labor* was not preordained, even in Bernie Sanders land. Despite the much-changed political culture of the Green Mountain State, it took a very long time for progressive trade unionists to turn their labor federation into a model for equivalent bodies throughout the country.

Over the last half century, the main locus of union democracy and reform campaigns in the US has been individual local or national unions. Trying to change the leadership, structure, or functioning of any single workers' organization—not to mention a multiunion labor council—is a very hard task. Rank-and-file reformers have been most successful when they have agitated for stronger contracts, effective strikes, and more militant leaders within their own union.

At key junctures, the most successful of these insurgents—Miners for Democracy, Teamsters for a Democratic Union, and Unite All Workers for Democracy—helped win greater membership control over the national headquarters of the United Mine Workers, Teamsters, and Auto Workers respectively, when reform slates ousted some or all old-guard officials.

Prior to 1995, few modern-day dissidents ever tried to revitalize city labor councils or state labor federations in the exemplary fashion described by David Van Deusen. These AFL-CIO-affiliated bodies can be no less bureaucratic or dysfunctional than some of their affiliates. But structurally, they are just too far removed from workplace struggles to generate many electoral challenges to incumbent AFL-CIO leaders at the local, state, or national level. Even when labor radicals have objected in the past to how a portion of their union dues were spent as "per capita" payments to the AFL-CIO, they usually lacked any effective electoral mechanism for changing the controversial program or policy involved.

In the 1980s, such grassroots frustration led to the formation of Jobs with Justice (JWJ), a national network of community-labor coalitions, which provided a much-needed alternative to moribund central labor councils (CLCs). In that era, as labor journalist David Moberg reported, "only half of all union locals in the country even belonged to their CLCs," because the latter were so "focused on banquets, golf outings, breakfasts with business leaders, and photo opportunities with politicians collecting a campaign check." Backed by restive industrial unions like the Communications Workers of America (CWA), JWJ provided real grassroots solidarity, via direct action and rank-and-file participation. In Atlanta, Cleveland, and a few other cities, new CLC leaders embraced JWJ-style activism and made it part of their official program.

New Voices in Washington?

In 1995, the national AFL-CIO finally had its first contested leadership election in a century. The winners were John Sweeney, president of the Service Employees International Union (SEIU); Richard Trumka, president of the United Mine Workers (UMW); and Linda Chavez-Thompson, a Texas-based leader of the American Federation of State, County, and Municipal Employees (AFSCME). Sweeney's "New Voice" slate pledged to work with state and local labor federations to make their political action and strike support work more effective.

As Moberg reported in *In These Times*, Sweeney sought the help of the nation's few "innovative local labor councils" in promoting strategies like "involving members more in decisions" and engaging in direct action protests (aka "street heat"). By 2001, about 130 of the nation's 600 CLCs—representing about half of all US union members—were formally enrolled in a New Voice program called "Union Cities." However, only several dozen of the most active councils—in states like Washington, California, Nevada, Iowa, Wisconsin, and Massachusetts—fully embraced the longtime JWJ approach of mobilizing workers and their community allies to help rebuild labor clout.

To accelerate the pace of change, the AFL-CIO then unveiled its "New Alliance," a top-down attempt to better coordinate the work of the national federation, its affiliated unions, and local CLCs. Critics of this initiative opened fire on it from multiple directions. On the left, activists objected to the proposed consolidation of smaller labor councils into larger ones and the replacement of their elected leaders with appointed "executive directors." Unions with a history of operating outside the AFL-CIO, like the Teamsters and the United Auto Workers, also balked at New Alliance encroachment on their own decisions, good or bad, about resource allocation for new organizing.

Nevertheless, CLCs in Los Angeles, Milwaukee, and Seattle did succeed in fostering more coordinated recruitment of new members. "It's about becoming a labor movement again," explained Ron Judd, then president of the Seattle labor federation. "People are slowly understanding that individual organizational identity and collective identity represent two different paths. We have for so long had an individual organizational path, but we can't win on this path."

Changing to Win?

Such hopes for "labor unity" were dashed a few years later when some of the most organizing-oriented national unions—the SEIU and UNITE-HERE—decided they could "change to win" by creating a rival labor federation with that name. In 2005, John Sweeney's AFL-CIO suddenly found itself with 5.5 million fewer per capita dues payers because five well-known unions, including his own (SEIU), had defected from the AFL-CIO. State and local labor councils around the country were then thrown into turmoil about how to deal with longtime local affiliates of the SEIU, UNITE-HERE, the Teamsters, the Laborers' Union (LIUNA), the United Food and Commercial Workers (UFCW), and the United Farm Workers (UFW) after their national leaders withdrew support for Sweeney's stalled reform efforts.

Hailed by some as the second coming of the Congress of Industrial Organizations (CIO)—the left-influenced industrial union formation of the 1930s—Change to Win had a short shelf life as a new labor "brand." Within a few years, UNITE-HERE, LIUNA, and UFCW all returned to the

AFL-CIO fold, leaving SEIU, the Teamsters, and a tiny UFW still outside it. (Change to Win has since downsized itself into a "strategic organizing center," a modest four-union alliance that now includes the always AFL-CIO-affiliated Communications Workers of America.)

In 2011, John Sweeney passed the torch to his second in command, sixty-year-old Richard Trumka. Two years later, at the AFL-CIO convention in Los Angeles, Trumka highlighted the federation's "solidarity partnerships" with immigrant worker centers, the Sierra Club, the NAACP, and the National Council of La Raza. In a flurry of speechmaking, resolution passing, and side meetings, left-leaning delegates and guests again dutifully embraced the need for community-labor coalition building, greater union independence in politics, and, of course, organizing millions of new members.

Trumka's recycling of nearly twenty-year-old "New Voice" themes did not sit well with several influential AFL-CIO executive board members. Harold Schaitberger, then national president of the International Association of Fire Fighters, denounced any renewed effort to turn the AFL-CIO into what he called "the American Federation of Progressive and Liberal Organizations." According to Schaitberger, if organized labor became "an extension of one ideological part of our society," it would fail in its primary "responsibility to represent workers' interests on workers' issues."

This criticism was echoed by Laborers' International Union president Terry O'Sullivan. He questioned why the AFL-CIO should be forging alliances with environmentalists, who had earned "solidarity partner" status despite their opposition to the Keystone XL pipeline project backed by his union. "We came here to talk about a new movement," he declared at the convention. "But let's not forget about the old movement."

Throughout Trumka's twelve-year reign as Sweeney's successor, such "old movement" figures—representing conservative public employee or craft unions—wielded far greater AFL-CIO headquarters influence than any liberal or progressive forces. However, two years before his death in 2021, Trumka had a rare opportunity to support a grassroots insurgency in the Green Mountain State that featured some "new voices" who believed that "the old labor movement" was not performing well locally.

These rank-and-file activists were frustrated by the ten-thousand-member Vermont State Labor Council's lack of militancy and creativity, as well as its inability to aid new organizing, contract campaigns, or strikes. So, in 2019, they created an opposition caucus called Vermont AFL-CIO United! In a rare contested election, fourteen United! candidates won—taking all the top officer jobs and becoming a majority (fourteen of fifteen) on the state fed executive board. AFSCME representative David Van Deusen, the author of this book, became the new state AFL-CIO president (and was reelected two years later) while continuing to work as a full-time representative of public workers in Vermont. Since then, as described so well in this book, organized labor in the state has pursued an exciting new agenda, which stresses internal democracy and transparency, social and environmental justice, and greater independent political action.

AFL-CIO executive board meetings are open to all union members, not just elected delegates, and annual state fed conventions have had their largest turnouts ever. The new leadership's savvy use of social media, radio shows, and local TV appearances has enabled organized labor to reach a bigger nonlabor audience—and build stronger relationships with community allies. For example, Vermont is now the only state labor federation in the region involved in the Renew New England alliance. This six-state "Green New Deal" coalition is campaigning for the creation of thousands of good union jobs—building affordable housing, installing rooftop solar panels, cleaning up pollution, and slashing the carbon emissions responsible for climate change.

In 2020, the Vermont AFL-CIO tried, without success, to get its parent organization to back Senator Bernie Sanders's second presidential campaign. The labor council gave the Vermont Democratic Party a long-overdue dope slap by endorsing far more Progressive Party candidates for state and local office. As part of their truly unusual outreach to militant members of the state's non-AFL-CIO unions, United! slate organizers helped rally hundreds of rank-and-file teachers and state workers against a public employee pension cut favored by top Democrats in the state legislature and Republican governor Phil Scott. And that same year, the state fed also used Vermont's annual May Day rally in Montpelier to build support for the state's immigrant workers.

Misconduct or Model Behavior?

In anticipation of Donald Trump's likely rejection of the 2020 election results, Vermont labor council delegates issued a call for "a general strike of all working people in our state" in the event of any right-wing Republican coup. Three years later, as Trump is the front-runner for the Republican nomination in 2024—and the threat of "fascism" weighing more heavily on the minds of millions of Americans—this action was both timely and ahead of its time. In late 2020, however, it was not well received in Washington.

AFL-CIO president Trumka first tried to block any democratic discussion of a general strike contingency plan—in the event of a constitutional crisis (of the sort which did occur, shortly thereafter, on January 6, 2021). When Vermont labor leaders debated the question anyway, Trumka ordered an official probe of their alleged noncompliance with national AFL-CIO rules applying to local affiliates. In response, Van Deusen urged the AFL-CIO headquarters to investigate "how the example we are setting in the Green Mountain State could serve as a model for what a more engaged, more member-driven, more democratic, more antiracist, more pro-immigrant, and more organizing-centered labor movement . . . could actually look like in other parts of the country."

As readers will discover, this tug-of-war had a happy ending. Vermont AFL-CIO reformers survived the threat of a national takeover of their council that would have resulted in the removal of elected leaders and their replacement by a Trumka appointee. Relations with AFL-CIO headquarters under Trumka's successor took a turn for the better. But the national AFL-CIO still wasn't singing the praises of this Green Mountain insurgency, despite three decades of convention resolutions passing (and new program unveiling) about the need for CLC revitalization.

In 2023, the insurgency continued even after the author stepped down as labor council president and supported Katie Harris (now Katie Maurice) as his successor. Harris is a thirty-one-year-old AFSCME activist and Democratic Socialists of America member who works as a mental health worker in Burlington. In a hotly contested and relatively close race, Harris and her running mate, Ellen Kaye, were elected president and executive vice president respectively.

Their United! slate won a majority of the seats on the executive board, an outcome that Harris hailed as "affirmation of our desire to continue to focus on rank-and-file organizing within the state of Vermont over political lobbying." Kaye, who is copresident of an AFT-affiliated campus workers union at the University of Vermont, believes "we've made history here in Vermont by electing a three-woman leadership team," which includes Danielle Bombardier, a working electrician who serves as secretary-treasurer. At the convention it was reported with pride that new organizing and a major affiliation with the long-independent Vermont State Employees' Association had doubled AFL-CIO membership in Vermont since 2019.

This impressive record of internal democracy and organizational growth offers a lesson for all trade unionists who would like to improve their local labor council. Do not look up (as in inside the Beltway) for top-down solutions. The power to make change is in your own hands, at the city or state level. You will find this book to be a unique and invaluable guide to uniting the best of organized labor, old and new, to meet the challenges facing labor in Vermont and every other state.

Working-Class Unity, Union Power!

Let's drink to the hardworking people
Let's drink to the lowly of birth
Raise your glass to the good and the evil
Let's drink to the salt of the earth
—The Rolling Stones, "Salt of the Earth"

The story of the Vermont AFL-CIO (American Federation of Labor and Congress of Industrial Organizations), from 2017 to 2023, is one of struggle, experimentation, praxis, and ultimately of showing a way toward a new and revitalized labor movement. In this time, we have:

- Advanced union democracy by expanding the number of elected executive board seats and more than doubling the number of rank-and-file delegates affiliates can send to annual conventions (our highest decision-making body);
- Worked with the building trades to pass responsible contractor ordinances (RCOs) that require prevailing wages on major public construction projects in multiple Vermont cities;
- Taken money out of lobbying and, with those resources, created a pool of on-call organizers to support our affiliates;
- Created distance between the neoliberal Democratic Party and ourselves, instead allying with the democratic-socialist-oriented Vermont Progressive Party (and won real elections along the way);
- Taken the principled stand of unequivocally supporting Black Lives Matter and become the only AFL-CIO state labor council in the country to call for Black self-determination;
- Not hesitated in becoming the only AFL-CIO state labor council in the

United! leaders on field at the Vermont Green Football Club game for Labor Night, 2022. Holding the Vermont AFL-CIO banner are Katie Harris (left) and Liz Medina (right). Just behind Medina is Ellen Kaye. In center is Local 1674 president Andy Blanchet.

United States, in 2020, to see through a general strike authorization vote in the event of a neofascist Trump coup; and

- Grown from ten thousand AFL-CIO union members in Vermont to over twenty thousand (thus becoming one of the only states in the nation to see union membership and density actually increase, all while advancing a more radical and militant working-class agenda).

The path we walked was not easy. While our actions have been far reaching (and much needed), we also recognize that our unorthodox approaches have made us powerful enemies along the way (old-guard unionists and Democratic Party politicians, to name but two). But much more important than creating conflict with the forces of the status quo, our bottom-up, labor-first approach has gained us the support and the respect of our rank-and-file membership base.

Our organizing arc, like too many other state labor councils, began with a state of decay—a place where our existence lingered in the shadows of irrelevance. But recognizing that a state of failure, even if familiar and seemingly entrenched, did not have to be our doom, dozens of union leaders from throughout the Green Mountains dared to imagine something different.

And it was in this space, between daily defeat and a self-evident need for change, that the United! slate takes form (and in 2019 takes power). With the arrival of United!, the Vermont AFL-CIO would come to position itself as the most progressive state labor council in the AFL-CIO, one grounded in a class-based politics aiming to amplify the collective voice and power of working people.

This book aims to show how an AFL-CIO state labor council in decline reversed such degradation not through doubling down on the failed strategies of the past, but rather by calling out internal and external institutional failures and by articulating a new working-class-left vision of struggle and victory. As the author, I have crafted this book because I strongly feel that our experience—why we did what we did, how we did it, what was weighed when formulating tactics—matters and has a direct bearing on the future of the labor movement well beyond the borders of Vermont.

The experiences I write about are all firsthand. For the last twenty years I have been heavily engaged in the Vermont labor movement, initially as a member (and cofounder) of the Green Mountain Anarchist Collective and later as an AFL-CIO officer.[1] I served as a Vermont AFL-CIO district vice president (first elected in 2007) and member-at-large (2011–12) during the period of relative decline, and in 2019 (and again in 2021) I was elected president as the head of the United! ticket aiming to deliver us to a period of renaissance. I say this simply to establish that I am no newcomer to the labor movement and, over decades, have seen all aspects of how the old ways of doing things have failed and where new approaches have shown promise. These were all experiences that helped inform me and United! as we sought the power to make progressive change.

This book seeks to map out these experiences, explain why we tried certain approaches, and then evaluate the results, the risks, the rewards, and how we can perhaps set the labor movement down a new course toward the achievement of real working-class power. Unless you believe that the decline of the national AFL-CIO and the labor movement is inevitable, is acceptable, or is simply our fate, readers throughout North America should find this work of interest insofar as it represents a new way forward—one of growth, militancy, and democracy within our unions.

A discerning reader will note that this book does not put focus on contract negotiations and related outcomes. While it is true that the winning of solid collective bargaining agreements, ones that provide good wages, family-sustaining benefits, safe working conditions, and more democracy on the job, is a cornerstone of what it means to be a labor movement, this is not a story about contracts. Rather, this is a story about seeking to change the political environment, the broad power relations between classes, and the internal structures and priorities of the labor movement itself, which underpin and give context to the environment within which individual union locals bargain contracts.

While I have personally bargained over one hundred contracts (being lead union negotiator for the lion's share of these), and while I can recount dozens of successful bargaining fights that resulted in major advances for specific groups of workers (like working with Damion Gilbert and Ron Jacobs in winning twelve weeks of paid FMLA for Burlington city workers in AFSCME 1343, or working with Dan Cornell in gaining $30.50 an hour plus the rate of inflation for DPW workers in Bennington for AFSCME Local 490), such tales are largely beyond the scope of this work.

Even so, if we are to consider the mechanisms and dynamics through which progressive reform within labor can occur, it needs to be plainly stated that union leaders cannot successfully advocate for change until and unless they earn credibility. And here credibility is earned, in part, through the demonstrated ability to deliver on the bread-and-butter issues. Thus, the winning of good contracts needs to be understood as not separate from the generalized effort to achieve progressive change.

All told, I did not write this book for union officials comfortably making a salary of $200,000 to $500,000 a year who believe things are working out just fine for them (and the members be damned). I did not write this book for the old guard or their apologists. Nor is this for those who value relationships with politicians and industrialists over those with the rank and file. And it is certainly not for anyone who cannot plainly recognize and admit that fifty-plus years of hitching our wagon to the Democratic Party and suppressing union militancy has resulted in anything other than radically reduced union density rates and a diminishing of union and working-class rights. And of course, this book is not for those who prefer to use the rhetoric of left unionism while actually supporting the status quo within the unions and without. This book is not for you.

But for those who do desire a true advancement of the collective interests of union members and the working class, for those who are unafraid to take on the entrenched powers that be, for those union members and leaders who are in it for more than their self-interest and personal rise through the ranks, for those who can dream of a future in which working people (as the great majority of the population) wield the power to define the social, economic, and political climate of our nation and the world, I assert that in our modest way, the Vermont AFL-CIO from 2019 (when United! took power) up to the present shows glimmers of how that change can begin to come about. It is for you that this book has been written.

I have no doubt in my mind that history will prove us right and that the unions and working class will prevail over the undemocratic forces of capital (just as we will also prevail over those internal forces that seek to keep us "in line"). I know that the great trajectory of history aims at a more equitable, more democratic, and more socialist society. But even as history unfolds, we must recognize that it does not do so as something external to ourselves, but rather through the collective action taken by all of us, together, willfully at each crossroads. Sometimes doing our part comes easy, but most of the time it is hard. The Vermont AFL-CIO is presently seeking to do its part.

We are not afraid of giants.

This is our story.

United!
David Van Deusen
President of the Vermont AFL-CIO (2019–21 and 2021–23)

CHAPTER I

Mass Labor Picket: Scott Walker and the Vermont Republican Party

Now is no time to think of what you do not have.
Think of what you can do with what there is.
—Ernest Hemingway, *The Old Man and the Sea*

Local 1343 president Damion Gilbert, blowhorn in hand, bellowed to the growing crowd that we had to stop this *now*; Scott Walker and the repressive anti-union ideology he represented could not be allowed to take root in our Green Mountains. "He is going to be Walker-ing his ass out of this city today after we go down and picket," asserted Gilbert. Hundreds of union members, now fired up, then followed a marching band down Battery Street in Burlington to the Hilton Hotel, where Walker was slated to address a fundraiser for the Vermont Republican Party. Not since the 2009 May Day demonstration for health care as a human right had so many union members come together in common cause for an issue not centered on a specific workplace struggle.

Chants of "Hey hey, ho ho, Scott Walker has got to go" and "Get up, get down, Burlington's a union town" rang through the crowd. Picketing in front of the Hilton, speaker after speaker denounced the Vermont Republican Party (who had invited Walker to the Green Mountains). Local 1343 member Dwight Brown, from Burlington's schools, stated, "In this brave little state, we want to send a message.... We want to tell our governor, who decided to side with someone who would be against labor, that we see it, we smell it, and we're not having it in the Queen City." I too spoke, as the AFL-CIO district vice president for the Northeast Kingdom and as an AFSCME (American Federation of State, County, and Municipal Employees) union rep.[1] I, like so many speakers before and after me, such as Danielle Bombardier, International Brotherhood of Electrical Workers

Union members picketing Scott Walker, Burlington, Vermont, 2019.

(IBEW), and Omar Fernandez, American Postal Workers Union (APWU), condemned Walker and the Republican Party for being anti-union and antiworker and called on our unions to be more assertive in defending and advancing the rights of labor.

The picket, which included a giant inflatable rat ("Scabby," representing Walker) and a truck equipped with a billboard flashing anti-Walker messages (both provided by the Trades), was electric. An anger and unity could be felt among the assembled workers; a general feeling pervaded the crowd that what had happened in Wisconsin could happen anywhere, but not if Vermont workers had something to say about it. At one point the AFSCME field services director, Steve Lyons, turned to me and said, "Not bad. When Walker came to New Hampshire, we had ten people on the picket line."

No one there that day came away with anything less than feeling inspired and optimistic about the Vermont labor movement's potential to unite and fight back if presented with an existential threat. Dissipated was the feeling of decline or powerlessness in the face of reactionary forces.

This was a turning point.

We were, in fact, *union strong*.

The picket against Walker was the result of months of organizing. Initially, the call to action came from eight local presidents from AFSCME. Early on, IBEW Local 300 and the Vermont Building and Construction

Trades Council AFL-CIO (headed by Tim LaBombard) backed the call and along with AFSCME Local 1343 (whose flagship unit was City of Burlington workers) constituted the core organizing committee.

As more and more unions endorsed the picket, 1343, the Trades, and I organized a planning meeting open to all unions and community allies. From this meeting, attended by over fifty persons representing organizations with a combined membership in the tens of thousands, key tasks were assigned, ranging from the production of event posters and lawn signs (AFSCME 1343 and the Trades) and the production of picket signs (AFSCME 1343) to securing props such as Scabby the rat (Trades), lining up the portable PA (Vermont Workers Center), and conducting a broad public outreach to gain widespread support (all). As the picket drew near, twenty-four hours before Walker was to arrive in Burlington, US senator Bernie Sanders sent out an appeal to his supporters asking them to stand with the unions and join the picket on May 30.

In the end, five hundred workers walked the picket line and fifty-six organizations, including thirty-six union groups, endorsed the action.[2] Community partners supporting the action included such diverse organizations as Black Lives Matter, Vermont Women's March, LGBTQIA Alliance of Vermont, 350Vermont, and Rights & Democracy (RAD). And with that, it was plain to me and a number of labor leaders that here we had found a broad nucleus of change and a trajectory that, if built on, had the potential to alter the political landscape of Vermont and to transform our unions back into the fighting force that the times demanded. If we wished to keep Scott Walker's brand of reaction out of the Green Mountains, we had to become the change we sought. Our rights as union members, as Vermonters, could not be guaranteed by an inactive and disengaged labor movement. Nor could labor realistically contemplate going on the offensive, to achieve more power for the working class, if we continued to rely on the polite and ineffective politics of the status quo. Rather, we had to rise up, chart a new course, strive toward alliances with social justice organizations, and be unafraid to call a spade a spade when it came to naming our friends and enemies. And here the picket against Scott Walker showed that when asked, when the issue was right, the rank and file were ready, able, and willing to take to the streets. The picket also showed that when AFSCME and the Trades chose to work together (themselves then representing the second- and third-largest blocs within the

Vermont AFL-CIO) there was much that could be accomplished. Thus, by the evening of May 30, 2019, fresh from the picket, my mind filled with the possibilities that could be realized within the Vermont State Labor Council and beyond, should we build on this moment.

CHAPTER II

Rock Bottom: The Near Death of Vermont Labor

You know, looked like ten thousand people
Were standin' around the buryin' ground
I didn't know I loved her, until I let her down
—Son House, "Death Letter Blues"

Return to the Proverbial Salt Mines

In August 2017, after a five-year stint as a union rep with the independent Vermont State Employees' Association (VSEA), I returned to the AFL-CIO fold, becoming AFSCME's union rep for Vermont (and a member of Local 2413). Two months after being back, I received an evening call from the state labor council president, Jill Charbonneau, National Association of Letter Carriers (NALC). Jill asked me if I would accept an appointment to a vacant executive board seat representing the Northeast Kingdom. I told her I would (six years previous, I was elected to the executive committee as member-at-large), but the fact that they had vacancies on their leadership board, given that they had just held their annual convention (which I did not attend), concerned me. I asked how the convention went. When she responded that it had drawn only twenty or so total delegates, and that at the banquet dinner (an annual tradition) they had all fit at the same table, I was nearly speechless—twenty or so delegates representing seventy-eight locals and ten thousand members. And of those delegates, a number seemed to be retirees or close to retirement.

For context, when I left the AFL-CIO five years previously for a position at VSEA (ultimately becoming the union rep for Agency of Transportation workers), conventions typically had fifty to sixty delegates and alternates. And back then, fifty to sixty delegates and alternates was considered a historic low (and area of concern), compared to decades past. Further,

while half a decade ago all the executive board seats tended to be filled, the leadership was aging. In fact, as the district VP for Washington County in 2010, at thirty-six I was the youngest member on the executive board. So even in 2010 it was clear to me that the Vermont AFL-CIO was not healthy. But by comparison to what I was hearing in September 2017, the less-than-ideal situation half a decade earlier seemed like a bright spot to aspire to.

This state of near collapse was predictable. Over years and decades, even as attendance at conventions declined, and even as the Vermont AFL-CIO increasingly failed to demonstrate power or the ability to consistently mobilize its base, there was never any serious effort to radically rethink its priorities, organizing methods, or means of political engagement. Instead, year in and year out, the labor council, without significant thought, largely put its eggs in the basket of a Democratic Party that neither adequately heard nor concerned itself with the demands of unionized workers. And even while union-backed candidates won election after election, a pro-union agenda never moved in sufficient levels in the Democratic Party–controlled statehouse.[1]

Meanwhile, the Vermont AFL-CIO sank most of its resources into endorsement mailings (during elections) and polite (and ineffective) lobbying in the statehouse. With few context-altering wins being registered, and with communications with the rank and file being near nonexistent, it should not take Columbo to figure out that the state fed was becoming something less than an afterthought (if that) for thousands of unionized workers.

Also demoralizing the state labor council was the recent experience whereby a former Vermont AFL-CIO president, Ben Johnson, also a former president of AFT-Vermont (American Federation of Teachers), publicly switched sides, opened a pro-management consulting firm, and engaged in a round of public statements against core union values such as fair share dues requirements.

Johnson, back in 2011, previously positioned himself as a reform candidate in his successful bid to become president.[2] A few short years later, he transitioned into being a corporate stooge and shill for his right-to-work backers, which speaks volumes to the shallowness of recent efforts aimed at change and certainly contributed to the increasing confusion and disengagement of the grassroots membership. It was a sorry state of affairs.

This is not to say that Vermont was devoid of effective and dynamic organizing. It's just to say that that effective organizing was being done by organizations such as Rights & Democracy, Migrant Justice, and the Vermont Progressive Party.

And where good organizing was being done in labor, it tended to occur within the silos of separate internationals or locals—not by the Vermont AFL-CIO as such. And frankly, this weak and aimless state that the Vermont AFL-CIO found itself in circa 2017 could serve as a stand-in for countless state labor councils across the US. This web of failures was not just a Vermont problem but was truly one of a national scale.

Point being, decades of subservience to the failed politics of the Democratic Party, coupled with disproportionate allocation of resources in support of Democratic Party candidates and dead-end legislative lobbying efforts, translated into the AFL-CIO being unable to assert its own social and political vision on a national or statewide scale.

Reaping in harvest after harvest of failure, the national AFL-CIO presided over a rightward drift of American politics led by their "friends" in the Democratic Party. To name but a few results of this drift:

- Job-killing free trade deals such as NAFTA;
- Reductions in social welfare programs; and
- Mandatory minimum prison sentence guidelines (largely targeting Black, Latino, and Native American people).

And at every turn of the screw, too often, it was Democrats such as Bill Clinton who led the charge in these antiworker attacks (while Republicans cheered them on). And then under President Barack Obama, also a Democrat, the AFL-CIO's Employee Free Choice Act (card check) went exactly nowhere. And still national AFL-CIO presidents Sweeney and Trumka pressed on orchestrating endorsements for the Clintons and Obamas of the world, and never once was a radical break with this suicide cult of a labor strategy contemplated as worthy of real consideration, not at the national level and not at the Vermont state level. Rather, the only thing the long-serving AFL-CIO political and social strategy was effective at achieving was the mass alienation and disengagement of its own rank and file. Unfortunately, in this regard, it delivered toward that depressing and unintentional end remarkably well.

Thus, from the high-water mark of 35 percent national union density in 1954, we fell to a rate of 20.1 percent in 1983 and then to a sad 10.3 percent in 2019. Not surprisingly, and not without support from working-class Americans, neofascist Donald Trump, after saying the system was broken and that Democrats had failed working people, won the electoral college vote in 2016 (even while losing the popular vote), becoming president of the United States of America. Even while Trump, who attacked unions once in office, did nothing more than to uphold the interest of his reactionary billionaire backers, he was able to tap into this mass alienation by stepping into the political void left by a silent and retreating labor movement. And even while the AFL-CIO lamented the politically motivated *Janus* decision by Trump's Supreme Court[3] and the unprecedented rollback of other core labor rights during Trump's presidency, the national AFL-CIO proved itself incapable of recognizing its own culpability in being the architect of its own demise by creating the political wasteland in which this more reactionary—even fascist—politics took root. As Malcolm X reflected, American politics are often a case of "chickens coming home to roost."

During my September 2017 phone conversation with President Charbonneau, I expressed my grave concern. I also told her that over the next 365 days I would work up a plan whereby AFSCME participation at the next convention (2018) would be maximized to stop the bleeding and to insert some energy into the broader labor movement. This would matter, as AFSCME, with 1,800 members, was the second-largest affiliate in the state fed (behind AFT). I had my work cut out for me (and so would other AFSCME leaders).

Defending Collective Bargaining Rights against NEA

As I got deeper into broader Vermont AFL-CIO politics through the end of 2017 and throughout 2018, the state of decay within the labor movement became an ever more pressing source of concern. Even though we were part of a lobbying-centered coalition with the National Education Association (NEA) and VSEA (Working Vermont), in winter 2018 NEA apparently thought so little of us that they unilaterally had a bill introduced in the Vermont Senate that would *end* collective bargaining over health care in the schools.

NEA had something over twelve thousand members in the public schools. The AFL-CIO, through AFSCME, represented some hundreds of support staff in the larger school districts. But in NEA's wisdom, they concluded that the right to bargain locally over health care could very well be eliminated by a legislative act of the Democratic Party–dominated general assembly, so they decided to pull the plug on their own by advocating that this benefit instead be universally imposed by a government commission (in theory half being NEA members or staff and half more oppositional in nature).[4] And they factored the AFL-CIO's weakness and nonassertiveness as such, whereby they did not even bother to tell us they intended to do this, let alone ask our opinion.[5]

Meanwhile, for some years, our other coalition partner, VSEA, had not put meaningful emphasis on broader social and economic issues that would more generally have a positive impact on unions or the working class as a whole.[6] While they occasionally would attach their name as supporters to unsuccessful bills that would establish paid family medical leave or free college tuition, they rarely if ever assigned their organizing staff to be proactive on such issues, nor did they commit union resources to movement-building actions like May Day demonstrations or support for migrant farmworkers. It had also been some years since VSEA had demonstrated willingness to meaningfully work with the Vermont AFL-CIO on our priorities.

Together, our coalition partners in Working Vermont (NEA and VSEA), like the Vermont AFL-CIO in years past, consistently endorsed and campaigned for Democratic Party candidates, who often turned on them after they won their elections. In addition, their organizing strategies were also heavily reliant on professional lobbyists advocating for minor reform in the statehouse (with member involvement often limited to requests to "contact your legislator"). VSEA, for their part, further had a tendency to perpetuate a toxic internal culture in which significant energy was focused on repressing the activity of their own members when such activity looked to veer from the path defined by their executive director and top officers. But none of this was news; I knew going back years that this was par for the course.

But when NEA came after the right to collectively bargain over health care in the schools, I immediately informed our AFSCME officers and school-based members and (through my role as a district vice president) demanded that the Vermont AFL-CIO withdraw from Working Vermont as an act of protest. And here I found a staunch ally in AFSCME Council 93 executive board member Karl Labounty (who himself was employed in the Property Services Department in Burlington Schools). President Charbonneau, for her part, deferred to AFSCME on this (as the only AFL-CIO affiliate with members in the schools). And following our next executive board meeting, the Vermont AFL-CIO was officially out of Working Vermont (and would remain out in the years to come).

On the ground, the Vermont AFL-CIO (and AFSCME) then went about pushing back against conceding our bargaining rights on health care in the schools. But given that NEA had opened the floodgates toward major (and negative) structural change, holding the line on local bargaining rights (school by school, contract by contract) was no longer tenable. Falling back to a position of establishing a statewide (unified) collective bargaining process was the winnable fight. And fight we did.

I worked with AFSCME's Karl Labounty (AFSCME's top-ranking officer in Vermont and at the time the executive vice president of the Vermont AFL-CO) in crafting a public op-ed on the issue clearly stating that even the thought of eliminating collective bargaining over school health care (without a universal single system first in place) would amount to an assault on core labor rights—and further, that any politician who went along with such a move would forever be viewed as an enemy of organized labor by the AFL-CIO. The op-ed was published in a number of newspapers around the state, and we also produced copies and distributed them to every lawmaker in the statehouse. The Vermont AFL-CIO, through President Charbonneau, also arranged for meetings between us and key lawmakers in the Vermont House and Senate, including the Democratic speaker of the House (and unreliable labor backer), Mitzi Johnson, in which our grave concerns were bluntly expressed.[7] Here we instead advocated for a statewide collective bargaining process, with NEA having four seats on a union bargaining team and AFSCME having one. We also organized a modest informational picket at statehouse entrances on a day when we had school-based members from Montpelier (the state capital) come in to speak with legislators directly on what it means to be union and why our right to bargain must be defended.

In the end, the Vermont AFL-CIO and AFSCME won. The law that emerged provided for the school health care benefit to be bargained by a statewide bargaining team composed of a majority of NEA members with one AFSCME member. Any negotiated agreement would have to be democratically ratified by NEA and AFSCME members, and if an impasse could not be resolved at the table, a last best offer from the unions and the Vermont School Board Association would be subject to binding arbitration.

While there were (and continue to be) plenty of problems with this new system, the outcome was a world more desirable than having a benefit undemocratically imposed. And with this, I like to think that the Vermont NEA learned the lesson that the Vermont AFL-CIO and AFSCME are not labor entities to be lightly considered.

As this fight to preserve collective bargaining rights in the schools unfolded in winter 2018, so too did my efforts to engage AFSCME members in the Vermont AFL-CIO. With the 2018 convention slated for August, getting that effort underway was imperative if we were to reverse the dangerous trend of nonparticipation.

Bringing AFSCME Rank and File into the AFL-CIO

At the same executive board meeting where Labounty and I successfully achieved the AFL-CIO's withdrawal from Working Vermont, I also proposed (with Labounty's backing) that we experiment with the convention structure that year. In brief, I sought executive board support in having all the decision-making at the convention happen on day two (Sunday). On Saturday (day one), I proposed that AFSCME hold their own one-day conference, bringing together members from all nine Vermont locals at the same location, though be it in a different room. My thought was that AFSCME members in Vermont, historically, never came together in the same place and time, but that the myriad of common issues to work through lent itself to a potential rank-and-file interest in participating in such an event. And with that, we could piggyback the Vermont AFL-CIO convention onto this, having the same members serve as delegates and alternates on Sunday with the AFL-CIO. During discussion, I pointed out that all our local AFSCME presidents had already been approached with this idea and supported it. When asked how many AFSCME members I projected would attend if we tried this method, I said fifty would be a reasonable estimate. A fellow executive board member, District Vice President Traven Leyshon, Office and Professional Employees International Union (OPEIU), ever the pessimist, scoffed at that projection and said we would never see fifty AFSCME members at a convention (as most recent conventions had included only two to five AFSCME delegates).[8] I told Traven he was wrong and offered to place a wager on it (an offer he did not accept). But skepticism aside, the executive board voted to go with this new approach.

With approval in hand, over the next few months I worked hard with several local AFSCME presidents and vice presidents to generate excitement with our base around the prospect of a Vermont AFSCME conference (timed to go along with the Vermont AFL-CIO convention). Instrumental in helping to build this mobilization was not only Local 1343 president Karl Labounty, but also 1343 steward Damion Gilbert, 490 president Dan Cornell, 1201 president Tom Franzoni, 1674 president Dan Peyser, 2413 president Rubin Serrano, 2413 vice president Jeremy Fortin, 3977 president Brittany Rhodes, 3977 vice president Sarah Williams, 1369 president Randy Edmonds, and Barre Town DPW chapter chair Tom Baily (of 1369). All our Vermont locals voted to financially support contingents of workers attending the AFSCME conference and Vermont AFL-CIO convention (paying for the hotel rooms of their members and AFL-CIO registration fees), and the AFSCME International organized a great training on shop-floor organizing (facilitated by organizer/trainer

Tracy Monahan). In addition, AFSCME Council 93 supported this effort to the hilt, allowing me (as their union rep) to commit significant staff time toward building it. Also, top Council 93 leaders, such as Executive Director Mark Bernard and Field Services Director Steve Lyons, committed to attending themselves.

Organizing participation in the convention and conference started with buy-in from local AFSCME presidents. This took me giving one-on-one explanations as to why we, as AFSCME, had a self-interest in a functioning and strong Vermont AFL-CIO. Here the point was hammered home that the state labor council is the body that all (or most) of the unions come together through. For example, when we fought in the statehouse to protect collective bargaining rights, with their support, we were truthfully able to say that we spoke for ten thousand workers (and not just the 1,800 AFSCME workers or the hundreds of school-based workers in our ranks). This obviously provided additional credibility (or sense of power) to our assertions, and likewise, any future political or social struggle we engaged in would benefit by including the many union members as opposed to the few. Thus, having a healthy and engaged Vermont AFL-CIO would only help to amplify our own power (and the power of other affiliated non-AFSCME unions).

Also, by building in the AFSCME conference to the convention, I was able to highlight that the event would serve as a means to train our AFSCME stewards in more effective shop-floor organizing and that we could provide multiple opportunities for AFSCME members and leaders to communicate directly with each other concerning shared experiences and challenges. Finally, it would also provide our nine Vermont locals a chance to informally register our collective priorities concerning the union over the next year (whether concerning internal policy or political issues). All told, all our AFSCME presidents came to understand the value of organizing in support of this event.

With vocal support from our presidents (which was expressed at local meetings), I then spent time visiting our union shops to talk with the rank and file directly about the convention and conference. Coordinating with our presidents, I created shop-level sign-up sheets for members to register interest. While talking with members I found that there was significant interest in taking part in organizing and stewarding workshops, and in the chance to meet other AFSCME members. In addition, the prospect that the convention and conference would be fun, with anticipated nighttime drinks with folks from around the Vermont, was certainly a draw. All told, it was clear to me that an excitement was building and that the prospects were high that this would be a success.

Of course, none of this was rocket science. No union leader or union rep worth their weight in salt needs to read this account to know how to build or maintain an engaged membership. Frankly, these are all simple tasks that should have been done all along, by reps and union officers alike. But these kinds of activities and discussions, unfortunately, had not been happening in recent years, at least not to the extent that they should have been. It was about time they started to.

Even so, this process was far from utopian. One fact that I discovered, when I brought up the need to build the Vermont AFL-CIO, was that a majority of members had no idea what the AFL-CIO was, let alone understood why growing its power mattered. Mind you, everyone knew exactly what union and local they belonged to, AFSCME, and generally identified their union as an important aspect of their work life. Remarkably, though, very few had any idea what the AFL-CIO was.

Think on that for a moment. The state labor council was so far removed from their day-to-day reality that they did not even recognize the name. Of course I explained it all, and after I did so members generally expressed interest or support, but this further realization of how divorced the AFL-CIO was from the rank and file (after so many years with their heads buried in the sand of ineffective lobbying and Democratic Party election support) made plain to me the overall state of weakness of the labor movement in Vermont. Things had to change.

The 2018 Vermont AFL-CIO Convention and a Political Shift from Below

Come August 2018, as a fruit of our organizing, we had *over* fifty AFSCME members, representing all our Vermont locals, attend the convention in Burlington. Combined with delegates and alternates from non-AFSCME locals, just over seventy-five member-leaders were at the convention. While seventy-five-plus was still too low by my count, it made it the best-attended convention in years.

On day one, after opening remarks from President Charbonneau, the fifty-plus AFSCME members left the main convention room to attend to their own conference across the hall. The trainings and internal debates went phenomenally well. Many common issues experienced by different shops were discussed, and members even openly brought up perceived shortcomings of the union. At one point, a nonbinding resolution was debated concerning how AFSCME should relate to nonmembers who refused to pay dues in this post-*Janus* environment. The resolution called on Council 93 to impose a substantial fee for service to what many called scabs, should they require union assistance. This topic generated serious debate. Here some members of Local 1674 and Local 3977 (both composed of mental health workers) argued that a fee for service would be the ideological wrong move to make, and rather that providing nonmembers with quality representation in disciplinary and grievance hearings would be the more impactful way to recruit them back into the union fold.

On the other hand, most of our blue-collar workers, many of whom drove snowplow trucks or worked in water and wastewater plants, bluntly stated that "Scabs should get nothing from the union dues everyone else pays," and, essentially, "Fuck those free riders when they come to us with their problems. Make them pay." Call me old school or even vindictive against those who would break solidarity with their fellow union members, but I agreed that nonmembers should be made to pay a fee for service. I vocally sided with our blue-collar members. In the end, the vote culminated in majority support for such a fee for service.[9]

Another highlight of this first day, on the AFSCME side of things, was a guest speaker, University of Vermont (UVM) Medical Center nurse Philip Bowler. In July, two-thousand-plus nurses, members of AFT, had conducted a powerful two-day strike in support of fair wage increases and safe staffing ratios. Many AFSCME members from Local 1343 (city workers) and Local 1674 (Howard Center workers) joined the nurses on their picket line in solidarity. Also during the strike Local 3977 members (Lamoille County mental health) organized a day of solidarity with the nurses whereby union members wore red while on the job as a sign of support for their struggle. Thus, the guest speaker told the story of how the nurses organized internally to build for the strike, with strike captains and contract campaign captains being assigned to every wing of the hospital in order to advance internal communication and better carry out actions. The nurses' contract negotiations were still unresolved at this point, so the talk included updates on the bargaining process. Our

AFSCME members were very interested to receive this information and were eager to offer solidarity, again, should the need arise. Unfortunately, this nurse was one of only a few AFT members to attend the convention. Nevertheless, it was one of the highlights of the day.

On day two, AFSCME members joined with other AFL-CIO delegates and alternates to consider endorsements in the upcoming general election. A number of political candidates came and spoke to the members prior to any decisions being made on who, if anyone, we would back. The two major candidates for governor were incumbent Phil Scott, a moderate Republican and longtime owner of a nonunion construction company, and Christine Hallquist, a moderate Democrat. Scott, in the previous legislative session, had vetoed bills that would have established a fifteen-dollar-an-hour livable wage and paid family medical leave for all Vermonters, and he was not viewed as a friend of organized labor. Hallquist, for her part, was the former CEO of Washington Electric (an IBEW shop) and the first transgender candidate for governor from a major political party. She had also endorsed Scott two years previously in his last run for governor. On the campaign trail, just days before the convention, Hallquist made public statements in support of a more regressive tax structure. Before becoming a candidate, she had no history of ever walking a union picket line or involving herself in union or progressive politics. But these shortcomings aside, she had recently won her primary against Brenda Siegel, Ethan Sonneborn, and AFL-CIO-backed candidate and left-leaning populist James Ehlers.

After Hallquist addressed union members, one of our AFSCME leaders from the Northeast Kingdom, Local 2413 vice president Jeremy Fortin, stood up and asked what her stance was on gun control. With that question, I perceived many of our members suddenly paying close attention. This was a hot-button issue, as Vermont, a very rural state with some of the lowest violent crime rates in the nation, traditionally has fewer gun restrictions than just about anywhere. To this day, Vermonters have a right to carry a handgun, concealed if they like, by right of citizenship. However, despite an average of only eleven murders a year in the entire state (not all with guns), Governor Scott had recently come out in support of some minor gun control measures that did not fundamentally alter the right to own and carry. Even so, this caused a good deal of anger in gun-rights circles.

So when Fortin brought up gun control, I knew that with so many blue-collar AFSCME members in the room, this was a loaded question. I also knew that other than raises and contract negotiations the number-one thing talked about in many (if not all) highway garages and water plants was hunting and guns (and opposition to any thought of gun control). I also happened to know that in Fortin's own garage, in Newport, the union bulletin board at that very moment included a flyer for a gun raffle. So what Hallquist said next would likely determine her fate.

But Hallquist either did not read the room or did not care what the room said back to her. In short, instead of redirecting the question or making a brief statement and then pivoting back to a core union issue, she proceeded to talk at length about her support for gun control and her desire to ban so-called assault rifles. And while this may have played well to the very small minority of white-collar Burlington-based union members, it was another nail in the coffin for the many more blue-collar folks also present.

After the politicians left, union members considered all they had heard and motions began to be made to back this candidate or another in a number of races. Unsurprisingly, the democratic socialist candidate for US Senate, Bernie Sanders, received a unanimous endorsement. David Zuckerman, a strong pro-union candidate for lieutenant governor from the Vermont Progressive Party, also was endorsed. When it came to the contest for governor, however, IBEW members stood up and reported that Hallquist had not been a friend of union workers when she was CEO of Washington Electric, and that IBEW members neither liked nor trusted her. One of the few delegates to stand up and speak in favor of a Hallquist endorsement was from United Steelworkers (USW) Local 4. After they encouraged support for her, I asked the speaker which USW shop they came from. With that, they had to state that they were a Vermont Democratic Party staffer (who was organized with Local 4).

In the end, it was the overwhelming vote of members, for the first time in electoral memory, to make *no* endorsement in the race for governor.[10] Our members rejected both the Republican and the Democrat and viewed with clear eyes that neither of these candidates were inclined to advance the interests of organized labor after Election Day. This was a big step forward in the collective political understanding of our rank and file.

The lessons I drew from the 2018 Vermont AFL-CIO Convention boiled down to this: First, it was possible to engage members from various unions prior to the convention to grow interest and excitement. And with some nudging from the local leadership, and with a program that is viewed as relevant to the struggles they face at work, they would attend. If this could work with AFSCME, it could work within other internationals.

Second, when a critical mass of members attends conventions, and when those members are allowed and encouraged to engage in open and free debate, these members were ready and able to make decisions that ran counter to the dull and played-out logic of the old guard.

And third, if this approach was used in 2019, a year when we would hold internal elections for all Vermont AFL-CIO officer positions, it was possible that we could orchestrate a revolution in leadership—creating one that was ready and willing to take a deep dive into the political orientation of the AFL-CIO and to explore new ways to engage in politics that did not rely on replicating the same failed strategies, ultimately producing the same failures of outcome.

Change was possible.

CHAPTER III

The United! Campaign: From Ashes Rise

I want to affect people like a clap of thunder, to inflame their minds with the breadth of my vision, the strength of my conviction and the power of my expression.
—Rosa Luxemburg

Launching a Movement for Change

After the success of the May 30, 2019, picket against Scott Walker (discussed in chapter I), there was zero question regarding the 2019 elections; I would run for Vermont State Labor Council president and seek to build a progressive slate around a unified working-class-left program. Significant change needed to come to the Vermont AFL-CIO if we were to realize the class power that had been absent for too long. We needed to take a left turn, one that put focus on empowerment of the rank and file. This was clear to me. We also needed to run a campaign that signaled to the members that this year, this election, was different, that it was not another irrelevant vote to place one personality or another at the top, but rather a referendum on the core direction of the labor movement. This had to be about a defined program of action and a full slate aimed at fundamental change, not just one candidate getting more votes than another. The platform that would soon emerge would be a radical embrace of internal rank-and-file democracy, a commitment to a broader struggle for a more direct participatory democracy in society as a whole, an active antifascist stance, a rejection of any alignment with the Democratic Party, an advocacy of a more robust social system benefiting the working class, support for a Green New Deal, and a commitment of more resources toward organizing.

On June 5, less than a week after the Scott Walker picket, I began sending emails and making calls telling AFL-CIO leaders I was close to

Vermont AFL-CIO United! campaign materials, 2019.

announcing a run for president. But I also made clear that this would have to be about more than just me or a few names on a ballot. We needed to articulate a comprehensive progressive platform, and we needed to put together a full slate of reform candidates from a wide cross-section of affiliates. As a starting point, I listed a number of issues I saw as a priority (like the need for us to put a clear focus on internal and external organizing and a recognition that the Democratic Party was not a reliable ally). I also asked for feedback concerning what they would like to see in a campaign platform and if they would be willing to put candidates forward to run on a progressive slate.

As I geared up for a campaign, so too did a candidate from AFT: Heather Riemer, executive director of AFT-Vermont.[1] Riemer, a longtime union staffer with twenty years of experience with the UE (United Electrical, Radio and Machine Workers of America) and AFT before becoming director, was (and remains) a very good organizer. She was left-leaning in a much less radical way than me (*liberal* perhaps being the better descriptive word) and favored keeping the Vermont AFL-CIO largely pointed in the same general direction (i.e., more effective lobbying and a stronger electoral approach in backing our endorsed candidates), but doing a better job at those tasks than we had always done (and with more emphasis on new organizing).

She was also a member of the Democratic Socialists of America (DSA, which I too am a member of), served from 1995 to 2001 as chair of the Vermont Progressive Party (again, a party which I am also a member of), and ran (and lost) as a Progressive for the Vermont House in 2006. So clearly this would not be a black and white election whereby a progressive candidate faced off with a hard conservative candidate. Rather, it would be one in which the members would decide if we took a radically new approach and significantly turned left or if we stayed the course but with potentially (if you bought what Riemer was selling) more wind in our sails.

Riemer, to judge her fairly, would have been a pro-reform candidate if the election had taken place ten years earlier. And a decade before, a Riemer victory unquestionably would have represented progress within the Vermont AFL-CIO. In many ways, her politics felt close to those of Ben Johnson (before he became a traitor), the last Vermont AFL-CIO president to come out of AFT. But we were not running in the past. The election would be in 2019, and what was to the left now was not the same thing as what had been to the left before.

My opponent, who had always worked within the labor movement (right out of college), had never to my knowledge been a rank-and-file union member after leaving grad school, nor suffered the firsthand challenges of being an hourly worker in recent decades (her one job outside of being a union staffer was as an HR manager for Draker Laboratories from 2007 to 2009). But she did have a proven track record of being part of successful new organizing drives with the UE (1996–2007) and AFT (2009–present), and her largest AFT affiliate, Local 5221, UVM Medical Center nurses and staff, in 2018 engaged in a successful two-day strike. She also would have the massive advantage of heading a Vermont union composed of eight locals that included roughly 40 percent of the total Vermont AFL-CIO membership. And here, if she was able to draw support from the Building Trades (with a thousand members) or to co-opt even a few midsized locals (especially if they cut into my natural AFSCME base), and if she was able to maintain support from all her AFT locals, she would win. In short, Riemer could only be beaten by building an unprecedented level of unity and momentum for radical change among nearly every Vermont affiliate not within the AFT. And just as I began to gear up my efforts, so did Riemer. As a starting point, based on the numbers alone, a betting man would not be wise to wager against her unless they secured ten-to-one odds. I and any slate I ran with would come out of the gate as the clear underdogs.

From the start it was my estimation that, once a progressive slate was put together, it would take a strong inside and outside game for us to prevail. We would need to reach out to key local leaders and give them reason to send delegates to the convention who would support us. More importantly, we would also need to generate awareness and support from the rank and file themselves, creating the sense that the progressive slate was a manifestation of their own desires for change.

In short, the election strategy had to be maximalist in nature, aiming to have as many union members at the convention as possible in order to challenge the conventional math whereby a few delegates, carrying the votes of a limited number of large locals, would determine the outcome. But such an approach to a contested election had not been carried out in recent memory (if ever) within the Vermont AFL-CIO (nor were contested elections, let alone ones that included an organized slate united around a common platform, even typical in any state labor council election).

Such a grassroots approach to building momentum for progressive internal change was perhaps more possible within the Vermont AFL-CIO due to its rural scale, a plethora of small locals, and a limited labor bureaucracy in comparison to many other state labor councils. The fact is, in Vermont a great number of our affiliated locals are run by full-time workers (and not staffers or paid officers), and even though many affiliates still have gatekeepers between potential reformers and their rank and file, the problem is less pronounced than in other regions of the US. Point being, the opportunity existed for us to make an appeal to the members themselves and in fact to reach them and move them with an effective working-class-left program.

Thus, from June forward, what followed would be two months of discussions with various affiliates and union activists. To help facilitate meaningful and focused discussion, I floated a draft platform to potential allies that, among other things, committed the Vermont AFL-CIO to supporting internal, member-driven, democratic reform; increased resources toward organizing (internal and external); expanded social benefits for the working class generally; promoted a Green New Deal; and took a step back from the Democratic Party.

Talking Change with Affiliates across Vermont

With this draft platform in hand, I met with AFSCME locals, the Building Trades, IATSE (International Alliance of Theatrical Stage Employees), UAW (United Auto Workers), and AFT–United Academics activists. Talking with AFSCME members, I was again reminded that prior to the efforts by myself and local presidents to build for the 2018 convention, a majority of the rank and file did not even know what the AFL-CIO did, or that they were members. When faced with instances of such understandable ignorance, I affirmed to members that the reason they did not know about the AFL-CIO was because of how ineffective the labor council had been for so long, thus not being relevant in our lives. From there I would pivot, asserting that this fact in and of itself was reason for us to take the AFL-CIO back and make it be something that supported us in our struggles (and this approach seemed to ring true to members).

With other affiliates, time and again I was told that no other candidate for Vermont AFL-CIO office had ever come and spoken with them in person about their issues and asked for their support in an internal election. So already, for many, this felt very different than in past years, when it typically didn't even register that there was an election coming, let alone having knowledge beforehand as to who the candidates were and what their visions for the future of labor amounted to.

Early on, the leadership of the Vermont Building and Construction Trades Council invited me and Riemer to meet with them separately. The Trades wanted to offer both candidates an opportunity to talk before deciding if they would back a candidate (and if so who). For me, support from the Trades was crucial if I was to have a chance at winning and if we were to forge a critical mass of affiliates committed to internal reform. Hence, as soon as the Trades extended the offer to meet at their South Burlington union hall, I told them to pick a day and time and I would be there.

In some regards, Riemer, all things being equal, should have had the edge in securing their backing. In general, the Trades were less inclined to take a step back from the Democratic Party than I was. They also invested in traditional lobbying efforts and were, at this point, aware of my support for Green New Deal legislation and having labor engaged in climate issues. This mattered, as the Trades had two hundred good-paying union jobs on the Vermont Gas pipeline that was then under construction, and would therefore be wary of the Vermont AFL-CIO going down any environmental path that could threaten those jobs. But all things were not equal.

In fact, the recent organizing around the successful picket against Scott Walker was largely a collaboration between AFSCME and the Trades. Here our unions worked closely together, and myself and Trades Council president Tim LaBombard (IBEW) especially so. AFT, on the other hand, while they endorsed the action and took part in the picket, were absolutely MIA during all the prepicket organizing. Further, just the previous winter the Trades were unable to get legislation passed in the Democratic Party–dominated statehouse that would have established a fairer means of enforcing worker misclassification by contractors on job sites. Thus, their frustrations with the Democratic Party and the limitations of traditional lobbying were also fresh in their minds (even if they were not naturally inclined to commit to a hard break from those approaches). Finally, they also carried with them the perception that the Vermont AFL-CIO, for the last decade, had largely ignored the struggles of the Trades in their political work. So when I sat down with them to discuss the 2019 election, I was able to draw from the goodwill banked in recent months and was able to speak directly to their areas of concern, offering a new approach that did not have past shortcomings baked in.

When we met, some of their leaders grilled me on my views of the Green New Deal and the Democratic Party. I did not flinch but rather stated my firm support for a Green New Deal, adding that I was not intending to head a slate that would support the elimination of union jobs on projects like Vermont Gas or that would seek to get rid of unionized industries where we had members in Vermont. Rather, I stated that what we should be doing is talking about the *new* green union jobs we wanted to create through the construction of new wind farms, solar arrays, energy-efficient buildings, and the like. Further, I stated that our political activity should be geared toward building support for positive incentives aimed at green projects that would generate those new jobs, and not toward regressive measures that could directly threaten existing union positions. I also argued that if we supported the Green New Deal, we would be in a better position to see to it that union concerns were built into it. I also offered that if they supported me and ran candidates as part of a progressive slate, they would carry serious influence within the Vermont AFL-CIO concerning any and all policy positions we took relating to the details of the Green New Deal and all other decisions that could impact their members in construction.

Concerning the Democrats, I talked about the fact that neither the Trades classification enforcement bill nor card check (an AFSCME bill) passed in Montpelier in 2019, despite the Democrats being by far the largest party.[2] Thus, I questioned the value of us backing nearly all of their candidates, election after election, and seemingly getting nothing in return. Here I suggested that the only rational response would be a reevaluation of our relationship to the Democrats and for us, at minimum, to be much more intentional regarding which candidates we backed. After all, when the sum of our experiences in the statehouse in 2019 was failure, that did not leave us with much to lose if we took a new approach.

All told, leaders of the Trades seemed to appreciate me being forthright and candid in stating my views. They also seemed to indicate to me that they agreed that now was the time to try a different kind of political approach with the state labor council, as the approaches we had engaged in recently had failed. But they were not going to make an endorsement on that day. They wanted to wait and meet with Riemer and then weigh their options.

However, weeks went by and that meeting with Riemer did not materialize. According to Building Trades Council president LaBombard, Riemer had consistently failed to coordinate a date for the offered meeting. This delay did not sit right with the Trades, and by late July LaBombard called to say they were endorsing me, would run as part of the slate, and would mobilize their voting delegations for the September convention. Riemer would eventually settle on a date to meet with them, but that fell after they had issued their endorsement. Given that the Trades were not interested in second-guessing their decision, that meeting had no impact on the events that would follow.

I was also invited to meet with the leadership of the International Association of Fire Fighters/Professional Fire Fighters of Vermont (PFFV). Attending this meeting, in addition to PFFV president Bradley Reed, was their contracted lobbyist. Not unexpectedly, the firefighters, with their lobbyist doing most of the talking, asked several questions about my more critical stance on the Democratic Party. In the end, the firefighters, who politically have been more conservative than a number of our other unions, would endorse my opponent, Riemer, and would oppose our progressive slate. If all ten of their Vermont unions and all 250 members were active in the Vermont AFL-CIO, this could have presented a challenge. But only one small local (Local 2934, with nine members) and the PFFV as a labor association were paying their per capita dues and were therefore eligible to vote in the September election. Thus, Riemer getting the nod from this body, in addition to being predictable, did not alter the playing field.

Early on, I knew that the United Steelworkers Local 4, representing about thirty-five union shops with 225 members, was lining up behind Riemer. I was told as much, point blank, by Local 4 president Ray Bettis. Bettis, in no uncertain terms, told me his "hands were tied" and that he had already received a phone call from the chairman of the Vermont Democratic Party, Terje Anderson, who informed him that Local 4 had to line up behind Riemer. Upon learning this from Bettis, I reminded him that politicians who claim to support labor should be getting their marching orders from us, and that there is a serious problem when it is the other way around. But Bettis was not moved, and he further stated that he represented Democratic Party staff members and that they would compose a significant portion of Local 4's convention delegates.

I found Bettis's backing of the relative status quo confounding. Over the previous year, I had often met with Bettis both for drinks and at his union hall in Barre to talk shop and provide advice about various grievances he had brewing. Bettis, on many occasions, had also expressed frustrations to me regarding his international and the general irrelevance of the Vermont AFL-CIO over recent leaderships. When the former came up, I would say how we needed to change the state fed in such a way to help locals like his grow through organizing new shops. Bettis had always seemed to agree. With such a personal relationship banked, I assumed United! would have support from Local 4 when the time came, or at least that Bettis would go to bat for us with his members. But I was wrong.

Local 4 had recently organized Vermont Democratic Party staffers, and these four or five staffers (and the Democratic Party leadership as a whole) seemed to be holding unreasonably significant influence within the local. Further, Vermont AFL-CIO political director Dennis Labounty (no relation to 1343's Karl Labounty) was also a member of this local and served on its executive board. Labounty, at the time the state labor council's only staffer, was primarily a statehouse lobbyist, a Democrat, and very much part of the old guard. As a lobbyist he believed very strongly in the need for us to prioritize our relationship with the Democratic Party (even though we got very little in return). Labounty also ran (and lost) twice as a Democrat for Vermont state representative (Caledonia 4). Further, it also seemed apparent to me that Bettis had little to no infrastructure in place for the local and had less than measurable participation from his rank and file. Thus, over fifteen years, the local did not just stagnate, but fell from about a thousand members to the 225 it had then. And here, it seemed that Labounty and Democratic Party staffers were the major players involved and informed about broader labor issues or AFL-CIO matters. All this, coupled with the Vermont Democratic Party chair apparently now dictating the local's politics, drove them to the opposition's side. As such, it was their inclination to support Riemer and internal candidates less likely to challenge or upend relationships with figures in the Democratic Party.

However, once it was clear to me that they were allying themselves with AFT and the firefighters, I still made an attempt to get them in our camp (as I wanted to leave no stone unturned). Through my good friend Conor Casey, himself the former executive director of the Vermont Democratic Party, I arranged for a meeting with Democratic Party staffer Spencer Dole, who I knew was going to be a delegate at the convention.[3] We met in a working-class tavern in Montpelier. Over a drink I told him that I and United! had increasing support from locals from across the state and that if we won, we would pressure the Democrats from the left, perhaps making them a better, more pro-union party as a result. And through AFL-CIO pressure we would be in a better position to see the party live up to its own campaign promises on issues like single-payer health care. Dole replied that personally he was not much of a supporter of single-payer. In fact he did not seem too interested in advancing a platform that placed a priority on expanding social programs. Toward the end of this meeting, I took a folded piece of paper out of my pocket and slid it across the table to Dole. I told him that if he and the other Democratic Party delegate from Local 4 supported United! at the convention I could promise the Democratic Party everything on the list. He picked up the note, slowly opened it, and saw that it was blank. He looked at me. I told him supporting United! was the right thing to do for the labor movement, no more and no less. The meeting ended. Local 4 would not be backing United!

A more significant meeting was had between me and activists from United Academics Local 3203 at UVM (an AFT local with more than 630 members). Early on, I reached out to a professor, Nancy Welch, a former member of the International Socialist Organization (ISO). Through Nancy, I arranged for a meeting with the local vice president, Sarah Alexander, who I was told supported union reform, and Helen Scott, also a former ISO member. The three of us met and talked for over an hour at Alexander's house. Here Scott and Alexander agreed that a strong and uniting progressive platform (and full slate) needed to be a central part of any campaign effort. Scott also stated that many of their members, college professors, would be more inclined to support candidates or a slate that promised to be engaged not only in core union matters, but also in social justice issues ranging from antiracism to solidarity for undocumented farmworkers to expansion of social benefits for all. On this assertion I agreed with Scott and affirmed organized labor must turn toward social justice unionism in all aspects of its work (from political activity to contract campaigns) if we were to build sufficient community support and power needed to challenge the oppressive politics of the mundane.

Scott and Alexander also indicated that by their estimation the members of their local could be won over, away from Riemer, given that they had heard very little from her since she had become executive director of AFT-Vermont (their parent body), nor had they seen much support coming from AFT on their issues. But they also cautioned that the fix seemed to be in.

When they asked their United Academics union staff about the upcoming convention, they were informed that Riemer had already contacted them to say they should send two or three delegates (presumably to carry the votes for her). There was zero talk of engaging with the members about the convention, let alone holding a vote to choose delegates. Keep in mind that this local, due to its larger size, was allowed thirteen delegates.

In the end, it was agreed that pending the final crafting of the platform, they would personally work to build support for our slate, and they would engage their rank and file in such a way that they would seek to force the local to hold elections for all thirteen delegate positions and make sure candidates for delegate were informed about the different candidates and were not simply ready to toe the AFT party line. But when invited to run on the slate with me, they were circumspect. Scott indicated that she was reluctant to take that step due to health reasons. Even so, they did not slam the door on this possibility.

Another key one-on-one meeting took place with a UAW Local 2322 leader Liz Medina (a member of DSA). Medina, who worked as staff at Goddard College (a UAW shop), was recommended to me by Green Mountain Central Labor Council president Traven Leyshon (OPEIU).[4] Medina and I sat down at a tavern in Montpelier and had a wide-ranging conversation about the state of the labor movement. We also touched on the draft platform I had previously provided her with.

Coming out of this discussion, Medina agreed, like the AFT activists, to personally back my candidacy and the slate and to work to build support within her local. But like the AFT activists, she too was noncommittal when asked if she would run as part of the slate for a district vice president position. Looking back, this first conversation with Medina would prove to be an important moment. As will be discussed in a later chapter, Medina would go on to become the first Vermont AFL-CIO executive director under United! less than two years later.

Through National Writers Union UAW Local 1981 member Ashley Smith (a former ISO leader, current *Spectre Journal* editor, and partner of AFT's Helen Scott), a meeting was arranged between myself and AFGE (American Federation of Government Employees) Local 2604 member Tristin Adie. Adie was then a nurse at the VA. However, in the recent past she had been a member of AFT Local 5221 when she was employed at the UVM Medical Center. With Local 5221, during their 2018 strike, she served as one of their chief stewards and had been a longtime militant within AFT, so garnering her support would be huge.[5]

Adie and I met in a Burlington coffee shop and talked politics for more than an hour. During the course of the discussion, she expressed skepticism to me about the prospect of Riemer being able to lead the Vermont AFL-CIO toward a radical break from the failed past approaches. She also confided that even as Riemer seemed to bank on the momentum of the contract victories achieved by UVMMC nurses through their recent strike, behind closed doors Riemer advocated with local leaders against engaging in the work stoppage. Thus, in Adie's mind Riemer was being disingenuous in her public posturing. Adie, also like a number of union activists I had previously met with, believed very strongly not only that the labor movement needed to embrace the strike as a major weapon in the arsenal of change, but also that social justice unionism needed to be a foundational element of how we were to move forward. By the end of this meeting, Adie agreed to support the progressive slate and further agreed to consider running for office with us.

Concurrently with all these meetings, I also engaged heavily with all nine of our AFSCME locals in Vermont. I attended local meetings to talk about what I was seeking to do and asked our presidents to maximize their convention delegations to help win the vote. I also had a number of AFSCME members agree to run with me for district vice president positions, including Dan Cornell of Local 490, Eric Steele of Local 1201, and Rubin Serrano of Local 2413. I also believed I had the support of the Vermont AFL-CIO executive vice president and recently retired AFSCME Local 1343 president Karl Labounty.[6] In fact, Labounty told me he would run as part of the progressive slate. But more importantly I had the support of the current 1343 president, Damion Gilbert, who was elected to office the previous winter in anticipation of Labounty's retirement.

Gilbert was an important figure in all these election efforts. The winter before, he had been elected as the new president of 1343 representing (largely) town and city workers in Chittenden and Franklin Counties, with their flagship being the City of Burlington. With four-hundred-plus members, this local was sizable for the Vermont AFL-CIO. Gilbert, at the time, saw with clear eyes that organized labor must become more active, more militant, and more aggressive in the fight for union power relative to the bosses and the politicians. He also was one of the major organizers of the picket against Walker in May. Without Gilbert and the support of his local, the Scott Walker picket would not have been nearly as successful as it was. And now that union attention was bending toward the September convention, Gilbert put his full focus to the matter and made sure that 1343 would send its full complement of delegates and alternates to the convention, and that to a person they would be in support of the progressive change the election was capable of helping to bring about. More will be said of Gilbert later.

The United! Slate and Ten-Point Program for Union Power

Coming out of this multitude of meetings and discussions with members and affiliates, by late July we put forth a comprehensive and final platform

that incorporated all those concerns, suggestions, and demands that were
articulated and expressed by members and leaders who pined for labor
to become a force, again, in the struggle. The platform, a detailed 3,500-
word document, was called the Ten-Point Program for Union Power (and
later, postelection, after it was adopted as the official Vermont AFL-CIO
platform, it would be known as the Little Green Book).[7] As a companion
to the full document, we also produced a summary version and used this
throughout the remainder of the campaign. This summary was as follows:

Vermont AFL-CIO United!
Ten-Point Program for Union Power
Summary of Platform for Change
UNION DEMOCRACY!
We shall seek to amend VT AFL-CIO Constitution to allow ALL
members an equal vote in electing Union officers. Seek to involve
the rank and file in collective decision-making.
WORKING CLASS UNITY!
We oppose fascism and discrimination in all its forms. We are strong
when we are united as Union members and as one working class.
OUR SOCIAL PROGRAM!
We believe that if you work forty hours a week, you should not have
to struggle to pay your bills and make ends meet. We will fight for an
expansion of social programs that benefit all working class people,
and we will fight to make sure these programs are paid for through
progressive taxation (and not having new burdens placed on working people).
POPULAR FRONT!
We will seek to coordinate on social and political efforts with allied
Unions outside the AFL-CIO and with community organizations
when and where those Unions and organizations interests reflect
our own. We recognize that we, as a people, are stronger together
than apart.
GREEN NEW DEAL!
We support investment in our public infrastructure that results in
a healthy environment. We assert that all such projects involving
public money must guarantee prevailing wages, good benefits, and
that Union labor is utilized.

ELECTORAL POLITICS!

We will NOT support candidates that do not actively support us; we do not care what party they are affiliated with. We recognize that the politicians in Montpelier have not been representing our Union interests. We will therefore explore new, more effective ways to approach electoral politics.

WORKING-CLASS DEMOCRACY!

We assert that working people, as the majority, should have a direct vote and say concerning the priorities and laws of the land. We therefore will fight to implement a Town Meeting–based referendum system of government.

PRIORITY ON ORGANIZING NEW SHOPS!

We know that by Unionizing new shops, we grow our Union power. We shall therefore dedicate real resources to organizing, and these resources shall support the organizing efforts of affiliated Unions.

WE ARE NOT AFRAID OF STRIKES!

We unequivocally assert that without our labor, Vermont cannot work. Therefore, one of the most powerful tools at our disposal is the withholding of our labor. When strikes occur, we shall provide support to striking workers. During contract negotiations of affiliated Unions, we shall also provide assistance by way of model contract language which, when implemented, helps build a stronger Labor Movement.

BUILDING A MORE POWERFUL LABOR MOVEMENT!

We stand with those Union members that stand with us. We further recognize moving a progressive working-class program forward will take not only the participation of AFL-CIO Unions, but also that of the NEA, VSEA, UE, and other non-AFL-CIO Unions. We therefore invite like-minded members from within those Unions to adopt this ten-point program, to join us, and to seek to implement this program in every Union in Vermont. We further recognize that it is not enough to capture the leadership of Unions; to win, we will also require rank-and-file engagement and action. Thus we will work to increase the involvement of the rank and file at every level.

On August 1, I announced a provisional list of candidates who would compose the progressive Vermont AFL-CIO United! slate. However, at that time I was still waiting for confirmation, or a final yes or no, from a number of potential candidates (including a number of women). So this provisional list was incomplete and less than ideal. It was top-heavy with men and still retained executive vice president incumbent Karl Labounty as my running mate. Almost immediately Riemer and her backers, such as AFT-Vermont president Deb Snell, started making statements attacking us for our lack of women on our slate. And to be frank, this was a fair criticism. While I knew that it was likely we would have several progressive women join us on the slate in the weeks to come, right or wrong, I decided to move forward with announcing the provisional slate (with the final platform) so as to allow us six-plus weeks to fully campaign.

Then, on August 13, a remarkable thing happened. Riemer announced that the executive vice president, Karl Labounty, had defected and issued a public statement endorsing her. I know that from Riemer's point of view this probably appeared as the coup de grâce. Looking from the outside, one could see how it would be thought that Labounty switching sides could logically bring over a number of AFSCME delegates into her camp. After all, for years Labounty was the highest-ranking AFSCME officer in Vermont, serving on the Council 93 Executive Board. But what Riemer did not know was that after Labounty had retired the winter before, the new Local 1343 president (and new Council 93 Executive Board member), Damion Gilbert, uncovered thousands of dollars in checks issued by the local that did not have receipts or invoices associated with them. The checks were issued by Labounty's treasurer, Caroline Gauthier (who had also recently retired and who was also presently serving as the Vermont AFL-CIO secretary-treasurer but who was not seeking reelection). The books Gilbert inherited were a mess, and there was much suspicion within the local regarding possible corruption. Thus, an internal investigation was in the works, and the rank and file were briefed on the situation. I knew about all of this as it was unfolding. I expressed to Gilbert that this was clearly a problem and that I would have to speak with Labounty and drop him from the United! slate. There was nothing else to do. However, I knew Labounty well and could not believe that he would personally be involved in any act of corruption. But I also recognized that he was local president and partially responsible for the actions of their treasurer, and there was a growing appearance that his treasurer, at best, had engaged in questionable and unauthorized spending. United! could not tolerate any cloud of alleged corruption to hang over our reform effort. So Karl had to go, and I was close to having that uncomfortable conversation with him when it was announced that he had switched sides. His switching was an absolute gift to United![8]

Labounty leaving our ticket was huge on several accounts. First, the taint of corruption (talk of which was known within AFSCME locals) would now land on Riemer's side (thus locking down our unanimous support from within the nine AFSCME locals). Second, Labounty, perhaps unfairly, was viewed as part of the more moderate old guard by several leftists within the affiliates. His position as number two on the slate always felt a little odd, given the break with the past we were looking to implement. Thus, having him allied to the other side suited our narrative. Third, his alignment with Riemer allowed me to go back to former AFT chief steward Tristin Adie (now a member of AFGE) and ask if she would serve as my running mate. (At the time, she was considering running as one of the lesser district vice presidents.)

Forty-eight hours after the Labounty announcement, already having a number of new candidates committed, I released a public statement listing our full and final slate of United! candidates, including Tristin Adie (AFGE) for executive vice president, Danielle Bombardier (IBEW) for secretary-treasurer, Helen Scott (AFT) and Sarah Alexander (AFT) for Chittenden County district vice presidents, and Liz Medina (UAW) for Washington/Orange/Lamoille County district vice president. Never before had so many women run for top office within the Vermont AFL-CIO. Having these five outstanding women union leaders running as part of United!, while at the same time Riemer was proudly trumpeting support for Karl Labounty, eliminated the charge of gender imbalance as any kind of meaningful attack from our opposition from this point on, and having Adie in the number-two spot called into question the loyalty of Riemer's base much more than Labounty's defection did concerning my AFSCME base.

Also announced as part of the slate were Dwight Brown (AFSCME) for Franklin/Grand Isle County district vice president, Omar Fernandez (APWU) for volunteer-in-politics, and Rubin Serrano (AFSCME) for Caledonia/Lamoille County district vice president.[9] Brown and Fernandez were Black men (Fernandez also being Latino, with roots in the Dominican Republic), and Serrano was a Latino (from Puerto Rico). Upon victory, this would make the majority of the Vermont AFL-CIO leadership, for the first time in our long history, women or members from

BIPOC communities.[10] Suffice to say that United! represented the most diverse slate ever to seek office in our state labor council.[11]

From August 15 forward, United! became not only a slate of candidates, but in effect an organizing committee within the Vermont AFL-CIO. No longer was I to be the person unilaterally making decisions. Rather, we began to hold conference calls to make collective decisions regarding our campaign efforts. At the same time, activists with AFSCME Local 1674, headed by local president Dan Peyser (a former member of Progressive Labor), produced a United! trifold campaign pamphlet for us that included a summary of our Ten-Point Program for Union Power and listed all the United! candidates. They also made United! campaign posters. These materials, in addition to being posted in 1674 shops, were used widely by us in our outreach efforts targeting other affiliates.

The Strategy of Maximum Participation and Public Engagement

During these final weeks of the campaign, our United! strategy was as follows:

1. Understanding that local leaders and member delegates are influenced by public opinion and secondary persons outside the AFL-CIO, we ran a public campaign as if it were a general election. Here we leaned on public social media as a tool to reach people.
2. With allied affiliates we pushed hard for them to send the full complement of delegates afforded to them by our constitution. This mattered, as our bylaws stated that the election to office would be done by a majority vote of the delegates (one delegate, one vote) unless there was a motion for weighted voting supported by 20 percent of the delegates present.[12] If it went to weighted voting, in theory, a single AFT delegate from Local 5221 could cast two-thousand-plus votes even if they were the only delegate present for that local. Thus, if we had 80 percent or more of the delegates supporting United! at the convention, and those delegates voted against any motion to go to weighted voting, we could remove the uncertainty that such a representational model would carry with it.
3. We would conduct a high-road campaign that talked about the issues and the differences between ourselves and our opponents (i.e., we would not engage in low-road personal attacks).

4. We would also conduct more traditional outreach to affiliates via emails and phone calls to local leaders.

5. We would position our United! platform front and center of all our combined efforts (and would seek to not allow the election to be about individual personalities).

At this point, from the perspective of United!, it appeared that Riemer was trying to ally herself with old-guard incumbent candidates, thus creating what felt like an AFT-led slate of their own. However, Riemer was also making calls to United! candidates such as Tristin Adie (AFGE), Danielle Bombardier (IBEW), Omar Fernandez (APWU), and Ron Schneiderman (UFCW, United Food and Commercial Workers), suggesting that they, like Karl Labounty, should switch to her side and that they all could work together after the election. Of course, the discussions were reported back to me in detail, and they resulted in no new defections. But what Riemer was doing was in effect setting herself up as beyond any slate. She wanted to maintain support from old-guard incumbents while also signaling to progressive insurgents that she was ready to work with them too, should they prevail. But in taking this approach, she risked being viewed as yet another personality seeking union office without committing to a true break from the past or being a candidate seeking to embody a new, more radical vision of the future.

However, Riemer was not just engaging in discussions with AFL-CIO affiliates. Like United!, it appeared as if she was also doing outreach to secondary targets outside the AFL-CIO (presumably to have them influence their contacts within the state labor council). Thus, past VSEA vice president Michelle Salvador, herself being a progressive union reformer, reached out to me around this time to report that Riemer had cold-called her to say that what United! was doing was for nothing, that the election math dictated that the vote was already a foregone conclusion, and that she would emerge as Vermont AFL-CIO president on September 15. I told Salvador that we were looking at the math too and assured her that the contest was far from over.

Riemer, on August 22, also put forward her own platform. While her positions were by no means conservative, and while she did express some progressive tendencies (compared to AFL-CIO officers or candidates in other states), unlike ours, hers were short on detail, fit on a single sheet of paper, and boiled down to:

1. Engage members so that we have an effective power in the legislature;
2. Engage in electoral politics in a principled way that builds power for working people;
3. Support organizing the unorganized;
4. Support local unions that have not been able to sign up a majority of their members;[13]
5. Coordinate solidarity for contract and grievance struggles;
6. Provide inspiration and support for building membership and leadership in our local unions.[14]

In the same public statement, Riemer also indicated that she and allied affiliates would put forward multiple resolutions at the convention. These resolutions therefore indicated her position on different issues, including support for a Green New Deal. However, her campaign position on the Green New Deal came long after I and United! had already made this a centerpiece of our platform and after the Building Trades had joined United! So there was no potential risk in Riemer taking this position at that point of the campaign.

In addition, other resolutions would also call for the Vermont AFL-CIO to once again join the Working Vermont lobbying coalition with VSEA and NEA (a staff-driven lobbying coalition we left after NEA's unilateral decision to introduce legislation that would have eliminated collective bargaining for school workers concerning health care) and to engage in the electoral process in a "principled" way. Other resolutions would support of a number of pieces of legislation (including a fifteen-dollar-an-hour livable wage, card check, and federal support for the US Postal Service) that was already widely supported by Vermont labor.

Her positions on rejoining Working Vermont and engaging in the electoral process were dog whistles intending to signal that under her leadership there would be no radical change regarding our relationship with the Democratic Party. And here these whistles were heard loud and clear by Democratic Party acolytes.

On August 29, the Professional Fire Fighters of Vermont issued their endorsement of Riemer.[15] So too did Democratic Party hack and former losing candidate for lieutenant governor Steve Howard. Also issuing a Riemer endorsement was State Representative Joanne Donovan (a Democrat, and cochair of the Legislative Workers Caucus).[16] Riemer also had the clear support of all of her AFT locals minus United Academics Local 3203 (which was still up for grabs), along with the United Steelworkers Local 4 (who, as previously discussed, represented Vermont Democratic Party staff) and the AFSCME retiree group (who had authorized Labounty to be their convention delegate prior to him switching sides). I suspected that she would also earn backing from the Sheet Metal Workers Local 63 (as their delegation would include incumbent district vice president for Caledonia/Lamoille County Bart Wilder). IBEW Local 2326 (representing 169 Consolidated Communications workers, not electricians from the Trades) was uncommitted at this point and could go either way. It also seemed apparent that she was receiving secondary moral support from the Vermont Workers' Center (an organization, like DSA, of which we were both members, and of which she had long-established relationships with staff members).[17] But on United!'s side of the nonunion leftist ledger, we had the backing of the Burlington-based Bread & Roses Collective.

The fact that she had active support from the old guard, the chairman of the Vermont Democratic Party, and unionized Democratic Party staffers (USW Local 4), as well as endorsements from other high-profile Democrats, while she was also supporting a return to the Working Vermont coalition and a normalization of our electoral approach, all played marvelously into United!'s hand concerning our public narrative. We were the slate of foundational change, and those with a perceived vested interest in maintaining the liberal status quo were with Riemer and the old guard. I don't know if Riemer was cognizant of this emerging perception, and I do not know if it was an intentional strategy on her part (although it was increasingly hard not to view it that way). All I do know is that at best it was incredibly foolish for her to allow this narrative to take root, and it ultimately worked against her personal self-interest. But just as one should never look a gift horse in the mouth, United! did not question her larger motivations on these points and simply used these talking points to our own advantage as we continued to do outreach with affiliates, with members, and in the public. But even as the ground was increasingly favorable to our labor insurgency, it was clear that the election could prove to be very close, with even a few delegates deciding the outcome.

As Riemer racked up establishment backing, United! briefly explored nationalizing the campaign (so to speak) through prominent progressive endorsements of our own. I personally spoke with Sara Nelson, well-known president of the Association of Flight Attendants–CWA (Communications Workers of America), and asked if she would consider endorsing United! I also spoke with Vermont's lieutenant governor, David Zuckerman of the Vermont Progressive Party, about the possibility of issuing his own United! endorsement as a counterbalance to recent Democratic endorsements of Riemer. However, both Nelson and Zuckerman expressed that while they supported what United! was seeking to achieve, such endorsements did not seem appropriate. Nelson indicated that if she came out for us, it could be viewed as a national progressive labor leader unfairly seeking to alter the outcome of a regional democratic process. Likewise, Zuckerman told me that while he found Democratic Party interference in an AFL-CIO election to be deplorable, he would not be inclined to have the Progressive Party go down that same path. Both Zuckerman and Nelson's reasoning rang true to me and United! and the matter was dropped. We would win or lose on our own efforts and how well our platform resonated with Vermont union members.

From the start, United! sought to run a clean campaign based on the issues. But as Election Day drew near, our opposition increasingly took a negative and personal tone. I received multiple reports from AFL-CIO leaders such as Tim LaBombard (IBEW) that one of the talking points Riemer would use with them was that I was too far left, too radical to effectively serve as Vermont AFL-CIO president. I was essentially being red-baited by a fellow DSA member. Then, on September 3, just twelve days before the vote, AFT-Vermont and AFT Local 5221 president Deb Silmser Snell (Vermont's top AFT officer and close Riemer ally) made public statements to the effect that the only reason we had women on our slate was to defang accusations that United! or myself was gender biased. She also attacked me for using public social media forums as campaign platforms and asserted that I would, in essence, be an unhinged president, more apt to blow off meetings with legislators or talk over them rather than effectively work with them.[18] She further claimed that I had failed to reach out to AFT locals to seek to learn about their issues or engage them in the election process. One did not have to read too far between the lines to see that Snell sought to plant the seeds of doubt in members' minds that I was perhaps a sexist and certainly a loose cannon capable of little more than banging on tables.

In reality, I had personally reached out to AFT locals and leaders many times throughout the campaign (and of course we had two AFT members, Scott and Alexander, running on our United! slate). I offered to meet with AFT locals to talk. But, as is a problem with union democracy throughout the nation, it was gatekeepers like Snell and Riemer who shut down meaningful dialogue with significant numbers of rank-and-file AFT members beyond those activist contacts we were able to make through leftist channels. In fact, on at least a half-dozen occasions I reached out to Riemer to offer to take part in debates in front of AFSCME locals, AFT locals, and in public on local radio. Each time I made such an offer, I was met with silence from Riemer.

By early September, Scott and Alexander were successful with their interventions within their AFT local at UVM. Through rank-and-file pressure and growing interest in the election, the local agreed to hold competitive elections for the thirteen delegate seats and, further, to invite both candidates to engage in a debate before their members. Even as my many offers to Riemer to engage in debates had previously gone unanswered, she could not ignore this one coming from one of "her" AFT locals. So we both accepted. The event was slated for September 10 (five days before the vote).

There were so many moments that one could argue were pivotal for the outcome of the election. But this one the most. The math at this point seemed clear to me and United!: to win we needed to hold on to all of our base, and we needed to gain overwhelming support from this single AFT local (the third-largest AFT local in Vermont). Whoever the majority of this local supported would likely decide who would win for Vermont AFL-CIO president. It was that close. So a strong debate performance was not just desirable, but could very well determine everything that would come next.

The debate drew a couple dozen members, many of whom were to be delegates at the convention. The opinions about the candidates that they walked out of the room with would be key. Riemer and I both gave opening statements and then began to field questions from the members, with back and forth between us as seemed appropriate. Both of us stayed to the high road and stuck to the issues. Riemer did well enough but missed the mark on a few occasions. When a well-liked AFT member (and delegate), Patrick Brown, a Black man originally from Jamaica, asked about how the labor movement should address discrimination and racism, Riemer's response was unfocused and rambling. She asserted, "Yeah, we need to do more of that." I assumed she meant, "We should be doing more to combat racism," but her intent was unclear and she failed to get across a policy position to the members. For my part, I said that we should make antiracism a strong priority within the Vermont AFL-CIO, pointed out that antiracism and antifascism was part of the United! platform, said that it was no mistake that United! was running the most diverse slate in Vermont State Labor Council history, and suggested that we should explore creating a BIPOC caucus within the Vermont AFL-CIO. My answer seemed to be well received by AFT members.

At another point of the debate, a member first recognized how I was running as part of a slate and then asked Riemer about her slate. She responded that she chose not to have a slate, failed to mention that she was backing Karl Labounty for executive vice president (which perhaps, even though Labounty was backing her, she now was not?), and said something to the effect that she did not want to put any candidates up against incumbents as there was a long tradition in the AFL-CIO of not running against people already in positions. This struck me, and surely other members, as a strange statement that if anything signaled support for the old guard or at least a continuity of sentiment on the executive board. During my response I sought to draw a stark contrast, arguing that the historic shortcomings of the Vermont AFL-CIO required us to make a break with the past and to replace existing executive board members with new members with new ideas. I also stressed that I was not here to simply ask for them to vote for me, but also for the entire United! slate, as we were all running together and shared a common progressive vision for the future of labor.

In the end, I walked out of the debate feeling like I had hit it out of the park. I felt confident that I did what had to be done and had secured enough support from the AFT local to give United! a chance at winning. And soon thereafter, I had this feeling validated by Scott and Alexander when they informed me that United! would receive full support from eleven of the thirteen AFT Local 3203 delegates at the convention.

CHAPTER IV

The 2019 Convention: United! Comes to Power

I want political action that counts.
I want a working class that can hold an
election every day if they want to.
—"Big Bill" Haywood

Election Eve

United! came to the September 14 and 15 convention ready to go and with firm support coming from twenty-three locals out of AFGE, AFSCME, APWU, CWA, GMCLC (Green Mountain Central Labor Council), IATSE, IBEW, the Iron Workers, LIUNA (Laborers' International Union of North America), NPMHU (National Postal Mail Handlers Union), OPEIU, UA (United Association of Journeymen and Apprentices of the Plumbing and Pipe Fitting Industry of the United States and Canada, or United Association), UAW, and UFCW, and we had majority support from AFT Local 3203. But even while we entered the convention with a strong and diverse base of support, Riemer had nine locals lined up behind her (six of them being from AFT) and undoubtedly would be working to subvert support away from United! if opportunities arose or could be created.[1] Furthermore, up for grabs (as far as we knew) was IBEW Local 2326 (one delegate and 169 members, representing workers at Consolidated Communications) and Sheet Metal Workers (SMW) Local 63 (one delegate and 100 members), along with the smaller OPEIU Local 45 (one delegate), OPEIU Local 277 (one delegate), and Professional Aviation Safety Specialists (PASS) Chapter NG3 (one delegate). Another uncommitted was President Jill Charbonneau (who served as the only delegate for NALC Local 521). But Charbonneau had repeatedly told us she would remain absolutely neutral in the election, so it was thought that her vote was not in play for either side.

Vermont AFL-CIO members at the 2023 convention, Northeast Kingdom, Vermont.

With all this in place, after months of organizing, United! knew that it was unlikely we could win over SMW Local 63, as their single delegate, Bart Wilder, was the incumbent district vice president running against one of ours (Rubin Serrano, AFSCME). But we factored that likelihood into our calculations and expected to lose that vote. We also knew United! could afford to lose IBEW Local 2326, but only if everything else broke our way; we had to hold on to all our supporters we entered the convention with and we needed to carry all the other small uncommitted locals. It would be tight, and much could change inside twenty-four hours if we did not play our cards just right, but a victory was within reach and we came to the convention prepared to do what we had to do to maximize the probability of success.

We had red campaign lawn signs out on the roads leading to the Burlington convention site. We had red campaign stickers ready to give out. We had flyers listing our slate alongside a summary of our platform. For each separate table, we also provided the long version of our Ten-Point Program for Union Power. And most importantly we had organized a record number of delegates to attend, who were largely in support of United! In total there were 105 delegates registered for the convention (IBEW Local 300 alone turned out 17), with perhaps 30 alternates, rank-and-file members without standing, and allied guests also present. Fifty-five AFSCME members were there, each and every one supporting United! This was the largest, best-attended Vermont State Labor Council Annual Convention in many decades.

Physically outnumbering our opposition by a large margin, our game plan was to have our United! delegates vote against any potential motion to go to a weighted vote (and again, if the opposition made such a motion, they would need to have 20 percent of the delegates support it for it to prevail). We also anticipated that the sitting president, Charbonneau, out of habit, might seek to go to a weighted vote as a first step, without a motion being made (as that is how voting had incorrectly been done in some elections past). United! preempted this possibility by filing a motion with the elections committee asking that they uphold the process laid out in our constitution and not allow for weighted voting unless a motion was made and passed by the requisite number of delegates. To bolster our assertion, we also included a written decision to that effect that we secured from the national AFL-CIO prior to the convention.[2] Furthermore, we gave every delegate at the convention a flyer from United! encouraging members to vote against any motion that may call for weighted voting. Here we argued that participatory democracy is superior or more desirable than a weighted representational vote, and further that rank-and-file participation at conventions should be encouraged, and to achieve that we should abide by one delegate, one vote.

In case AFT, on September 14 (the election was to be held on September 15), looked around and realized how outnumbered they and their few allies were and came to understand our strategy, United! also filed a motion with the credentials committee asking that no additional delegates be seated after the convention was brought to order if their paperwork had not previously been submitted. If accepted by the committee, this would put the kibosh on Riemer and AFT from rapidly making calls and filling out paperwork for the dozens of delegates to show up after the convention had begun (as by United!'s thinking, they had already had months to organize their members and if they had not done it by now they should have to face the consequences).[3]

As is tradition in contested elections, President Charbonneau invited Riemer and me to both have one of our supporters appointed to the elections committee. Riemer had Snell put on this committee, and I had AFSCME Local 1343 president Damion Gilbert appointed, effectively making him my top lieutenant for the convention.

All told, it was plain from the start that pro-United! delegates would massively outnumber Riemer's supporters. And Riemer, almost like she had never read the election rules in the constitution or otherwise anticipated that we would seek to block any move to go to weighted voting, stuck to her approach whereby very few AFT delegates would attend but these delegates (with the exception of Local 3203) would be unwavering in their commitment to her. Thus, of the twenty-three total registered AFT delegates, thirteen were from Local 3203, with eleven of those AFT delegates supporting United! (one short of United! actually having a majority of all AFT delegates).

United! also appointed Danielle Bombardier (IBEW), our candidate for secretary-treasurer, to serve as what amounted to our whip at the convention. Danielle did an outstanding job talking with members about United!, making sure members knew who the United! candidates were, preparing friendly delegates to oppose any eventual motion to go to weighted voting, and handing out United! campaign stickers.

The first day of the convention went as expected. After Charbonneau brought the convention to order, AFSCME members, as they had done in 2018, left to take part in AFSCME-driven trainings and organizing discussions across the hall. In the main hall, the remaining union members not from AFSCME locals were largely talked at by politicians and their staff (something we would change in 2020).

As the day grew old (and night unfolded), United! candidates and I took every opportunity we could to talk with members, shore up our support, and seek commitments from delegates who had entered the convention undecided. My lieutenant, Gilbert, and Local 1343 vice president Jesse Greeno also organized a well-attended United! happy hour before dinner in their adjoining hotel rooms. By the time the vote approached the following day, United! had secured support from OPEIU Local 45, OPEIU Local 277, and PASS Chapter NG3, thereby bringing the number of pro-United! locals up to twenty-six.

A Road Not Taken

At one point during the convention, as I fretted over various possible outcomes, I took Damion Gilbert and AFSCME Local 1674 president Dan Peyser into my confidence. I relayed to them, truthfully, that I had information about one opposition local president who had previously reached out to me wanting to know if there was a way they could disaffiliate their local from their international and become part of AFSCME. For a union officer to be heard even whispering about decertifying or inviting a raid is a mortal sin within the AFL-CIO (and is not allowed), so the request was unusual to say the least, and after being approached with this request I rapidly filed a report on the encounter with AFSCME Council 93 that included the name of the local president in question and some possible (nonraiding) courses of action we could engage the international with if we so chose. Not surprisingly (all being AFL-CIO affiliates), nothing ever came of it. But I still had that report. I told this tale to Gilbert and Peyser and pointed out that if I was to ever make the report available to their international, this president undoubtedly would be removed from their post and the local would likely be put in trusteeship until their next election. The president would be ruined. I told Gilbert and Peyser all this and mused that I could tell this president that I expected them and their local to support United! or this could be their fate.

Gilbert, without hesitation, said I should tell this local president that I had the report in hand and that I fully expected them to vote the right way. By Damion's reasoning, I did not need to actually make a threat; the threat would be implied and would be enough to achieve our ends. For Gilbert, in this moment, it seemed his thinking was, "The object is to *win*, and if it means taking a lower road to get to victory, so be it."

Peyser, on the other hand, told me point-blank that if I did that, if I used a form of blackmail to prevail, I would be no different than the proverbial old guard that we opposed. He said we had to win or lose on the strength of our platform and our ability to organize, and not through dirty tricks of this nature. Dan's words rang true, and my moment of weakness and doubt passed. I get that real-life political battles sometimes need to go beyond pure principle and employ a skillful means in order for the right outcome to be attained. But this approach would be a bridge too far. There was no more talk of walking though such forms of darkness. Fortunate is the aspiring leader who has people of character (like Peyser) as trusted advisors.[4]

The Inside Game/Tactical Pressure

In attendance on September 14 and 15 was AFSCME Council 93 executive director Mark Bernard and their political director, Jim Durkin. Both came up from Boston. Throughout the convention they did everything they could to be supportive of me and the United! slate. Bernard expressed to me how crappy it was that Karl Labounty, as a delegate for the AFSCME retiree group, had publicly switched sides and was backing Riemer. Bernard was none too pleased with Labounty since AFSCME was compelled to open an investigation concerning him and his former treasurer for unaccounted-for expenditures while officers in 1343. In fact, just days before the convention Council 93 had issued a letter to Labounty (and Gauthier) demanding immediate action concerning the missing funds and making clear that an investigation was underway. It was also widely known (or should have been expected) that Council 93 would have key leaders at the convention. But as day one drew to a close, so far Labounty was a no-show.

Following the banquet dinner, after I made the rounds to all the tables and shared some whiskey with a number of members whose support we would need the next day, Council 93 field services director Steve Lyons suggested it would be a good time for me to sequester myself in my hotel room (as the election outcome was still uncertain, and one wrong move encouraged by bourbon could spell trouble for United!). With that, Damion Gilbert walked me back to my room. As we were going through the lobby, Riemer and Snell were sitting in chairs adjacent to each other. As we passed, I said to Riemer, "Whatever happens tomorrow, should United! win, know that as far as I am concerned we are all *one* labor movement the next day." To that, Riemer replied something to the effect of, "And I hope the same holds true for AFSCME after I win."

Back in my room, I decided to reach out to Karl Labounty by phone.[5] Mind you, I knew Karl, and I never believed he had it in him to purposefully misspend union money. Frankly, I believed that the investigation, if anything, would cast aspersions on his former treasurer. This is not to say that Labounty, as local president, did not bear some responsibility for the acts of his officers—he did—but that is not the same as him putting his hand in the till.[6] I also knew it would be close the next day, and while Labounty was publicly backing Riemer I thought he could be brought over once again. The fact that Riemer almost went out of her way to *not* state her support for him at the AFT debate on the UVM campus struck me as something worth having a conversation about. Here I was prepared to ask that he place his vote for me, along with other United! candidates. But under zero circumstances would I step back from publicly or privately supporting my running mate, Tristin Adie, who would face off against him for the number-two spot. But Labounty did not answer his phone, nor did he return my message. And ultimately Labounty would never show up to the convention at all. No one had stopped Karl from coming, and no one had told him not to come. I suspect he did not show up because he knew Council 93 officers from Boston would be there and that he also sensed that no other AFSCME delegates or leaders had followed him to the Riemer camp. These factors, coupled with the letter from Council 93 just days before, gave him stress and reason to not walk into a union space where confrontation was likely and where he would feel like an outcast among his own union. So by intention or not, Council 93 did United! a service regarding the timing of the investigation letter. Labounty would not be a factor at the convention or in determining the election outcome.

Also while I was alone in my hotel room, the elections committee met. Gilbert was there representing me, and Snell was there representing Riemer. Gilbert asked Vermont AFL-CIO political director Dennis Labounty to demonstrate how he determined that delegate and voting-strength calculations were made, as some locals, such as IBEW 300, believed that they had more members than was factored into their delegate allotment. Labounty was unable to provide a clear answer. Gilbert then called into question the underlying accuracy and fairness of the vote that would take place in the morning. Snell, Riemer's second, irate at Gilbert's questioning of the process, began to raise her voice, called it bullshit, and soon stormed out of the meeting. This was no more than foreshadowing, or a dress rehearsal, of what would take place on the 15th.

The Election and Fights from the Floor

First thing in the morning, the convention hall filled up. Close to 90 percent of the people in the room (not all being delegates) had red United! stickers on their lapels. There was excitement and tension in the air. After President Charbonneau brought the convention to order, we went about considering various resolutions. At one point, a non-AFL-CIO person who was present, Andrew Sullivan from the UE, was recognized and spoke on a matter under consideration. This drew some objections in that this was not a UE event but an AFL-CIO event.

At that point, I raised my hand to be recognized. After being called on, I made a motion to allow nondelegates and guests to speak (but of course they would not have a vote). The motion seemed benign to me, and I made it without giving it much thought. But to my great surprise, after I spoke, President Charbonneau flipped out. Immediately, she went off the rails, yelling at me and the members generally, saying in essence that she was sick and tired of so many motions and delegates seeking to alter convention process and in doing so challenge her authority. And when I say she was yelling at everyone, I am in no way exaggerating.

Truth be told, President Charbonneau was under a good deal of stress. She and Political Director Dennis Labounty were accustomed to running conventions of twenty to fifty people, typically with no contested elections, little ideological divide, and no tactical maneuvering. This convention, which included all such factors, was unlike any they had navigated before and was significantly larger than any they had previously managed. Further weighing on President Charbonneau was the absence of her top officers (Executive Vice President Karl Labounty and Secretary-Treasurer Caroline Gauthier), so the weight of convention fell on her alone.

Furthermore, United!'s motions to various committees the day before, along with the adversarial nature of the elections committee meeting the night before, undoubtedly added to her stress. So too did two other United! motions brought forth by Omar Fernandez from the floor that compelled the officer elections to allow each candidate to briefly speak before the vote, starting with district vice presidents before moving to executive committee positions, with president going last.[7]

After a five-minute rant aimed at the members generally, Charbonneau, reaching her breaking point, resigned on the spot and left the convention. Such a resignation was unprecedented.

Immediately, the ranking officer in the room, Member-at-Large Traven Leyshon, assumed the role of convention chair (not without first removing his United! sticker from his shirt). With Leyshon at the podium, after some commotion, considerations of the resolutions resumed.

One resolution advanced by AFT sought to define the Vermont AFL-CIO's political relations and included a direct challenge to United!'s platform, compelling us to rejoin the Working Vermont coalition with NEA and VSEA. This resolution was being backed by Riemer and her allies. Thus, passage or nonpassage of this clause would serve as a test of United!'s strength. Knowing this, from the floor I objected to it and again used it as an opportunity to talk about why it was that we had left the coalition to begin with and why United! opposed rejoining until and unless certain changes were made within Working Vermont that were favorable to the AFL-CIO. In response to my concerns, Marty Scanlon (AFGE) proposed an amendment that would allow the new executive board to, in essence, set conditions on such a rejoining and to stay out until said conditions were met by the NEA and VSEA. Riemer's backers opposed this amendment. Debate ensued. In the end, the amendment was overwhelmingly adopted and the resolution passed.

After resolutions, the time came for elections. Leyshon opened by relaying to the members the concerns expressed at the elections committee meeting the night before. He stated that since the membership strength of the locals could not be confirmed with documentation the night before, should the election go to weighted voting, if it was close, the final results may not be confirmed until after a more accurate review was conducted concerning voting strength (or after the listed voting strength of the locals was confirmed). He also verified that weighted voting would *not* be utilized unless a motion to do so came from the floor and, per the Vermont AFL-CIO constitution, was supported by 20 percent of the voting delegates.

At this Riemer's second, Deb Snell, became irate, stated to the packed room that she could see what was happening here, said again that this was all "bullshit" and that no results from today would stand, and led a walkout of the great bulk of Riemer delegates (all fourteen of them).

I could see what was happening too. The facts were that ninety-nine registered delegates were present. Eighty of them were committed to United! Riemer needed twenty delegates to support weighted voting for her sparsely represented AFT locals to have their membership strength be a factor. She simply did not have the numbers to get that done. Further, even if she did, we still had them beat. Given the delegates in the room, we had firm support from eighty delegates representing 3,851 members. Riemer had firm support from eighteen delegates representing 3,575 members (including from Bart Wilder of SMW Local 63, who were one of the few locals potentially up for grabs coming into the convention). The only uncommitted delegate present at this point was Sandy Tumaso from IBEW Local 2326 (169 members). If she would have gone with Riemer (and perhaps she would not have), Riemer still would have failed to reach the 20 percent threshold to get to weighted voting (she needed twenty delegates

and Tumaso would only bring her to nineteen), and even if the numbers
did somehow get there, even if Riemer got the votes from Local 2326, I
would still win in the race for president, overcoming Riemer by a vote of
3,851 to 3,744—a clear United! victory by a one-hundred-plus vote margin.

As for the other contests, at this point they were in the bag under
nearly all circumstances. For the other executive committee seats, the
opposition candidate for executive vice president, Labounty, was a
no-show, thus Adie was a shoo-in (and as a former AFT nurse would likely
get votes from core AFT delegates otherwise behind Riemer). The opposition also failed to put forward or campaign for the secretary-treasurer
and member-at-large positions. Thus Bombardier and LaBombard (both
IBEW) appeared to face no obstacles. Further, the district vice president
positions were each voted on by geography, whereby members must live
or work in the county the VP would be elected to represent. And given that
Riemer's relative strength centered around Chittenden County (Vermont's
most populous and least rural county), and given that the majority of AFT's
Chittenden County delegates were United! supporters from Local 3203,
and finally factoring in that two of the three United! candidates for these
seats, Scott and Alexander, were themselves 3203 members, there was
not a reality where they would lose. Therefore United! was on the cusp
of a sweeping victory, and there was no way that was unclear to Riemer
and her supporters. Plain and simple, we had them beat and they knew it.

At the end of the day, United! did the effective organizing needed
in the months prior to the convention to put a comprehensive win well
within reach. And we further came to the convention prepared to engage
on a number of fronts where we could gain a tactical advantage leading up to this moment. On the other side, simply put, Riemer and her
allies were never able to find a compelling rationale for their campaign,
and by vaguely trying to appeal to progressives while also seeking to
retain support from the old guard and the Democratic Party and telling
members I was too radical to lead the Vermont AFL-CIO, she played into
United!'s hands, allowing us to delineate the two camps as the relative
status quo versus a new left. Further, Riemer and her allies did not grasp
the implications of United!'s maximum participation strategy concerning
the weighted vote, or they wrongly assumed we could not reach the level
of 80 percent delegate support. Thus, their minimal participation strategy (whereby they seemingly put all their eggs in the basket of sending a

small number of unwavering pro-Riemer delegates to the convention to carry the votes of their members) was inadequate and further decreased any feeling of momentum that could have gone in their favor. And with United! clearly being the only driving force resulting in the largest convention in decades, it was easy for us to convert that perception into gaining the support of the three small uncommitted locals during the convention itself. In short, while Riemer, by any objective measure, was and remains an excellent union organizer when it comes to bringing new shops into the labor movement, her organizing specifically geared toward the election was well off the mark.

Getting back to the walkout, Snell brought with her a number of AFT delegates who were behind Riemer (nine in total), the firefighters (three delegates), and the two Democratic Party staffers who were delegates for USW Local 4 (their president, Ray Bettis, was unexpectedly a no-show). Of Riemer's supporters, the two AFT Local 3203 delegates that came into the convention backing her remained, as did the delegate from SMW Local 63. Riemer also lingered for some time, but she left before the vote for president could take place.

Once the reaction to the walkout dissipated, the convention continued on with elections. United! won every race it ran in for district VP positions (including United!'s Rubin Serrano beating incumbent Bart Wilder for Caledonia/Lamoille County). By acclamation, we further captured all the executive committee seats. For president, I was nominated by David Feurzeig, a member of AFT Local 3203, and AFSCME Local 1201 president Tom Franzoni seconded my nomination. In the spirit of union democracy, I stood up and nominated my opponent, Heather Riemer. However, at this point Riemer, on her own volition, had left the convention hall and could not be found to accept the nomination. I therefore withdrew my nomination of Riemer, and facing no other nominations, delegate Steve May of the National Writers Union UAW Local 1981,[8] with a second again from Tom Franzoni of Local 1201, moved to make me president by unanimous consent. The motion passed by acclimation. With these sweeping wins, United! captured the leadership of the Vermont AFL-CIO, and with that the Vermont State Labor Council took a hard left turn.

CHAPTER V

From Opposition to Governing

Election days come and go. But the struggle of the
people to create a government which represents all
of us and not just the 1 percent—a government based
on the principles of economic, social, racial, and
environmental justice—that struggle continues.
—US Senator Bernie Sanders

Machinist Strike

With victory for United! achieved, we hit the ground running. On September 30, 2019 (just fifteen days after the election), seventy-five machinists from Local 2704 employed at the Velan manufacturing plant in Williston went on strike. The strike represented a rejection of the bosses' demand for draconian cuts to their health care benefits and the right to bring in more nonunion temp workers, coupled with an insulting 1 percent raise offer. Velan was a Canadian company based in Montreal.

Immediately on learning of the strike, I headed to the picket line. There I spoke with Local 2704 president David Littlefield, who briefed me on the conflict and what workers needed to see in a new contract before they would agree to go back to work. For my part, I offered Littlefield and Local 2704 the full support of the Vermont AFL-CIO in any way that may be requested.

In the coming days, the Vermont AFL-CIO did everything it could to amplify the voice of the striking workers and called on community support for the struggle. I personally walked the picket line as often as I could, and I made sure we had at least one AFL-CIO representative on the line every day. I also worked with Local 1343 to have City of Burlington workers come out, with their green AFSCME shirts on, to walk the line.

Vermont AFL-CIO president David Van Deusen (second from left) speaking at a demonstration in support of a Green New Deal, with executive board members Marty Gil (holding banner, left) and Omar Fernandez (third from right) and Secretary-Treasurer Danielle Bombardier (holding banner, right) in Montpelier, Vermont, 2020.

Further, through AFL-CIO appeals for solidarity, community groups such as Democratic Socialists of America, Vermont Women's March, and the Bread & Roses Collective came out on different days to show their support. The Vermont Women's March brought coffee, and the Bread & Roses Collective brought lunch for the strikers. Lieutenant Governor David Zuckerman (from the Vermont Progressive Party) also came out in solidarity. And on day two of the strike, in an act of international class solidarity, union members from CSN (Confédération des syndicats nationaux) in Montreal, also employed with Velan, staged a noontime walkout at one of their Quebec facilities in support of Local 2704's strike.

A week into the picket, the company folded and agreed to double the raises, also backing away from their demands for health care cuts and increased use of temps. As a result, a new collective bargaining agreement was ratified and the strike came to an end. The union won.[1]

Following the victory, I attended the next 2704 meeting and, on behalf of the Vermont AFL-CIO, presented the local with a check for $500 to help defray some of the expenses they had suffered during the work stoppage. I also congratulated members for standing together against the bosses and for not being afraid to utilize the strike as a weapon in their collective self-defense.

Local 2704 did not take part in the 2019 Vermont AFL-CIO Convention. But after showing our solidarity with them on their issues, they would send a delegation to both our upcoming December political summit (more on that later) and to our 2020 convention. Thus, solidarity again showed itself to be a two-way street.

New Progressive Platform, Bringing in Organizers

With the machinist strike fresh in the win column, on October 6, 2019, in the capital city of Montpelier, we held our first Vermont AFL-CIO Executive Board meeting since the convention. Here it should be noted that before United! came into power, executive board meetings took place at most four times per year, and often three times per year. Further, it was often a struggle to reach quorum, agendas were not made known to rank-and-file members, there was zero effort to make the meetings inviting to members, and very few people ever saw any of the minutes from the meetings, let alone knew about any decisions that were made. As far as the average member was concerned, the meetings may have well never taken place. From the start, our new executive board sought to change all this, meeting on a monthly basis, making the agenda and minutes widely available to members via social media, and explicitly inviting any and all interested persons from our rank and file to attend (and speak) if they were so inclined. And that is exactly what we would do for the duration of United!'s time in the majority. And never once have we struggled to reach quorum.

At this first meeting, on the agenda was consideration of making the United! campaign platform (Ten-Point Program for Union Power) into the platform of the Vermont AFL-CIO. Here, without prompting, the single district vice president who did not run on the United! slate, Ed Smith of OPEIU (we did not have a candidate running against him), made the motion. It was seconded by District Vice President Liz Medina of the UAW.[2] The motion passed unanimously. Having Smith, who was not on our slate but who did commit to supporting United! as a delegate at the convention, do this was significant. With the passage of this motion, the Vermont AFL-CIO formally adopted the most progressive platform of any AFL-CIO state labor council in the country. But of course words on paper are just that. What would matter would be *how* we transformed those words into action over the coming years.[3]

Adoption of a progressive platform was not the only major action of this meeting.[4] We also voted to deduct funds from the budget dedicated to paying for an outside lobbyist and to reallocate them into creating a stable of part-time on-call organizers who we could assign to affiliates to help with internal or external organizing efforts or to work on broader campaigns driven by the Vermont AFL-CIO as needed. We further decided that when a local made a request for such organizing support, and when it was approved by Vermont AFL-CIO leadership, in some cases we would ask the local to match funds dedicated to paying the organizers a livable wage of fifteen dollars an hour (in order to extend the number of hours we could provide for organizers). At the discretion of the leadership, we could also choose to waive such matching funds. Once organizers were assigned, we would place them under the direction of the local (thus preserving the local's autonomy). This first stable of organizers consisted of Scarlett Moore, Cobalt Tolbert, and Caleb Freeberg, all three being members of the Bread & Roses Collective (and all of whom recently did part-time organizing for AFSCME Local 4802—Home Healthcare Providers).[5]

Creating this organizing resource for our affiliates as one of our first actions as United! mattered. In a concrete way, it showed that our commitment to prioritize organizing over lobbying (given that our resources were finite) was more than rhetoric. Further, never before had the Vermont AFL-CIO been able or willing to deploy organizers in support of our affiliates, and so this marked an important step in transforming the state labor council into a body with relevance to the locals. From 2019 to 2022, we utilized this new rank-and-file resource on five campaigns: (1) we deployed them to key communities to help build support for card check legislation; (2) we assigned them to AFSCME Local 1674 to go door to door to help sign up new members from within their bargaining unit; (3) we had them work directly with AFT Local 3203 (UVM) to assist the local in their fight-back campaign after university management announced massive program cuts that would result in layoffs; (4) we deployed them to help with a new UFCW

Local 1459 organizing effort at a dairy-processing plant in the Northeast Kingdom; and (5) we assigned them to our effort to build alliances with other progressive unions and labor councils across the US. While our effort to pass card check is ongoing (as well as the UFCW organizing effort and national alliance building), our efforts concerning Local 1674 helped this seven-hundred-plus worker bargaining unit grow their membership from 17 percent (2019) to 42 percent (2022).[6] The overall efforts at UVM's Local 3203, along with increasing enrollment, caused management to significantly scale back its proposed program and job cuts.[7]

More generally, we also aimed to be supportive of new organizing and bringing in more affiliates to the Vermont AFL-CIO. Thus, starting from 2019, we signed solidarity charters with an SEIU (Service Employees International Union) local and two carpenters locals, as well as affiliated a new UFCW local seeking to organize supermarkets in Vermont and affiliated new CWA and SAG (Screen Actors Guild) locals.[8] Over this time, we also became one of the few state labor councils in the nation to increase membership through organizing new units and contractors with the IBEW (Current Electric, Danda Electric, Devino Electric), LIUNA (Towns of Georgia and Calais), National Writers Guild CWA (*VTDigger* staff), and UFCW (Springfield Co-op), and by way of AFSCME gaining 250-plus new members through affiliating Community and Economic Development Office workers and South Burlington workers into Local 1343; organizing Rights & Democracy staff, Soteria House workers, and Burlington Schools clerical employees (all also into 1343); organizing the Rabble-Rouser retail shop into Local 1369; more than doubling membership at the Howard Center (Local 1674); and further building membership among homecare providers (Local 4802).[9] Further, AFT-Vermont, regardless of political disagreements between their leadership and United!, from 2020 to 2022 did a remarkable job organizing well over a thousand workers into their ranks with newly established bargaining units at UVM (clerical and technical workers), Planned Parenthood staff, and various hospital employees.[10] And as of early 2021, the Vermont AFL-CIO set up a web form for workers interested in forming a union at their job.[11] Such tips now come in on a regular basis and are referred to a jurisdiction committee for later assignment to an affiliate.[12] Through these efforts from 2019 to 2022, we have seen the Vermont AFL-CIO grow from 10,000 members to over 11,500 members (in May 2022).[13] This represents progress, especially when many if not most state labor councils in the US continue to see a decline in their union density, but the Vermont AFL-CIO, and the labor movement in general, still has a long way to go.

The Green New Deal

Early on, the executive board set out to make real United!'s commitment to building solidarity with external organizations and movements. One important aspect of this effort was outreach to the environmental justice community.

From its inception, United! recognized the need for labor to engage on environmental issues. After all, workers live on this planet and rely on clean air and water as the basic foundation in making life possible. Thus, it was understood that union members have a direct interest in environmental sustainability. We also saw that there was opportunity for the creation of new union jobs through programs potentially created by a Green New Deal, especially concerning building out a renewable energy infrastructure and making existing buildings more energy efficient. Further, if we were to be able to come into common cause with sections of the environmental movement, and if they supported progressive financing for new or existing programs and supported organized labor in demanding the incentives be created to make sure newly created jobs were union jobs (or otherwise carried with them prevailing wages and family-sustaining benefits), we would stand to see our political power multiplied. And conversely, if labor were to join with the environmentalists in calling for such new sustainable approaches to development, they too would see their power multiplied. So there was a potential win-win to be had here.

As a first move in this direction, United! honored a resolution passed at the 2019 convention and gave its support and endorsement for the climate strike called for on September 20. While actions took place across Vermont on the 20th (and in fact around the world), the largest Vermont demonstration occurred in Burlington. There, over three thousand people rallied for climate action. Joining UVM students in a mass walkout were also the professors, members of AFT Local 3203 (who, one will recall, were key United! supporters). While the great majority of the protesters were students, union members, including myself, were present as well, as too was the Vermont AFL-CIO banner. Speaking for labor was AFSCME Local

1674 member (also a United! supporter and former ISO member) Nolan Rampy.[14] Rampy, addressing the crowd, stated, "This global climate strike is so significant because it represents one of the first steps toward harnessing the power of unions and the working class to fight climate change!"

Further seeking to create trust and dialogue with environmentalists, I accepted an invitation from 350Vermont to speak at a September 25 rally in Montpelier that sought to demand action on climate change while also decrying the influence of highly paid corporate lobbyists at the statehouse. And later, on January 9, 2020, I again accepted an invitation from 350Vermont (this time also with Extinction Rebellion) to speak at another climate action, this one in front of the statehouse in Montpelier. At this rally, flanked by members of IBEW, United Academics/AFT, UAW, APWU, and IATSE, I called for a union-led Green New Deal and asked that just as we stand with environmentalists when they demand climate action, we ask that they stand with us when it comes to making sure new green jobs are union jobs. But demonstrating the challenges of labor working with environmental groups, it was not lost on me (or the IBEW) that a speaker who took to the podium before me had dedicated a portion of her speech demanding that the Vermont Gas pipeline project be shut down—a project that had over two hundred good-paying IBEW union jobs on it. Shutting down of projects that provided jobs to our members was not the direction we, as United!, were willing to go. For us, we sought to maintain unity by talking about the new green (union) jobs we wanted to create, not those we were willing to lose.

In 2020, we were also invited to become founding coalition partners with the Renew New England partnership. The invite came from the Burlington-based Rights & Democracy (RAD) group.[15] Renew was seeking to build a New England–wide coalition of community organizations that would seek regional action on climate issues from a community-needs-based approach. Further, this effort envisioned mutual cross-border support in advancing legislative objectives on a state-by-state basis. Renew partners in each state would exercise autonomy and the ability to define the details of their respective programs in order to best represent the needs and political realities of their respective areas. In brief, Renew, like the Vermont AFL-CIO, sought to advance what amounted to a Green New Deal for New England.

The Vermont AFL-CIO, along with the Nulhegan Abenaki Tribe and Rights & Democracy, were the first to join in Vermont.[16] We appointed Danielle Bombardier, IBEW, as our representative to the coalition, and we soon got down to work defining our program and making sure the objectives in Vermont included very clear pro-union priorities as well as advocacy for any and all new programs to be funded through progressive means (and not regressive taxation on workers). Later, other environmental organizations such as 350Vermont and the Sunrise Vermont also joined. To date, of the six involved New England states, the Vermont AFL-CIO is the only state labor council to join Renew.

But even as we have sought to bring the Vermont AFL-CIO into alliance with aspects of the environmental movement, we have still found ourselves at odds with a number of mainstream liberal organizations, especially when they advocate for nondemocratic or regressive ways to impose climate action. One such source of conflict has been around the Northeast Transportation Climate Initiative (TCI). This regressive scheme would have, in effect, resulted in a sizable gas tax. In theory, the revenues generated by this project would have then gone to good or progressive programs. However, our United! platform (and now our Vermont AFL-CIO platform) clearly and unambiguously rejected union support for any new regressive taxation (instead asserting that it was time the rich and corporations paid their fair share). Further, TCI had zero components that would have guaranteed a single union job be created through this revenue redistribution, and beyond that, all we saw this program doing was forcing working-class people to pay significantly more to commute to work. By our mind, working people were already struggling, and we did not need to put more burdens on them to solve environmental problems caused by the policies of the 1 percent who reaped profit off of environmental degradation. Thus, it was odd that some TCI supporters from the liberal side of the aisle were surprised and even angry when we came out forcefully against this proposal.[17] Here it struck me that some folks were just so used to campaigns in which promises are made and never kept that it did not even dawn on them that we would run on a program that rejected regressive funding mechanisms and then after winning actually stand by that.

Our rejection of TCI was jumped on by conservative groups in Vermont, such as the Ethen Allen Institute, who themselves opposed any new carbon tax, in an attempt to discredit Democratic politicians who supported it (and in order to keep up pressure against Vermont joining in the scheme).[18] We also garnered national and regional media attention via publications like *Forbes* and the *Boston Herald* as an oppositional voice to the proposed pact (and as the only major labor body taking a public stand on TCI), thus increasing regional trepidation on the program. Further, us not playing ball or remaining silent on this issue (as were the other unions, such as VSEA and NEA) pissed off plenty of liberal politicians in our state capital, but pissing off Democratic politicians who rarely delivered for union members did not concern us. However, when we did get pushback from several Vermont Progressive Party politicians, we took notice. Not because we had any intent of altering our position (our platform was clear on our stance concerning regressive taxation), but because we were interested in developing a deeper relationship with them, so we wanted to understand how some of them came to support such a regressive measure while, essentially, espousing a democratic socialist political approach. We also wanted them to hear directly from us as to why we found the proposal disagreeable from a class-based lens. And finally, we viewed dialogue with this third party, and any other environmental groups who may also have an interest in talking, to be positive in and of itself.

Thus, Lieutenant Governor David Zuckerman, a Progressive, arranged for a meeting between Vermont AFL-CIO leaders, representatives from environmental groups like the Vermont Sierra Club, and key Progressives elected to the Vermont House and Senate. And in January 2020, we met in Zuckerman's office in the statehouse. There, Senator Chris Pearson, who was a strong union ally, expressed frustration that organized labor seemingly did not flag our concerns with TCI earlier in the process (hence Progressives keen to support measures aimed at combating climate change moved forward with TCI while not being aware of potential labor objections). To that I pointed out that we had never been asked our opinion by Progressives or legislators who were engaged in climate issues. So it was not until the process got further along (and not until after United! had come into power just a few months prior) that we came to understand the potential impact on workers and came out forcefully against it as a result.

The meeting was constructive insofar as we all agreed cross-movement communications needed to be better and in the future such dialogue on the left needed to take place earlier on. Toward that end, I assigned our political director to attend the weekly Climate Caucus in the statehouse for the remainder of the session, and Rob Kidd, staffer for the Vermont Sierra Club, offered that he would attend the weekly meetings of the Legislative Workers Caucus (the pro-union grouping of Vermont lawmakers).

In the end, Vermont's Republican governor, Phil Scott, gave signs that he would veto any legislative effort to join TCI. With the AFL-CIO actively opposed, reaching a two-thirds veto override vote seemed unlikely, and the effort did not advance. And even the Vermont Sierra Club, who began as TCI advocates, by January 2021 pulled back and became neutral on the issue out of respect for the Vermont AFL-CIO concerns on its impact on workers. What momentum was left in Vermont for TCI, with liberal environmental groups (with little or no class analysis) like VPIRG and Vermont Natural Resources Council still pushing for joining TCI through administrative action, utterly died in fall 2021 when just about every northeastern state signaled that they too would not join. TCI was dead, and the Vermont AFL-CIO helped kill it.

Likewise, in winter and spring 2022 the Vermont AFL-CIO actively opposed liberal legislation in Montpelier that would have established a regressive, market-based home-heating fuel-pricing penalty scheme aimed at fossil fuels. Called the Clean Heat Standard, as with TCI, the program would have driven up home-heating costs for tens of thousands of working-class households who did not have $10,000 to $15,000 of disposable income to invest in a new, more sustainable heating system.[19] This time we were joined in public opposition by our allies in RAD and 350Vermont. While the bill passed the Vermont House and Senate, it was vetoed by the governor and the override failed by one vote. Here our public resistance contributed to the defeat of this false and regressive climate solution.[20]

But our opposition to TCI and the Clean Heat Standard occurred alongside our public advocacy for the Green New Deal. As such, from 2020, we vocally supported a Vermont bill (introduced by State Senator Anthony Pollina, a Progressive) that would have advanced green projects through recouping tax revenue from the wealthiest 5 percent of Vermonters (those who disproportionately benefited from the Trump tax cuts), and here we were proud to attend a press conference with Pollina in solidarity with the effort. We also continued our work within the Renew New England coalition, which also sought to advance a regional (progressively funded) Green New Deal. While the Pollina bill failed to gain majority support from the Democratic Party–dominated statehouse, the Renew efforts are ongoing.[21]

Supporting the Vermont Building and Construction Trades Council

As the Vermont AFL-CIO supported the Green New Deal and action against climate change, in order to hold United! together it was also important that we engage on the more bread-and-butter issues important to the Building Trades (something past Vermont AFL-CIO administrations had failed to do consistently or effectively). On that, after the 2019 election, we actively supported the Trades effort to pass a fairer system of worker classification enforcement on construction sites through statewide legislation that gave the office of attorney general (as opposed to the Vermont Department of Labor) enforcement authority. We made this one of our top priorities for 2020, and we managed to see this legislation pass (where it had failed in 2019, prior to United! ascending to leadership). We also backed another Trades-led effort to pass a responsible contractor ordinance in Montpelier. The ordinance would require contractors to pay prevailing wages on all major city construction projects as a condition to bid on public work, and in doing so would give union contractors, who already paid good wages with family-sustaining benefits, an advantage in the bid process (as opposed to the race-to-the-bottom approach that otherwise incentivized low pay as a factor in providing low bids). While the Trades were the lead on this effort, the Vermont AFL-CIO actively supported it. With Democratic city councilor Conor Casey shepherding it through the deliberative process,[22] and with support from Progressive mayor Anne Watson,[23] the ordinance passed.

Pivoting from this victory, in 2021, we had a similar ordinance introduced in our largest city, Burlington, by Progressive city councilor Jack Hanson. On this effort, the Vermont AFL-CIO was more of an equal partner with the Trades in seeking its passage and took the lead in gaining and maintaining support from Progressives (who constituted half of the council). We were also pleased to have AFSCME Local 1343 (representing a large portion of public workers in the city) come out in favor of the measure.

In January 2022, in another major victory, the ordinance passed, and it is now in effect in Burlington. It is the intent of the Building Trades and Vermont AFL-CIO to fight to get it passed in the City of Barre (where we also have progressives on the city council).[24]

Also in Burlington, working with Tim LaBombard, president of the Building Trades and, in 2020, a key United! member on the Vermont AFL-CIO leadership, the Vermont AFL-CIO opened a dialogue with the developer of the stalled CityPlace project. CityPlace was to be a major downtown development project in which hundreds of residential units with storefronts at street level would be built in a multistory building. The $100 million–plus project recently lost its financial backer and was in need of financing. Seeing this as an opportunity, I reached out to the developer, Devonwood, and over a number of conversations laid the groundwork for financing to be arranged through the AFL-CIO Housing Investment Trust (HIT), with the money being contingent on 100 percent of the labor being done by the unions and at least 20 percent of the housing units being "affordable." If we closed on the deal, this would be years of good work for our members in the Trades. However, Devonwood had a long history of shady dealings, and they were a far cry from being a reliable partner. In fact, the city was presently in the process of suing Devonwood for breach of a previous agreement.

Working with LaBombard, over a period of months, we secured interest from HIT, had HIT line up Devonwood with a union-favorable mortgage banker to navigate the HUD underwriting process (which was a requirement of HIT financing), and, when told that Devonwood had the disadvantage of not previously doing HUD projects, generated interest from another major developer (with HUD experience) to buy a small interest in the project in order to check that box. However, as a settlement with the city drew near concerning the pending legal dispute, Devonwood, when pressed, would not sign a formal agreement with the Vermont AFL-CIO or Trades committing themselves to the HIT financing and union labor.

So, in the eleventh hour we marshaled our supporters on the city council and asked them to *not* settle their legal dispute until we had commitments from Devonwood on key labor issues. As a result, on February 16, 2021, our friends on the council took the action of delaying the legal settlement for a week. This led to seven days of frantic action in which we sought to rally our allies and drive calls and emails to Mayor Miro Weinberger (Democrat) and City Council President Max Tracy (Progressive) demanding labor commitments on CityPlace as a precondition of any legal settlement. Behind the scenes, LaBombard and I communicated with the mayor and key city council members such as Brian Pine (Progressive). In the end, we secured a commitment to have the future jobs created by the project paid at prevailing wage rates, with priorities being put toward hiring women and workers from BIPOC communities. The prevailing wages was a major victory (one that gave the unions an advantage in the bidding process). But even so, I thought we should have gone further and held out until we had hard guarantees that union jobs were to be a component of the construction. But ultimately this was a Trades issue, and LaBombard felt we should take the win and move on. So, following his lead, that is exactly what we did.

Thus, on February 23, 2021, we told our friends on the city council we now wanted them to resolve the legal dispute with Devonwood with the prevailing wages on CityPlace built in. And with a unanimous vote, it was settled and the improvement was locked in.

While a number of the issues United! has tackled on behalf of and alongside of the Building Trades may not be particularly sexy in a political sense, and while myself and United! would certainly rather see major housing projects (like in the case of CityPlace) be public projects that would ultimately be owned by the city or collectively by the eventual residents, we are dealing with a world that has certain immediate realities to it—private development projects being one of those realities. And here our members in the Trades need to be able to put food on the table for their families.

So even while we agitate for a more forward view of public development, one well beyond the limitations of contemporary capitalism, we also must seek to secure the livelihood of our members in the here and now. And further, by aggressively supporting the Trades on issues they define as priorities, and by doing so in a focused way not previously seen by the state labor council, we were able to signal that United! was committed to having the back of our construction workers. And with this came credibility, and with such credibility came a flexibility in our ability to stake out more leftist positions on other issues without the risk of losing support from the Trades. At the end of the day, the Trades want to know that the Vermont AFL-CIO stands with them where it matters, and if that road is consistently traversed, we will continue to have their support even while we dare to redefine labor politics in many areas where previously a progressive shift was thought untenable.

Alliance with Migrant Justice and Undocumented Workers

One such area where United! has sought to redefine labor politics has been in regard to our support for undocumented workers laboring on Vermont's dairy farms. Here an estimated two thousand workers, largely from Mexico and Central America, have built an organization called Migrant Justice. Migrant Justice is committed to securing better working and housing conditions on farms, winning better pay and benefits like paid sick days, and generally advocating for the fights and interests of the undocumented worker. In 2017, through their Milk with Dignity campaign, Migrant Justice secured an unprecedented agreement with Ben & Jerry's ice cream whereby all dairy farms selling milk to their plants would have to sign on to labor and housing standards set forth by Milk with Dignity, and alleged violations would be subject to review and binding arbitration. Among other things, the agreement made progress on wages, dignified housing, nondiscrimination, paid holidays and vacation, progressive discipline, and just cause. Participating farms would also be paid a premium from Ben & Jerry's that was intended to allow farms to implement the required improvements defined by the agreement. All told, participating farms through Ben & Jerry's constituted 20 percent of the milk produced in Vermont on seventy farms, directly impacting the lives of 260 migrant workers. In short, Migrant Justice was acting as the labor union of the undocumented. And in 2019, they decided to next target the Hannaford supermarket chain, demanding that they only source milk from farms who also sign up to the Milk with Dignity standard.

United! understood that for us to grow power we must break down movement silos and build partnerships of trust with nontraditional allies, and Migrant Justice represented one such group with which we hoped to build a political relationship. Thus, myself and Executive Vice President Tristin Adie reached out to Migrant Justice and arranged for a meeting. In fall 2019, we met with them in Burlington. At this meeting, they explained their struggle, their long-term objectives, and how they intended to further advance the interest of undocumented workers through organizing, political pressure, alliance building, and direct action. Both I and Adie were impressed with their vision and commitment. So, at our November 2019 executive board meeting, we discussed Migrant Justice and how they were essentially doing the work of a union and overwhelmingly voted (with support from Tim LaBombard of the Building Trades) to endorse the Milk with Dignity campaign and to extend a formal invitation to invite Migrant Justice to affiliate with the Vermont AFL-CIO.[25]

With this campaign endorsement in place, the Vermont AFL-CIO, over the coming months and years, would send speakers (including Executive Vice President Tristin Adie and vice presidents for AFT Helen Scott and David Feurzeig) to Migrant Justice rallies in support of Milk with Dignity and on other issues of interest to undocumented workers. We would also support Migrant Justice's demands during the COVID-19 pandemic for undocumented farmworkers to receive crisis pay from the state (which they were successful in securing). Together, the Vermont AFL-CIO and Migrant Justice would go on to jointly organize several actions and speak from the same podium (along with other partners), including the 2020 May Day car caravan for essential workers in Burlington and the 2021 May Day demonstration in Montpelier. And following the five-hundred-strong 2021 May Day action in front of the statehouse in Montpelier, I and a number of other union members were happy to walk a Milk with Dignity picket line at the Hannaford supermarket in Barre (and we walked their picket line again, this time at the Hannaford in South Burlington, on May Day 2022). And conversely, Migrant Justice would support various union actions, including a 2020 picket called for by City of Burlington workers (AFSCME Local 1343) against austerity. Thus, the Vermont AFL-CIO and Migrant Justice, since 2019, have worked in solidarity with each other, mutually amplifying our voices on issues important to workers (both documented and not).

Bringing the Fight to the Bosses: Pandemic, Picket Lines, and Member Action

In March 2020 (just four months after United! took office), the COVID-19 pandemic struck, and the economy would soon go into crisis.[26] Fear and uncertainty were on the rise among workers. Immediately, the Vermont AFL-CIO recognized the gravity of the situation and began to advocate for a greatly expanded social safety net to be implemented by the government and for employers to take steps to better guarantee safer working conditions. We demanded, among other things, that unemployment benefits be extended to workers not traditionally eligible, that an eviction moratorium be enacted for the duration of the crisis, that essential workers receive hazard pay, that essential workers (especially those in the health care sector) be afforded adequate personal protective equipment, that free childcare be provided for essential workers (in light of schools being shut down), that school food programs continue to keep lower-income children fed (through free meal delivery or pickup), that paid sick days be afforded to all, and that high-risk workers (even in essential fields) be afforded the right to stay home with pay. We further asked our members to express support for our demands to their elected government representatives (and we set up email actions to better facilitate such communications). And on March 18, 2020, in Burlington, as the statewide lockdown was going into effect, we took part in an outdoor (socially distant) press conference amplifying a number of pandemic-related action steps we saw as necessary to better safeguard the health and interest of workers with several allied organizations, including Rights & Democracy, Migrant Justice, the Vermont Progressive Party, and other left organizations.[27]

In short, the pandemic not only forced the Vermont AFL-CIO and the broader labor movement to recalibrate their immediate priorities, but also laid bare the contradictions and failures of contemporary capitalism as well as the weakness of our common social safety net.[28] Where many highly paid management positions were suddenly exposed as nonessential (or constituting work that one was able to do from the relative safety of the home), many more lower-paid jobs such as custodians and retail food workers were recognized as essential and a core element of maintaining the basic functioning of society. And even though we, together with countless allies, were largely successful in seeing government action carried out to meet our immediate demands, the fact that these steps were necessary highlighted just how hollow our social safety net was as a state and as a nation.[29]

Therefore, the Vermont AFL-CIO resolved not only to fight to implement temporary measures during the pandemic, but also to use the weaknesses exposed through the crisis to advocate for a new, more worker-centric social contract. We also saw with clear eyes that the pandemic-related economic crisis that emerged would carry with it a fight regarding austerity versus public investment. And here we knew that this struggle would be a defining conflict in the months to come. But even as we foresaw this coming conflict, the very real public health dangers in the prevaccine period compelled the labor movement to temporarily rethink how we conducted mass actions and exerted public pressure in such a way that our members' lives would not be unduly put at risk.[30] As such, rallies and pickets using personal vehicles became a mainstay for a period of months.

The first mass action in Vermont against austerity came in April, when the Vermont state college chancellor, Democrat Jeb Spaulding, proposed the shuttering of three state college campuses as the means to address lost revenue and chronic underfunding. Vermont state college workers were represented by AFT and VSEA. When the chancellor sought to close down campuses and eliminate five hundred good union jobs, the public backlash and union response was swift.

In a matter of days, students, alumni, and Vermonters generally circulated a petition against the closings, generating tens of thousands of signatures. The AFT further passed a no-confidence vote concerning the chancellor. Then, on April 20, thousands of Vermonters converged on the statehouse in Montpelier, all in their vehicles, demanding that the campuses remain open. Here hundreds of vehicles adorned with signs, flags, and banners circled in front of the capital, congesting the streets. The rally, the first major one in the pandemic era, was supported by AFT members and included AFL-CIO leaders (such as myself) who were apt to show solidarity. The message was received loud and clear by the politicians. The thought of shuttering campuses was rapidly shelved, and additional public money was allocated to keeping the colleges going. Not long after, the chancellor would resign.

Then, on May Day 2020, Vermonters engaged in a second car caravan, this one in Burlington and in support of essential workers.[31] Organized by a coalition of organizations including the Vermont AFL-CIO, AFT Local 5221, UE Local 203, the Vermont Workers Center, Migrant Justice, Black Lives Matter of Greater Burlington, Rural Vermont, DSA, 350Vermont, and Burlington Tenants United, some of the demands included hazard pay for all essential workers and a moratorium on evictions during the pandemic. The caravan, which included five hundred workers, drove through the city, stopping at various points and halting traffic to hear from speakers. The speakers delivered their messages through a blowhorn, with their words being piped into each car through a link accessible by way of a cell phone. In front of the Vermont Department of Labor, on behalf of the Vermont AFL-CIO, I said the following:

> We demand crisis pay for all essential workers. We demand a moratorium on evictions and mortgage foreclosures. We demand that we rebuild our economy through a New Deal, a Green New Deal, not through austerity and cuts!
>
> We will not go back to the status quo. We will not go back to business as usual.
>
> The ten thousand members of the Vermont AFL-CIO stand in solidarity with all of you. And we demand that the social benefits being offered during the crisis and after be extended to farmworkers regardless of immigration status!
>
> Now is the time to fight against neoliberalism! Now is the time to fight against austerity! Now is the time to fight, together, for a New Deal! ... Say *no* to politics as usual! Say *yes* to solidarity!

In the weeks and months following this May Day demonstration, the eviction moratorium was passed, and thousands of Vermont workers, including health care workers, first responders, migrant farmworkers, and thousands of home care providers (the latter of which were organized into AFSCME Local 4802) received hazard pay or other direct cash payments.[32]

Following May Day, on May 14, a third car caravan was organized, again in Burlington, by United Academics AFT Local 3203. At the time, the University of Vermont was looking to massively cut the hours of unionized adjuncts, which would have a devastating impact on their take-home pay. In fact, university management was seeking to reduce their pay by 25 percent. One hundred union members, including United! supporters such as District Vice President Sarah Alexander, and allies took part in this rally, which circled UVM administrative buildings. I too was there as state labor council president. In conjunction with additional actions carried out over the course of months, by the end of September 2020, management backed down and largely restored the paid hours they originally sought to claw back from adjuncts.

Come summer 2020, with mass uncertainty and public fear concerning the COVID-19 pandemic, and with the economy in free fall (and the City of Burlington projecting a $10 million budget shortfall), it was with great concern that AFSCME Local 1343 received a communication from Burlington's mayor, Democrat Miro Weinberger, requesting the city contract be opened in order to roll back planned raises and increases to on-call pay.[33] The mayor told AFSCME (and IBEW, firefighters, and police who also had union contracts with the city) that failure of the unions to agree to givebacks would result in layoffs.

While we had already seen attacks on union workers and public programs in higher education, we had not yet witnessed such assaults attempted on the municipal level. Thus, what began to take shape in Burlington felt like it could be just the first in a series of conflicts. How the unions dealt with this threat here could have reverberations across the state. This was not lost on me, the Vermont AFL-CIO, or AFSCME 1343.

AFSCME 1343's response, through local president Damion Gilbert (a key United! supporter) was unflinching: after months of struggling through the pandemic, there was no fucking way AFSCME was going to reach down into the pockets of members to balance the city budget. Rather, union workers would fight back to resist any givebacks and job cuts. COVID would not be used to advance austerity if 1343 had something to say about it, and the Vermont AFL-CIO would stand by AFSCME come what may. After all, Burlington prided itself on being a progressive city, and if we allowed the interests of our members to be rolled back in the Queen City it would set the tone for smaller communities throughout the state. We had to hold the line.

The mayor first made demands of the unions in May 2020. Rapidly Gilbert and 1343 vice president Jesse Greeno informed their members and began to educate the rank and file about how if they were to remain steadfast against opening the contracts, they needed to be prepared to take action if they were to effectively push back against the threatened layoffs. Thus, coming out of a local meeting, it was decided that Gilbert would remain a firm "no" on concessions while the local would set in motion an informational picket for June 9. Even so, recognizing the health concerns relating to condensed public gatherings due to the COVID-19 pandemic, it was deemed that the picket, as was utilized in previous actions, would be a "car picket," in which union members and supporters would remain in their vehicles while circling city hall. Further, the stationary aspects of the picket (at the start and end) would take place in more spacious outdoor areas where members could maintain social distancing while listening to speakers.

Gilbert, Greeno, and I moved quickly in building the action. We knew that a strong show of force would spook the mayor and give him reason to pause. We also knew that other communities would be looking to see what unfolded in Burlington as a predictor of what they could expect, on a smaller scale, in their towns if faced with a similar dynamic. From the start, we saw this as a first shot across the bow concerning the looming fight of austerity versus a New Deal approach to the worsening economic situation.

While the IBEW (who represented workers at the city-owned power plant), firefighters, and police unions, like AFSCME, all declined the mayor's request to open the contracts, they were not ready to take the confrontational approach AFSCME was planning as a means to defend their jobs. So even while Gilbert repeatedly reached out to leaders in these three unions, it was becoming clear that this would need to be an AFSCME undertaking. Even so, the 250 AFSCME city workers would by no means be alone in this fight. The local also represented support staff in Burlington Schools and workers in a dozen other shops throughout Chittenden and Franklin Counties. And here 1343 explained to those members that if the mayor was successful in pushing through austerity in Burlington, it would only be a matter of time before such austerity came to their cities, towns, and workplaces.

While Gilbert worked to mobilize his local members, as Vermont AFL-CIO president I went about seeking support and solidarity from other unions and community organizations. And within two weeks, dozens endorsed the picket. In fact, by June 8, the day before the picket, forty-five unions and organizations, including Migrant Justice and 350Vermont, supported us.[34]

As picket organizing got underway, as we did with the previous year's action against Scott Walker, we approached the mobilization in a very public way. In fact, we were happy to telegraph our every step to the mayor. We wanted him and his Democratic Party allies to clearly understand that there is a price to pay for attacking union workers and that AFSCME, the Vermont AFL-CIO, and the labor movement as a whole, after months of dealing with the dangers and uncertainty of the pandemic, was in a fighting mood. We also kept in close communication with city councilors from the Progressive Party (which was the largest party on the council and which 1343 and the Vermont AFL-CIO had endorsed as a slate in the previous winter's election). And as the pressure mounted on the mayor, certainly with thoughts of the huge Scott Walker picket of 2019, he backed down; at the end of May, he announced that he had found the means to balance the budget without the unions having to agree to concessions or job cuts. This was a win.

But when Gilbert asked the mayor to put a no-job-cut commitment in writing, he demurred, saying that while the immediate crisis had passed, he could not say what the future would hold. And with that, 1343 saw that the fight was not concluded; the battle may have been won, but the war was not yet over. Thus, the union would go forward under the premise that a show of strength now would serve as a deterrent to any future thought of attacking the livelihood of city workers. The local would also pivot to a more general footing whereby the picket, while still focused on the interests of city workers, would also seek to embrace the broader struggles of workers across Vermont as they struggled against the pandemic and the uncertainties of the economic crisis.

On June 1, 2020, Gilbert briefed the city council on the victory and the plans to move forward with the picket. Gilbert also relayed the union's support for a proposal coming out of the Progressive Party Caucus to change the city charter to allow for a wealth tax to better fund public services. The following, in part, were the words Gilbert spoke:

> AFSCME recognizes that the [COVID-19] health crisis has become an economic crisis. We see that. But if we are to enter a new Great Depression, we must be prepared to come out of it through a *New Deal*, and *not* through pay cuts and job cuts. Now is the time for increased public spending. Now is the time to ask the rich to pay their fair share. Therefore we support the proposed city charter change calling for the local ability to implement a progressive income tax on the wealthiest Burlington residents. And here we invite this city council and the working people of Burlington to agree.
>
> We further ask for the commitment of this city council to stand with us in *never* asking any union in the city to reopen a contract in

order to make concessions; *not* laying off any union workers; rehiring *all* seasonal workers and agreeing to recognize them as union members with access to our grievance procedure and just cause protection; no reduction of city services; no privatization of city services; no cuts to school staff or programs ...

At this point, Local 1343 and the Vermont AFL-CIO observed that dozens of different unions and organizations stepped up when city workers asked for solidarity. And wanting to return the favor, it seemed only right that the local (and the Vermont AFL-CIO) should recognize the validity and urgency of all the struggles being waged by our allies (and not only focus on our more narrow self-interests). Hence, I worked with Gilbert and Greeno in putting together a public statement that sought to link these fights being engaged in by allies and to articulate that in fact these were all one fight: justice and solidarity versus austerity and the interests of the elite.[35] So on June 3, 2020, the three of us signed a document stating twenty demands. This communication was as follows:

Demand a New Deal—No to Racism—No to Austerity—Union Yes!
An Attack on One Is an Attack on All
WE DEMAND A NEW DEAL!
NEW DEAL: We demand the federal government, the State of Vermont and municipalities commit to an economic recovery effort through a progressively funded NEW DEAL that puts the working class first and gives rise to a more directly democratic society free of racism, discrimination, oppression, and economic exploitation of the laboring classes;

IN BURLINGTON WORKERS & PUBLIC COME FIRST: We demand that the City of Burlington and mayor NOT cut (nonmanagement) wages, jobs, or public services—not now—not ever. The City of Burlington and the mayor must not ask or expect any of the city unions to open their contracts to make concessions. Where cuts must take place they will come from the top—specifically from political appointees, upper management, and police department brass first! Let it further be known that AFSCME Local 1343 supports the City of Burlington canceling any and all construction agreements with private nonunion companies and instead use in-house union labor or union labor from within the Vermont Building Trades Council of the AFL-CIO for any and all city construction or renovation projects. We further demand that the city and mayor sign a contract with IATSE Local 919 so that skilled union labor, paid at livable wage rates, are used to efficiently and professionally meet the city's performance needs. And finally, we require that any business or entity subject to the city's livable wage ordinance also be subject to a card check union recognition procedure;

UNION RIGHTS: We demand that the State of Vermont pass pro-union legislation whereby workers have the tools they need to form a labor union of their own. Here we require card check for all public sector workers. We further require that the state (and local governments) pass legislation that compels private businesses to also implement card check union recognition (and other labor rights) through a Labor Progress Agreement (LPA) whenever said private business seeks to gain government contracts involving public money and/or when said business gains advantages through tax benefits and/or when said business apply for a state or local license;

CITIES & TOWNS MUST HOLD THE LINE: We demand that all municipalities maintain their current jobs and public services;

MUNICIPAL WEALTH TAX: We demand that cities and towns seek charter changes to allow municipalities to implement a progressive local income tax and luxury tax only on their wealthiest residents to achieve adequate revenues;

PRIVATE EMPLOYERS MUST RESPECT WORKERS & UNIONS: We demand that private employers respect the rights of workers, honor all existing union contracts, and that management at all nonunion shops commit to voluntary card check recognition when their workers choose to form a union. Further we, like the Workers Caucus, support the Colburn-Kornheiser "Fair Jobs Recovery Plan" and call on it to be adopted by the Vermont House and Senate;

CRISIS PAY: We demand that ALL essential workers, including farmworkers regardless of immigration status, receive crisis pay;

SAFE WORKING CONDITIONS FOR HEALTH CARE WORKERS: We demand that ALL medical workers (and ALL essential workers) be provided adequate and free personal protective equipment;

ENACT COVID-19 WORKERS COMP: We demand that workers' comp cover any and all essential workers who may become sick with COVID-19;

NO STATE JOB CUTS OR CUTS TO SOCIAL PROGRAMS: We demand that the State of Vermont NOT cut nonmanagement or supervisory pay, jobs, or social services delivered on behalf of the public, and that the unionized state workers receive paid family medical leave as was agreed to during bargaining;

STATE AID FOR SCHOOLS, VERMONT STATE COLLEGES, & DESIGNATED AGENCIES: We demand that the State of Vermont increase spending on social programs and provide more robust economic support for local school districts, the Vermont state college system, and designated agencies.

NO CLOSINGS OF VERMONT STATE COLLEGE CAMPUSES: We demand that NO Vermont state college campus be closed, that VSC and UVM nonmanagement workers suffer no layoffs or pay cuts, and that the State of Vermont implement free in-state tuition for all Vermonters;

INVEST IN LOCAL INFRASTRUCTURE: We demand that the State of Vermont make significant additional funds available to municipalities and school districts for local public infrastructure projects with the requirement that any contracted services paid for with these funds be done only with employers that are union and pay prevailing wages. We further demand that Vermont municipalities pass responsible contractor ordinances whereby ALL major construction projects require workers to be paid the prevailing wage;

STATE INVESTMENT IN RENEWABLE ENERGY: We demand that the State of Vermont make significant public investment in renewable energy and efficiency, and that all construction jobs created by such projects be awarded to unionized contractors whereby all workers are provided a prevailing wage. We further support the intent that any new renewable energy plants built with public money remain publicly owned and maintained/operated with union labor after completion;

EXPANDING THE SOCIAL SAFETY NET: We demand that the State of Vermont commit to legislation that further builds a stronger social system whereby all workers, among other things, have health care as a human right, earn a livable wage, receive paid family medical leave, have adequate paid sick days, have access to dignified affordable housing, and do not suffer food insecurity;

NO TO RACISM AND DISCRIMINATION: We demand that the State of Vermont commit to combating racism and discrimination in all its forms and put an end to racial profiling, and other practices of discrimination based on economic class, gender, immigration status, sexuality, disability, or nationality;

WOMAN'S RIGHT TO CHOOSE: We demand that the State of Vermont remain steadfast in its commitment to defending a woman's right to control her own body;

FIRST NATION RIGHTS: We demand that the State of Vermont recognize and support the sovereignty rights of the four Abenaki Tribes;

TAX THE RICH, GREEN NEW DEAL BONDS, & STATE BANK: We demand that the revenue needed to fund these NEW DEAL projects be attained through the progressive taxation of the wealthy and on corporations (not on low-income and working-class people!). We further support the creation of Vermont Green New Deal bonds as a means to raise additional revenue. We also support the formation of a Vermont state bank so that we can better retain our public wealth and invest it for public good;

DIRECT DEMOCRACY: We demand that the legislature begin the process for adoption of a constitutional amendment whereby a directly democratic town-meeting-based referendum system of self-government be implemented throughout the Green Mountains. We require this expansion of democratic rights so as the gains working people make through this NEW DEAL can be effectively defended for generations to come.

United!

The Lead Organizers of the June 9 Picket:

Damion Gilbert, President of AFSCME Local 1343

Jesse Greeno, Vice President of AFSCME Local 1343

David Van Deusen, President of the Vermont AFL-CIO

Days after the statement was released, even as more organizations endorsed the coming picket, the Vermont AFL-CIO received communications from the VSEA, NEA and AFT-Vermont. All expressed concern and degrees of anger that I and 1343 officers would dare to issue such demands. Their argument was that their unions had endorsed the 1343 picket to protect city jobs and not to commit to a progressive program of this nature. During a call I had with Vermont NEA executive director Jeff Fannon, he expressed displeasure in the unilateral nature of the statement, while still adding that many of the issues listed were "good causes."[36] As a result, the NEA would not be putting any organizing behind the effort and, in essence, their members would not be attending (or so he said). I found it ironic that he would forcefully assert such a point about unilateral action less than two years after he, without first consulting with AFSCME or the Vermont AFL-CIO, had his union introduce a bill in Montpelier that would have eliminated collective bargaining rights over health care in the schools. VSEA, for their part, informed me that their planned speaker, First Vice President Aimee Towne, was no longer going to attend (although John Davy, president of VSEA's Chittenden chapter, who was outside the control of VSEA headquarters, would still be present along with a number of their more progressive members). AFT-Vermont also failed to mobilize a contingent for the picket (but again, rank-and-file AFT members would certainly be there regardless).[37]

What all these unions had in common was that they all took part in the Working Vermont coalition (a coalition the Vermont AFL-CIO left in 2018 but which AFT-Vermont unilaterally chose to still be part of anyway). And in the case of VSEA and AFT-Vermont, the official leadership of these groups actively opposed United! and the progressive unionism we advocated for in the lead-up to the 2019 election (and beyond). The fact that the backlash occurred within the same forty-eight-hour window made it plain that the response was coordinated.[38] It was also significant that we received *zero* complaints or concerns from any other union, endorsing organization, or even from a single rank-and-file union member, be they from a core United! affiliate, AFT, VSEA, or NEA. *Bottom line, these were objections coming from the top leaderships of those unions who were hostile to the kind of unionism United! sought to advance.*

On June 9, 2020, the day of the picket, we gathered in a parking lot across from the Department of Public Works building. There, 1343 members from the schools set up at the entrance, giving out AFSCME signs and shirts to all who entered. Over a hundred cars lined up, adorned with union signs and messages against austerity. A number of speakers, including AFSCME 1343 vice president Jesse Greeno, John Davy of VSEA, Ben Luce of AFT Local 3180 (state colleges), Progressive state representatives Selene Colburn (a member of AFT) and Brian Cina (a member of AFSCME), and Ashley Smith of DSA (a member of UAW Local 1981), addressed the crowd. The speakers, in addition to stating support for 1343 city workers, called on all Vermont unions to provide mutual aid when facing attacks (and not only focus on their narrow self-interests), demanded a New Deal economic recovery effort, and affirmed labor's unqualified solidarity with Black Lives Matter and the related longshoreman strike that had shut down US ports on the West Coast just days before. Following the speeches, led by a group of union members on motorcycles, the caravan left, heading toward city hall.[39]

Together our hundred-plus vehicles slowly snaked our way downtown. Each vehicle displayed signs demanding no layoffs or austerity in the face of the general economic decline. Union members leaned on their horns, and some chanted union slogans out their windows through blowhorns. We circled city hall a half-dozen times. There was not a person in downtown Burlington that day, including the mayor, who was not made aware of labor's presence (and power).

The caravan ended at the top of a city parking garage that itself was ringed by large green and white balloons marked with AFSCME and Vermont AFL-CIO messages of union power. Floating far above the city, they were visible to pedestrians down below on the streets to read. Vermont AFL-CIO district vice president Dwight Brown (also a member of Local 1343) got things started not only by demanding that the city not lay off workers or cut public services during hard times, but further by asserting that the union fight for economic justice could not be divorced from the fight for racial justice and declaring Vermont labor's solidarity with Black Lives Matter and the demonstrations going on throughout the county at that time following the murder of George Floyd.

After Dwight Brown, speakers included myself, Mike Leonard (a progressive member of the Vermont NEA), Rosie of Migrant Justice, Helen Scott of United Academics AFT Local 3203 (also a district vice president of the Vermont AFL-CIO), Andy Decelles of UE Local 203, Burlington

Progressive city councilors led by Zoraya Hightower, and Liz Medina of UAW Local 2322 (also a district vice president of the Vermont AFL-CIO). Medina, in fiery tones, called for a union-based Green New Deal to put America back to work and for the nationalization of key industries.[40]

A theme that ran through all the speeches was that an attack on one must be understood as an attack on all, and that organized labor needed to be unified in its struggle to see through a union-based New Deal economic recovery effort. All participating unions also confirmed solidarity with Local 1343 city workers.

Closing out this powerful display of progressive interunion solidarity was AFSCME Local 1343 president Damion Gilbert. Gilbert, at the time employed in the city parking garages, congratulated his members for a successful picket and thanked the many allied unions and organizations that had sent a delegation to the picket. Gilbert concluded by again affirming that 1343 would be there for other unions when they needed support and challenged union leaders to do more to fight against racial discrimination.[41] Union members left that day feeling fired up.

Following the picket, as I here put pen to paper, Burlington's mayor has never again asked that we open our contracts, nor has he threatened layoffs. Also, even as economic fear continued to grow in other communities, we did not see any attempts by municipalities to carry out mass layoffs or cuts in services.[42] And as the federal government later began to issue direct economic support to communities throughout the United States, the immediate danger passed. For unionized workers, the dooms-day we had seen on the horizon, and the mass fights that such would precipitate, did not come into being. Even so, the AFSCME 1343 Burlington picket was significant for two reasons. First, it set a fighting tone for public sector workers throughout Vermont. Second, through the struggle and by seeing solidarity extended to them on their specific issues from unions and organizations that did not have a direct self-interest in the outcome of this fight, 1343 came to better understand the interconnectedness of their fight and the many other fights being waged in different sectors. Thus, the local rallied not only for their own rights and dignity, but also for those of its natural allies, such as rank-and-file members of other unions, 350Vermont, Migrant Justice, and Black Lives Matter. And here, the broader movement for change took one step further down the road of oppositional unity to a status quo geared to serve the few at the expense of the many. Finally, the Vermont AFL-CIO observed that while the top union leadership in less progressive labor bodies like AFT-Vermont, VSEA, and NEA might push back against the Vermont AFL-CIO when it sought to define labor action beyond the more narrow self-interest of a specific bargaining unit, at the end of the day that would not prevent their rank-and-file members from supporting us and that which we sought to articulate and achieve.

CHAPTER VI

Concerning Elections: Rejecting the Premise of the Democrats and Building a More Direct Democracy

> It is better to vote for what you want and not get it
> than to vote for what you don't want and get it.
> —Eugene V. Debs

The 2019 Political Summit and a New Electoral Direction

It was no accident that United!, in part, won the 2019 election campaigning on a need to break from a Democratic Party that consistently failed to deliver on labor issues. And it was not a coincidence that powerful figures in the Democratic Party actively backed our challengers.[1] While it was clear to me and United! that, now in office, we had to follow through with this promised break, we also recognized that how we made the break mattered and that such a break would not be a turn toward the electoral right, but rather to the further left. It also felt clear that members were not interested in a total break from elections (as Vermont is a state with higher voter turnout compared to other states), but rather in a rethink of how elections were approached.[2]

United! saw the need for the break to come out of a rank-and-file-driven process, in which members would be asked to reflect on and provide guidance concerning any new political reorientation. Thus, as a first step, in fall 2019, we formed a political committee, chaired by our volunteer-in-politics, Omar Fernandez (APWU). This three-person committee would review the effectiveness and ineffectiveness of the state labor council's political actions concerning elections and political parties and would aim to provide recommendations for a new path. In addition, the executive board decided to rebrand the annual COPE (Committee on Political Education) Conference as a major "political summit" where the members would hear the recommendations of this committee and would

Striking UAW workers from Goddard College demonstrating in front of the Vermont Statehouse, spring 2023.

be asked to vote on a radically different way we would engage politically going forward. We set the date for this summit for December 7, 2019. The location would be the Old Socialist Labor Party Hall in Barre, Vermont. The slogan for the summit was "No More Politics as Usual."

On December 7, affiliates from across Vermont sent delegations, and over eighty members representing a wide cross-section of workers (from college professors to snowplow drivers) were present. By comparison, in

2018, the previous COPE Conference, in addition to being woefully boring, had about thirty members attend. And where previous COPE Conferences largely consisted of little more than elected politicians speaking at us for a day, telling us what a great job they were doing, and providing little meaningful space for members to define our political direction, this summit aimed to spark a wide-ranging conversation about the nature of politics, where various parties stood on unions and society as such, and how leaders of other unions and allied organizations thought about the broad question of political engagement. Here we allowed both allies and (sometimes) adversaries to address our members. The decision to allow for such a wide cross-section of viewpoints (and not just the hard left) was intentional, as United! did not want to be seen as seeking to stack the deck toward a preordained end. Thus, organizations slated to address our members included the Vermont Progressive Party (Lieutenant Governor David Zuckerman and State Senator Anthony Pollina, the party chair), the Democratic Socialists of America (State Representative Brian Cina), and even the Democratic Party (Terje Anderson, party chair; Representative Joanne Donovan, chair of the Legislative Workers Caucus; and Conor Casey, Montpelier city councilor).[3] Beyond parties, we also had the Vermont NEA (Tev Kelman and President Don Tinney), VSEA (John Davy), UE (Andrew Sullivan of Local 255), Vermont Workers Center (Amy Lester), and Rights & Democracy (Executive Director James Haslam).

In short, our goal here was for our members to hear a wide cross-section of political thought, not just ideas consistent with the United! platform, as a means to inform their position as the conference built toward a deliberative conclusion. We also made a priority of facilitating a question-and-answer session and discussion between our members and each speaker.

Of all the speakers, it was Democratic Party chair Terje Anderson who received the most fire from our members. To him, our members were relentless on questioning and attacking his party for insufficiently supporting labor legislation such as card check, a fair means of enforcing worker classification in construction, and not adopting universal livable wage standards for all. The frustrations and anger directed at him from our rank and file (unprompted by the United! leadership) were telling and foreshadowed that this conference would end with a new political path divorced from our record of uncritically backing the Democrats.

Last to go at the summit was Omar Fernandez. Fernandez reported the recommendations of the political committee. He argued that we, as a labor movement, must take a much more critical approach to endorsing politicians, that the number of endorsements we make be reserved for the few labor champions in the statehouse, and that we consider reaching out to third parties (including the Vermont Progressive Party and the Movement for a People's Party) as an alternative to Democrats and Republicans. After Fernandez spoke, the floor was open to broad discussion and debate.

The conversation among the membership was extended and passionate. While most seemed to support a break with the Democrats, some, including members of the Building Trades, cautioned against a hard break and worried that such a move would further weaken our ability to pass pro-union legislation. However, it was also argued that in 2018 we effectively got nothing passed, so risking a new approach to politics, at worst, would not diminish our returns below 2018 levels. After the general debate reached maturity, as president of the Vermont AFL-CIO, I took the floor.

I thanked members for engaging in this constructive debate, and I asked that they consider all they had heard on this day. I asked them to weigh the words from political figures against the measurable results we had witnessed over recent years. I asked them to consider which politicians and parties walked picket lines with us and which seemed to only take an interest in labor during election season.[4] I further stated my opinion that the Vermont AFL-CIO should not be choosing between two devils, but rather that we should only ever stand with those who have stood with us. And finally, I stated that in my view it was time for us to be telling the politicians what they need to do, and not them telling us what we should settle for.

With that, I read out loud a proposed resolution I had previously drafted that, if adopted, would commit the Vermont AFL-CIO to defining nonnegotiable priorities at the start of each legislative session. Then, any political party (not individual members of a caucus) that did not back these priorities or were responsible for said priorities not making progress toward being passed as part of legislation would face a two-year endorsement moratorium for all Vermont AFL-CIO election endorsements for the Vermont House and Senate. For example, assuming the Democrats were the majority in the state capital, if the Vermont AFL-CIO were to say that the minimum wage needed to be raised by one dollar an hour, and if the speaker of the House failed to advance the related bill, or if enough Democrats did not vote in favor to allow it to pass, then the entire party would suffer a two-year freeze in AFL-CIO endorsements and electoral support. Such a moratorium, if triggered, could only be overridden in select cases by a two-thirds vote of the executive board. The resolution also called for the Vermont AFL-CIO to seek to cultivate a closer alliance with the democratic socialist Vermont Progressive Party (while retaining our independence).

My thought here was as follows: enacting such a policy would allow all the parties (Republican, Democrat, and Progressive) to be first put on notice not only about what we needed to see pass, but also about what the consequence would be if they did not back us. Thus, although we did not come out of the gate full throttle, there was a built-in escalation should our legislative requirements not be met. In this way, the policy did not single out any one party, did not have as a starting point an action that would alienate our members who identified with one of the capitalist parties, and provided each caucus an equal opportunity to effectively stand with us or against us, and if the parties failed to back us, our backing away from them would be unavoidable. Further, this incremental (cause and effect) approach allowed for us to not get ahead of our membership. On the contrary, our members would see who our allies and enemies were and would become educated by how this process unfolded. Finally, this policy would also allow for exceptions to be made (by a two-thirds vote of the leadership) so that we could be pragmatic in specific instances (and not a slave to our own rules).

After I had made my case, and following more rank-and-file discussion, the resolution was overwhelmingly passed. It was further voted that our three legislative priorities for the session would be card check, establishing a fairer system of worker classification enforcement, and establishing a universal livable wage for all workers.

The executive board met immediately after the closing of the summit. Acting on the democratic will of our members as expressed in their votes, the executive board then formally adopted these positions (again by an overwhelming vote in the affirmative). With the adoption of this policy (and our three legislative priorities), the Vermont AFL-CIO took a major step in the direction of decoupling labor from the Democrats.[5]

Our political summit was a great success. Not only did it involve more rank-and-file members than any COPE Conference in memory, but it also asked members to help define a new political direction. It did not assume that what we had done in the past was what we should do in the future, nor did it serve as a soapbox for politicians asking for votes. Instead it sought to expand the understanding of the nature of political engagement itself and to put labor back into the driver's seat. The summit also included participation from affiliates like the machinists (who we supported on their strike), who were not present at the convention. We already were seeing growth in local participation. However, it was also of note that with the exception of the professors at UVM (Local 3203), AFT delegations were not present. Nor were the firefighters or USW Local 4. It seemed that AFT-Vermont president Deb Snell still had not walked back into the union hall.

The 2020 Legislative Session: Endorsement Moratorium Triggered

Soon after our political summit, in January 2020, the legislative session began. Over the next five months, with our new legislative and electoral policy in place, we succeeded in passing legislation creating a fairer way to enforce working classification rules on construction sites (placing oversight with the Vermont attorney general's office), and we worked with a plethora of organizations supporting legislation that resulted in the Vermont minimum wage going from $10.96 to $12.55 an hour by January 1, 2022. Both of these bills were supported by the Democrats and the Progressives.[6] And while we were successful in forcing the Vermont House to hold hearings on card check, this bill did not move under the Democratic leadership (and the Republican Party also failed to demonstrate support for it).[7] Thus, in May 2020 (at the end of the session), the endorsement moratorium was triggered against the Democrats and Republicans. The Progressives, for their part, did not suffer such a sanction, as to a member their caucus supported all of our priorities and worked closely with us throughout the winter.

While we had failed to move card check, progress on two of our three top priorities marked a great improvement over our 2018 record (before United! came into office). So even while we fell short of a trifecta, we did demonstrate that it was possible to take a hard line with the capitalist parties and to not go backward in our ability to see legislative progress on union concerns.[8]

Burlington City Elections: Backing the Vermont Progressive Party

As the 2020 Town Meeting Day approached (March 3), AFSCME Local 1343 president Damion Gilbert approached me about the upcoming City of Burlington elections.[9] Local 1343, you will recall, represented city workers. Gilbert expressed that he lacked confidence in the Democratic mayor and his party allies on city council.[10] Therefore, he was planning to invite both Progressive and Democratic candidates to one of his local meetings, with the hope of leading his membership toward an endorsement of the Progressive slate for city council. His calculation was that the Progressives, who are a democratic socialist party in orientation, had consistently stated their support for organized labor, and their caucus in the statehouse had stood with the unions, thick and thin, on issues like card check. So, if we could help grow their numbers on the Burlington City Council (Burlington, with a population of forty-two thousand, being Vermont's largest city), the unions would be better positioned not only in bargaining city contracts, but also in advancing local priorities that impact workers in general. Their candidates in 2020 were Zoraya Hightower (Ward 1), Max Tracy (Ward 2), Brian Pine (Ward 3), Nate Lantieri (Ward 5), Ali Dieng (Ward 7), and Jane Stromberg (Ward 8).[11] The idea appealed to me and I brought it to the Vermont AFL-CIO Executive Board.[12]

Then, on February 18, a week after meeting with the Progressive candidates face to face and gaining commitments on a number of union priorities, the Vermont AFL-CIO Executive Board voted to endorse their entire slate.[13] We rapidly followed the endorsement up with internal outreach to our members, a campaign ad on the side of a city bus, radio ads on five stations, and a social media ad buy. On Election Day, we also had members at polling stations supporting their candidates. The Vermont AFL-CIO was not alone in this effort. Local 1343 members also voted to endorse their slate on February 24. Also backing Progressives were the local DSA chapter, Rights & Democracy, and several other left organizations.

It is of note that part of United!'s thinking on the radio and bus ads was to give the Democrats reason for concern in a broader way. We wanted the Democrats, who were already aware of our new electoral policy and potential for endorsement moratorium, to see in a very public way that when and if the Vermont AFL-CIO chose to more fully ally itself with a party to the left that we had the will and the means to cause Election Day problems for them. We wanted this thought on their minds as the 2020 legislative session in the state capital played itself out. In short, the implied threat was that there is in fact a price to pay for a party to be insufficiently pro-union.

On Election Day, our candidates won a resounding victory, with five of the six members of the Progressive slate prevailing in their contests.[14] And with that, coupled with the two Progressive city council seats that were already secured in Perri Freeman (Central District) and Jack Hanson (East District), for the moment, the Progressives gained a majority on the city council for the first time in a generation.[15]

A Deepening Alliance with the Vermont Progressive Party

Helping to win these elections would matter over the course of the next two years. With the Progressives as the largest party on the city council, the Vermont AFL-CIO and Local 1343 were in a much stronger position to fight back (and win) against the mayor's threat of layoffs if we did not make concessions within the city contracts (summer 2020), and we were ultimately able to pass the Burlington responsible contractor ordinance (2021). Point being, our intervention in this election mattered.

For the rest of 2020, 2021, and 2022, with the Democratic and Republican endorsement moratorium still in place (as card check had still not been passed by the general assembly), the Vermont AFL-CIO continued to back the Progressives.[16] In the November 2020 general election, we, for the first time in our history, endorsed the entire Progressive Party slate for statehouse elections (and Progressive David Zuckerman for governor and Doug Hoffer for auditor).[17] Here we would see seven Progressives elected to the Vermont House, and two in the Senate.[18] In 2021, in Burlington, we again endorsed the Progressive slate, this time backing Perri Freeman and Jack Hanson in the reelection bids for city council (they both won) and Max Tracy for mayor.[19] Later in 2021, in a special election in Burlington, we would back Progressive candidate Joe Magee for city council (Ward 3). Magee would also win his contest. In 2022, again in the Burlington town meeting elections, once more we endorsed the Progressive slate and once more we won the bulk of these races, again helping the Progressives retain their status on the city council as the largest party in Burlington.[20] Finally, also in the 2022 general election, in addition to again backing the Progressive slate, we again endorsed Progressive David Zuckerman (who had lost his bid for governor in 2020) in the race for lieutenant governor (a contest he would win).[21]

Coming out of this closer alliance between the Vermont AFL-CIO and the Vermont Progressive Party, in fall 2021, two Vermont AFL-CIO leaders from within pro-United! locals, Katie Harris (AFSCME Local 1674) and Paul Wieshart (UFCW Local 1459), would win internal Progressive Party elections, giving them seats within the party's statewide leadership.[22] With this, labor gained more influence over a party that had already shown itself to be a reliable friend of the unions.

The Vermont AFL-CIO, by seeking to hold political parties accountable for their collective positions and by showing a willingness to walk away from a Democratic Party that declined to support us, showed that labor does not have to tether itself to the capitalist parties to build power. We gained more legislatively after playing hardball than we did when we played along to get along in 2018 and before. And whereas Vermont has an existing left third party in the Progressives, we recognize that the rest of the United States lags behind in this regard. The Progressives should serve as a model for the rest of the country.

After all, in a state that demographically should be the most right-wing Republican one in the nation (i.e., Vermont being extremely rural, aging, and lacking in racial diversity), the Progressives (and the broader social and labor movements) have shown that living in the woods and among farms does not have to translate into a right-wing creep. In fact, if you speak the language of the common people, if you give voice to their concerns, their values, and their needs and seek to democratically empower them, every place where working people are the great majority can be brought to the left. And further, if we desire a future beyond the crumbs of capitalism, one beyond the uneven playing field of the Democratic and Republican parties, we, on a national scale and as organized labor, must be willing to venture into the uncharted waters devoid of the parties of the status quo and risk alliances with new or third parties, be that the Movement for a People's Party (which the Vermont AFL-CIO endorsed in September 2020), a national Progressive Party, or something

entirely new.[23] But even here, even as we look for a change in our electoral alignment, we must also not lose sight of the fact that no party will
liberate us in and of itself. In the end, our liberation, the liberation of the
working class freed to realize its own power to shape society according
to the principles of equity and a more direct democracy, will only come
by our own hand. Point being, our true power will forever be on the shop
floor, in our unions, in our communities, and through our solidarity. And
where we lead, and where we make the politicians fear us, they will follow
or risk the final breakdown of a system that does not serve the needs of
the many. And toward this day, the day on which working people hold the
reins of transformative power, we endeavor.[24]

Beyond Elections and Parties: A More Direct Participatory Democracy

Even while the Vermont AFL-CIO engages in a leftist election strategy,
it must also be said that we do not view campaigns and ballot boxes as
the measure of democracy alone. Rather, a central point of the United!
platform (now the Vermont AFL-CIO platform) is also the reordering of
Vermont whereby government becomes more of a direct participatory
democracy. We support the passage of an amendment of the Vermont
Constitution through which the people themselves can direct and legislate their own future through an empowered town meeting system of
self-rule.

Since the founding of Vermont, a central element of our democracy
has been the town meeting. The town meeting is how local government
is arranged and through which all the citizens of a given community,
together, represent the legislative branch of government. The de facto
town meeting structure is for citizens to gather in the town hall to debate
any and all local issues of their day, be they the school budget, the buying
of a new snowplow truck, the setting of the tax rate, the management of
publicly owned land, or the setting of local ordinances. All such issues,
and resolutions relating to said issues, are subject to amendments from
the floor (from anyone) and ultimately are voted up or down by the people
themselves in full view of their neighbors. However, it should also be said
that communities, through a democratic vote, are also free to change how
they conduct their town meetings. Thus, some communities vote to take
certain money items off the floor in favor of placing the decision in a more

traditional ballot box. And a very few of the larger communities (nine, to
be exact) have voted to constitute themselves as cities, with an elected
mayor and city council and without any traditional town meeting. But of
Vermont's 243 municipalities, 75 percent of them, to this day, hold floor
votes utilizing a direct participatory democracy model.

Increasingly from the 1980s on, these town meetings, especially on
Town Meeting Day (the first Tuesday in March), have used this forum to
make the opinion of the people known to the politicians and the world by
the passage of nonbinding resolutions on state and world affairs. In more
recent decades, such Town Meeting Day resolutions have been used to
call for an end to the Iraq War, to show support for the establishment of a
single-payer health care system, and for a myriad of other issues. But the
way things stand now, such resolutions on matters beyond the scope of
the municipality are essentially symbolic. And this is something United!
and the Vermont AFL-CIO aim to change.

It is our intent that in the foreseeable future, through our Progressive
Party allies in the Vermont Senate, we aim to have a constitutional amendment introduced that will create a town-meeting-based referendum
system whereby the laws of the land can be changed when and if a majority of communities, representing a majority of the population, adopt any
given resolution.

On passage, such a change would mean that regular working-class
Vermonters and small farmers would attain the power to override or
go beyond the limited vision of our current representational form of
government and instead vest the final authority directly with the people
themselves.

If such were in place, the Vermont AFL-CIO believes we would be
in a position to make much more rapid progress on things like universal livable wages, health care, expansion of social benefits, and workers'
and union rights than we see now through our representational form of
government. And by basing such a process within the traditional town
meeting structure, we would also preserve and greatly expand the participatory element of our traditional rural democracy.

Even so, this Vermont AFL-CIO goal, the building of more democracy,
is a long-term goal. United! recognizes that the process of changing the
Vermont Constitution is a long-term endeavor. We anticipate that it will
take a number of years, at best, to elevate this idea among a critical mass

of Vermonters to the point where elected politicians feel the pressure needed to legislate such a change. And even then it is required to pass in the general assembly in two back-to-back bienniums before it is then voted on universally by Vermonters themselves. It is only then, after a majority of all Vermonters adopt it at the ballot box, that it would go into effect. So clearly this is not a short-term project. But public discourse must start in earnest at some point if we are to move this forward.[25]

CHAPTER VII

Black Lives Matter, the Police, and the Politics of Reality

> Black Power is giving power to people who have
> not had power to determine their destiny.
> —Huey P. Newton

Black Uprisings in the Wake of George Floyd's Murder

The murder of George Floyd on May 25, 2020, at the hands of the Minneapolis police force sent shock waves of unrest across the United States. The racist killing sickened me, but in the days immediately following I did not anticipate that its impact would be felt across the continent. It was not until some days after his death that the political magnitude of what was about to unfold started to hit me.

On May 28, I was talking by phone with AFSCME Local 1343 president Damion Gilbert. We were discussing some grievances in the City of Burlington, as we do on most days. Toward the end of the call, he asked if I was going to the demonstration in Burlington. I asked him what the demonstration was about, and he explained it was a response to the Floyd murder and that he and some other 1343 members were intending to go and would be meeting up with the local's Burlington Schools chapter chair Dwight Brown (who himself is a Black man and who was also a Vermont AFL-CIO district vice president from United!).[1] I told Damion I could not make it but was glad he would be there.

In the end, on May 30, over 1,200 Vermonters took part in this demonstration. Further, in communities all across Vermont rallies and vigils were being organized against the Floyd murder and in support of racial justice. Even in my small town of Cabot, population 1,434, a few dozen residents, including myself and my children, gathered in the town common for 8 minutes and 46 seconds (the time that a cop placed his knee on

Black Lives Matter banner on the side of the AFL-CIO headquarters in Washington, DC.

Floyd's neck) of silence. Nationwide protests were taking form daily. In many cities, such as Chicago and Washington, DC, the protests took on militant and violent tones against a racist status quo. It has been reported that protests occurred in over two thousand US cities and towns, with an estimated twenty-six million Americans taking part in one form or another. Looking at the actions as a single though dispersed event over some weeks, this marked the largest demonstration in the history of the United States. A rebellion against centuries of racism and discrimination seemed to be taking form.

In the nation's capital, as in many urban centers, demonstrations turned violent. Tellingly, one institutional target of attack, on the night of May 31, was Richard Trumka's national AFL-CIO headquarters (located close to the White House). The union HQ suffered smashed windows, fire damage, and graffiti. By intent or by happenstance, this attack highlighted that either:

1. The national AFL-CIO's seeming inability or unwillingness to meaningfully engage on issues relating to the fundamentals of US racism has in the eyes of the Black community made the union's HQ into just another symbol of status quo racism; or
2. The national AFL-CIO's perceived nonengagement on social issues aiming to change the political and economic foundations upon which America rests translated into average workers, Black people, and protesters not even knowing what the AFL-CIO is, thus the attack on their HQ was simply an attack on another corporate-looking structure in DC.

Both scenarios highlight the continuing failure of the labor movement to go beyond the lukewarm nothingness of Democratic Party politics and narrow shop-floor self-interest.

National AFL-CIO president Richard Trumka's public statements after Floyd's murder did not help. While paying lip service to antiracism and condemning the killing, Trumka refused to commit to any form of meaningful debate within the AFL-CIO concerning the role of police within the labor movement. Even while he engaged in a type of hollow virtue signaling, he also repudiated any and all protesters who engaged in violent or militant actions in this moment of national outrage.

In doing so, Trumka again made labor, on a national scale, irrelevant to the five-hundred-year struggle of Black people against systemic oppression. In short, he missed the mark, willfully misread the historic moment, and failed yet again in linking the struggle of the labor movement to the struggle and oppression suffered by tens of millions of Black Americans (millions of whom are union members).

Labor at a Crossroads on Black Liberation and Police Reform

With this unfolding political reality becoming clear to see, it was self-evident that the Vermont AFL-CIO could not be silent on the unfolding rebellions occurring in urban centers, nor could we ignore the intersection of labor politics and racial politics. Further, on June 8, the Writers Guild of America East (CWA) publicly called on the national AFL-CIO to expel the International Union of Police Associations (IUPA) from its ranks, asserting that the existence of a police union within the labor federation was antithetical to its goal of liberating workers. Further, on June 17, the seventy-five-thousand-plus-member MLK Labor Council (Seattle) voted to expel the Seattle Police Officers Guild for similar reasons.

The argument that advocates of these methods of racial redress made boiled down to this: Police too often kill working-class people, disproportionately Black men, and historically have acted as the armed wing of the bosses when it comes to strike-breaking. Conversely, police unions have defended their members from public outcry against such abuse of power and have not acted as a force willing to work with communities in order to provide meaningful accountability and public oversight. Concerning politics, police unions have opposed progressive change benefiting working-class and low-income people and often back far-right electoral candidates. *Thus, the entry of police into the labor movement has retarded progressive change, not expedited it.*

The conservative politics of police unions has compelled numerous labor leaders to tone down or blunt their social and economic demands to maintain a sense of forced unity by the least common denominator. But here, this watering-down carries the effect of alienating the progressive wing of labor and makes the articulation of a vision beyond minor reform and virtue signaling at worst impossible and at best uninspiring (especially to the millions of Black workers already in our ranks). And as labor fails to articulate a social vision counter to the rigged system that feels all-pervasive, and as workers from minority communities fail to see labor engaged on the issues and hardships they experience on a daily basis, the prospects of organized labor recruiting significant new members from their ranks declines.

But any thought of easily decoupling police from the labor movement is much more complex than expelling a few stand-alone police unions. The truth is that tens of thousands of law enforcement personnel are actually represented by amalgamated unions, be they AFSCME, AFGE, AFT, or IBEW. At a time when union internationals are struggling to maintain their membership numbers, let alone grow, and in a post-*Janus* world where anti-labor forces have sought to entice members to forgo voluntary union dues, any talk of further diminishing the membership lists in favor of more ideo-logical purity should be expected to meet fierce resistance from powerful players. And philosophical objections aside, less dues coming into a union means less resources for new organizing, and thus the struggle to grow becomes again impaired. This is the rock and the hard place the AFL-CIO finds itself in when considering the question of police within our unions.

That said, the situation in Vermont was different in summer 2020. By and large, Vermont cops were represented by the independent Vermont Troopers Association, the VSEA (which also represented prison guards and parole officers), and the right-wing New England Police Benevolent Association (NEPBA). None of these unions were part of the AFL-CIO.

All told, of the hundreds of unionized shops in our labor council, only five were police departments.[2] AFSCME represented three small-town PDs, and IBEW represented another. The Brattleboro PD was represented by IUPA, but to my knowledge this IUPA local never paid a penny in per cap dues to the labor council and never once sent even a single delegate to any convention or union action. Thus, although technically an AFL-CIO affiliate, they were well off any radar.

Thus, only four police departments, representing perhaps forty total cops, were the extent of our law enforcement membership (with none of them serving in any statewide union office). I say this to show that our starting point as the Vermont AFL-CIO was significantly different than that of other labor councils.

Given the lay of the land, and given massive public actions being taken in the nation and in Vermont against Floyd's murder and the continuing abuse of power by law enforcement, a critical mass of Vermont AFL-CIO leaders felt it imperative that we act and not remain effectively silent on such related community issues. After all, if we were to prove ourselves worthy of the social justice unionism approach that we had campaigned on in 2019 (and that served as a core principle of United!), nonaction from us on racism and police reform, while the country convulsed with protest, would have been seen as a betrayal and failure. Thus, action had to be taken, but in what form was yet to be determined.

Between Principle and Implosion: Vermont AFL-CIO Walks a Razor's Edge

Being right is often a different thing than being smart and effective. Our United! coalition, while having unity around a progressive program, was not and is not monolithic. The fact is the Building Trades, a key component of our ruling coalition, was much more conservative than our more liberal college professors (UA/AFT). Many blue-collar AFSCME members were not ready to make radical breaks with mainstream American culture, including a generalized support for unionized police. While the Vermont AFL-CIO is largely devoid of police unions, AFSCME represented three shops and IBEW another (AFSCME and IBEW, in 2020, both being crucial United! affiliates). This meant that any public position we took on race and police, if not strategically balanced and well thought out, could result in massive internal fracture and the end to our leftist ruling coalition, and with our two-thousand-plus AFT nurses already opting out of paying dues because of political differences (by an act of a few local officials, and not the rank and file), the state labor council could not afford any further divisions. Inviting such new fractures would be akin to conceding the absolute defeat of United!, the economic devastation of the state labor council, and the killing of all our social and political aspirations before a deep reform effort even got underway.[3]

Further, on a practical level, as I weighed the cost-effectiveness of possible courses of action, we also had to put on the scale that much of what we may say or do would be symbolic. The entire ten-thousand-member Vermont AFL-CIO had maybe forty police officers in it, and none in statewide leadership positions, so law enforcement had little to no direct or pressing influence on the scope of our broader social policies.[4]

It was in this context that I called for an executive board meeting largely to discuss the rise of Black Lives Matter–organized protests and the role, if any, the Vermont AFL-CIO should take in this movement. The meeting took place on June 15.

Here it is important to highlight that as a result of the protests filed by a number of AFT and firefighter locals concerning the 2019 election, following a preliminary investigation by the national AFL-CIO, in spring 2020 it was ruled that the entire convention was conducted under an old Vermont AFL-CIO constitution that was no longer in effect.[5] This unprecedented error (committed by the previous administration) meant that even as the election of president (myself), executive vice president (Tristin Adie), and secretary-treasurer (Danielle Bombardier) were upheld, all other leadership positions were invalidated, as geographic district vice president positions no longer existed by the constitution that was actually in force. These executive board seats were actually supposed to be elected based on an international's affiliated strength or by job groupings. Therefore, until a special election could be held (slated for August, and to be run by the national AFL-CIO), technically the entire elected leadership (with formal voting power) was composed of the three executive committee members. However, as soon as this decision came down from the national AFL-CIO, I appointed all our former United! executive board members to the presidential advisory committee, and we continued to conduct executive board meetings with all those leaders included. Informally, we continued to conduct leadership votes with all participating as if they still had standing on the executive board.

Given that the August special election was rapidly approaching, and given that it was crucial for United! to maintain solidarity in order to prevail in this special election, we had to act as if everyone had an equal vote and equal voice. Conversely, if I, Adie, and Bombardier (or a majority of any two of us) decided to muscle through major policy decisions on our own, United! would be dead from that moment on. That was the context in which the first executive board meeting concerning Black Lives Matter and police reform took place.

At our meeting, out of the gate, a number of the leadership were aggressively pushing for us to immediately expel all police from the state labor council. Chief among these was Sarah Alexander. Alexander, a professor at the University of Vermont, member of United Academics/ AFT, and a white woman, came to the issue with the passion and energy of a person who, perhaps for the first time, realized that racism exists in the world or at least the extent to which it is pervasive. Her zealous advocacy for radical and immediate action, consequences be damned, had a Paul-falling-off-his-horse-on-the-road-to-Damascus feel to it.

Also taking a hard line was Dwight Brown. Brown, one of two Black men in our leadership, was an AFSCME member and was an IT specialist in the Burlington Schools. His brother, years before, had been killed by a cop. He, along with 1343 president Damion Gilbert and others, had attended the recent protest in Burlington with his family. But Dwight, unlike Sarah, did not come across as a new zealot. Dwight, by virtue of his race, had dealt with and struggled against bigotry his whole life. However, even while demanding a comprehensive and principled response to the police killing of Black men and requiring that the labor movement be proactive in the fight against racism, Brown understood that major decisions should take into account potential fallout weighed against potential gain, or even justice.

On the flip side, some leaders, like Tim LaBombard, an IBEW member and president of the Vermont Building Trades Council, were firmly disinclined to take any action that would universally condemn unionized police, believing that kind of action would be alienating to a significant portion of our membership. Still others, like Eric Steele of AFSCME, were not comfortable wading too far into any critique of unionized police (and felt strongly that the members he represented in the more conservative Rutland and Addison Counties would reject any Vermont AFL-CIO moves in this direction). But here it is also important to point out that no one sought to justify or excuse the sickening actions of Officer Derek Chauvin for Floyd's murder. On the tragedy of that killing, all shared in a moral repulsion.

Two other BIPOC leaders, Omar Fernandez of APWU (Black and Latino) and Rubin Serrano of AFSCME (Latino), took more of a middle-road approach. While concerned about racism in America, neither seemed too eager to sanction actions that could not serve as a place of unity among their rank and file. Both, though, also recognized that racial problems were deep and real in America, and both were not agreeable to taking no action at all.

This first executive board meeting on issues relating to Black Lives Matter, the fight against racism, and police within the labor movement was contentious. Various and conflicting policy approaches were put forth on both sides of the issue. As debate continued, Alexander began to assert that any board or committee member not agreeing with her on the need to immediately expel all police from the state labor council were in fact white supremacists.

Executive Vice President Tristin Adie (AFGE) suggested that big issues like this should be debated and decided on by the rank and file directly, and not just by the elected executive board or presidential advisory committee. Thus, she proposed that an antiracist study and

education committee be formed to look more at how racism is embedded within society and how it can be more effectively combated. She
further asserted that action on racism and policing be tackled at our 2020
convention, by the members themselves, which was still some months
off. However, these ideas were rejected, with Brown leading the argument
that we don't need more education on racism, we need action, and that
that action needs to happen *now*. Alexander again aggressively pushed
that any decision or action that did not immediately result in every cop
being kicked out of the state labor council was damningly racist at its
core and that every executive board member or Vermont AFL-CIO leader
responsible for this failure must be understood as racists.

After two hours, the meeting concluded with tempers hot and no
consensus emerging. The only agreement was that there would need to
be a second meeting to discuss the matter and to see if a unified position
could be reached. But reading the room, it was clear to me that if push
came to shove, a majority would vote to expel the police. But the price that
would be exacted for the expulsion of forty members (none in leadership
positions) would mean that the United! coalition would be fractured in
irreparable ways and that a number of internationals would likely pull all
their per caps, thus leaving us not only with a weakened political base and
a leadership doomed to defeat at our next internal election (in August),
but also with a dangerously small war chest, on par with a midsized local,
and inadequate in funding for organizers or staff positions. In short, we
would be weak, fractured, isolated, and used as an example nationally of
why the left cannot and should not be put into leadership positions within
labor. So we faced a danger here that if this matter were handled poorly
or without thought beyond pure principles, what we did next could spell
our rapid downfall.

In the aftermath, Alexander provided me her resignation, stating
that the executive board and presidential advisory committee's failure to
agree with her showed that we valued white supremacy over antiracism.
Brown also offered his resignation, out of frustration with the leadership's
inability to agree on a principled position on police reform at a time when
the nation was erupting in protest. As president, I accepted Alexander's
resignation but not that of Brown.

My thinking was this: the situation we faced would not be the first
difficult political decision we, as the Vermont AFL-CIO leadership, would

have to navigate. Other very hard and very difficult crossroads no doubt lay ahead. Alexander's approach, by seeking an all-or-nothing gut check whereby you were either with her and right or akin to a fascist traitor, would be poison to our long-term project and the goal of moving labor to the left. And if she was ready to call those who disagreed with her now white supremacists less than a year after running on the same progressive slate as them, I had to assume this would be a recurring plotline with her. In my experience, this all-sum approach to defining policy positions did not lend itself to consensus building or reasoned compromise, but rather to an all-pervasive atmosphere of tension and factional infighting. In my mind, this kind of leftist fundamentalism would not be conducive to the creative cooperation and experimentation that the labor movement required at this juncture, nor would it allow United! to more effectively reach back down to our membership base to educate and effect a leftward trajectory of our rank and file. So I accepted her resignation.

Dwight Brown, on the other hand, was a different story in every way. Brown, a leader in his AFSCME local, had already proven himself effective in both leading his members in a more progressive direction and in finding common ground with a diverse rank and file on issues ranging from economic to social to political. I viewed his offered resignation as a statement of frustration not just regarding the leadership's inability to more rapidly chart a principled course on the issues of police reform, but also as an expression of the frustrations and hardships he and his family had personally experienced over his lifetime when it came to racism. I also saw Dwight as a person more than equipped to navigate difficult collective decisions without ultimately framing a debate as "you are with me or against me." So I rejected Dwight's resignation and instead asked him to give me a few days to try to work out a compromise whereby we would take a strong position in support of Black Lives Matter and against police abuse of power, but one that would minimize our exposure to factional implosion. Brown agreed. I bought myself a week to try to work this out.

With time bought, I privately called and messaged executive board and presidential advisory board members from both sides of the issue (minus Alexander, whose resignation I had accepted as final). I proposed that we not take any action to expel police but instead that we call for a moratorium on organizing any new police units into our ranks, state our solidarity with progressive activist efforts to decrease funding for state police and the Burlington Police Department (with savings going into social programs), give our unequivocal support for Black Lives Matter and the cause of Black self-determination in general, and provide direct financial resources to the local BLM organization and toward groups advocating for the release of Black political prisoners.

To those leaders like LaBombard (IBEW) and Steele (AFSCME), I said that the votes were there for a resolution to pass that would expel the police. And if they actively opposed the compromise I was suggesting, we would instead experience a firestorm of internal strife after the majority of the leadership voted to expel the cops. But also, by my calculation, if they tacitly supported this compromise approach, I could get the other side to agree (and drop the demand that the cops be kicked out).

To those who supported the expelling of police, I recognized that they could likely force through a vote on their preference, but if they did we would face the end of the United! coalition, we would fail to retain power at the next election, and a number of internationals would likely pull their dues (thus crippling us). But if they agreed to my compromise, they could hold their heads up high insofar as we would still be the first state labor council in the country with a police organizing moratorium in place, and we would be the only major labor body in the US, ever, to outright support Black self-determination.

As such private one-on-one conversations continued, I worked up a draft resolution. I further took the liberty of floating the draft to two key Black community leaders in Vermont: former state representative Kiah Morris, movement politics director of the Rights & Democracy organization, and Mark Hughes, director of the Justice For All organization.[6] I asked Morris and Hughes for their constructive feedback on the draft and told them that I would be happy to make changes, at their request, before it went out for a vote. As anticipated, I got some great suggestions for edits. From Morris I added sections on the need for Black and other impacted communities themselves to be central to the defining of reforming efforts and for inclusion of a section calling for a statewide civilian police oversight commission. I included all the changes that were suggested. At the end of the day, I achieved buy-in from these two key Black community leaders before it went to a vote.

I also worked closely with Dwight Brown on the elements of the draft resolution. I very clearly recognized that the hardliners within leadership would follow Dwight's lead. If Dwight opposed it, so would they, and we would end up with the dangerous expulsion route being the likely outcome. But if Dwight felt good about the compromise, so would they. Suffice to say that I kept the lines of communication very open in this regard, as nothing could be left to chance or the whims of debate.

All told, I knew that for the compromise to work, it would need to push the boundaries as far as possible and would need to expose us to the potential of some factional danger, but only to a degree that I calculated to be manageable (if even just barely). This was not an easy balance to strike. And frankly, understanding that the nine AFSCME locals in Vermont were parented to New England Council 93 (which in New Hampshire, Maine, and Massachusetts includes cops and corrections officers in its ranks), I anticipated major pushback on even this compromised stance. So to mitigate this threat, I called Council 93's executive director, Mark Bernard, the day before the meeting in which the resolution would be voted on.

This was an inoculation call. I point-blank told him that the votes were there to expel the cops and that I knew that if we did this AFSCME would flip out. I further explained that I recognized the divisiveness that such an action would carry and recognized that the third-biggest union in the Vermont AFL-CIO, IBEW, would likely be on the same page as AFSCME if this were to occur. So I was therefore working on a compromise that would fall just short of an expulsion but which would also be well beyond anything normally agreeable to AFSCME. We talked at some length. In the end, he seemed to understand my situation (although I was not under the illusion that he would agree with my course of action). We ended the phone call amicably.

Running concurrently with all these discussions within Vermont and the region, national AFL-CIO representative Dan Justice, who had been at our previous executive board meeting as the eyes and ears of President Richard Trumka, reported back to the national organization that we were poised to take controversial action concerning antiracism and police in the labor movement that was not in step with the marching orders coming from DC.

As a result, President Trumka had his lieutenant for the Northeast, David Driscoll-Knight, call me. Driscoll-Knight implored me, as state labor council president, to shut down any and all debate or action that would challenge, in any way, existing AFL-CIO policy concerning police,

police reform, or the relationship between police and the labor movement. After feeling pressure from the Writers Guild of America East (CWA) and from the MLK Labor Council (Seattle), Trumka and his establishment cronies did not want a new front to be opened against his leadership (or lack thereof). In Trumka's mind, he ruled the AFL-CIO and he saw us as vassals, no more no less. And the role of a vassal is to publicly parrot the party line handed down by the ruler.

Thus, Driscoll-Knight implored me to shut everything down at all costs. Being transparent (something I would learn is not always advisable in dealings with national AFL-CIO union bosses), I explained to him that I was looking to navigate our labor council toward a moratorium against new police organizing and that this would be an alternative to expelling law enforcement. He was not excited about either of these probabilities. Driscoll-Knight even went so far as to make the absurd and reactionary argument that "leadership is difficult, and sometimes a leader needs to make the hard decision," and as their Vermont leader I had to make the difficult decision to shut down all democratic debate on the police issue.

The funny thing about that argument is, as he was saying the first part, in my mind I was agreeing. Leadership is hard, and leaders do, at times, need to make the hard decision. And thus I *had* to invite the state labor council to make this hard decision, to risk our relationship with the national AFL-CIO, and to take a meaningful stance on the very real problem of police repeatedly murdering Black workers.

Supporting Black Self-Determination and Police Reform

Something more than a week later, on June 28, 2020, with all this back work complete, we held a second executive board meeting. I presented the draft resolution for review. I was further able to say that it was vetted by key Black community leaders in Vermont, that they expressed that should we adopt the resolution and that we would have made great progress in bridging the gap between organized labor and the Black community, and that it had their full support. Further, by involving Dwight Brown in the process of its crafting, he was also able to unequivocally state his support. After lengthy discussion, the following was adopted overwhelmingly:

Vermont AFL-CIO Stands with Black Communities in Resistance
- Self Determination for Black People in the US!

- Free All Black Political Prisoners!
- The Murders Must Be Stopped!
- Black Lives Matter!

Vermont AFL-CIO Position Statement on the Fight against Racism:
Now Is the Time for Unity and Action!

June 28, 2020, Montpelier, VT—Black Lives Matter. The Vermont AFL-CIO understands and recognizes that the United States of America is a nation which has long been governed by a ruling class whose power (social and economic) is rooted in slavery, racism, inequity, and oppression. We further see with clear eyes that Black people, whose ancestors were brought to this country in chains, have suffered (and continue to suffer) oppression on a massive and inexcusable scale. Such facts are made plain by not only looking at history, but also by looking at contemporary unemployment figures, poverty rates, average household income, incarceration rates, and through policing data. People who are Black are also murdered by American police officers with sickening regularity. George Floyd was not an exception. He, like Breonna Taylor, Michael Brown, Terence Crutcher, Eric Garner, and Freddie Gray (to name but a few), was one of the latest in a long line of martyrs going back hundreds of years (and accounting for thousands of taken lives). We must not become numb to these murders. We cannot accept that Black families must educate their children on how to not become the target of unprovoked police violence. We cannot allow systematic racism and police violence against Black people to continue as the regularity that it has always been. Rather, we must resist.

Vermont is not immune to racism and police repression. In our largest city, Burlington, Blacks were the subject of police use of force in 20 percent of all cases over the last seven years, despite composing just 6 percent of the city's population. And further, throughout Vermont Black people make up 8.5 percent of the prison population and account for 2.69 percent of all state trooper vehicle stops even though they make up only 1.4 percent of the total populace. These figures are deeply troubling.

The Vermont AFL-CIO, which of course includes members from all races and nationalities, seeks to be the united voice of Vermont's multiracial working class. As such, we cannot be silent while the Black community continues to be the subject of oppression and brutality both here at home and across the nation generally. And for us, this means that we intend to stand with Black Lives Matter. Conversely we will not and cannot stand alongside police organizations when they seek to defend the indefensible, namely the murder and brutalization of Black citizens. Therefore, the Vermont AFL-CIO affirms the following positions and actions:

1. We call on unions to stand with Black Lives Matter, to stand with the Black community, and to organize in these communities to widen and strengthen a united multiracial labor movement and to NOT organize any new police groups into the ranks of organized labor;

2. We support Black self-determination in the United States, as the fate of the Black community must be defined by the Black community itself;

3. We state our allegiance with those in the Black community who take action in their own self-defense;

4. We state our allegiance with all those who have and continue to engage in uprisings throughout the United States in resistance to racism, police brutality, oppression, and economic exploitation;

5. We ask our Vermont rank-and-file union membership to support Black Lives Matter and to take part in the demonstrations being organized across the Green Mountains against racism, against police brutality, and for adequate investment in the expansion of social programs as opposed to the funding of a system which criminalizes and brutalizes Black, Brown, Native American, and low-income people;

6. We call for a union-led Green New Deal economic recovery that advances the needs of Black, Brown, Native American, low-income, and working-class people;

7. We call on state and federal governments to release all Black and allied political prisoners incarcerated for actions alleged to have

been taken while fighting against racism and for Black liberation while serving in, or allied to, the Black Panther Party, the Black Liberation Army, and Republic of New Afrika. We further commit the sum of $1,000 to the Jericho Movement, an organization that advocates for and seeks to defend political prisoners within the United States. And here we encourage the national AFL-CIO to contribute a sum of $100,000 to the Jericho Movement;

8. We call for the State of Vermont to fundamentally rethink how we, as a society, approach public safety;

9. We call on the Vermont General Assembly to immediately pass meaningful police reform that includes the outlawing of choke-holds (with no loopholes or exceptions), and the creation of the nation's highest bar for any and all use of force (and we condemn any and all who oppose such immediate reforms as reactionar-ies on the wrong side of history);[7]

10. We call on the Vermont General Assembly to pass legislation creating a statewide Citizens Police Oversight Commission vested with subpoena power;

11. We further call on the Vermont General Assembly to reduce the state police budget in order to reallocate funds to social programs, especially programs that benefit Black, Brown, Abenaki, and low-income communities;

12. We call on the City of Burlington to reduce their police budget by 30 percent in order to reallocate funds to social programs, especially programs that benefit Black, Brown, Abenaki, and low-income communities;

13. We commit to supporting and advancing the creation of Black, Indigenous, and People of Color (BIPOC) caucuses within the Vermont AFL-CIO in order to better guarantee that the needs, desires, and concerns of Black and BIPOC union members are articulated and advanced by our state labor council;

14. We assert that all efforts and programs aimed at transforming society according to the notions of equity and antiracism which are advocated for herein, be led by those communities most impacted by the wrongs we are seeking to overcome, and who stand to gain through such a transformative process;

15. We commit an additional sum of $1,000 to Black Lives Matter of
    Greater Burlington in order to support their efforts to combat
    racism and to defend Black communities;

16. And finally we call on non-AFL-CIO labor unions in Vermont to
    join us in supporting Black Lives Matter, in more than just name,
    and adopt the commitments listed herein;

    The Vermont AFL-CIO, representing ten thousand working-class
    Vermonters, opposes all forms of racism and discrimination. We
    know what side we are on. We say without hesitation "Black Lives
    Matter."

    UNITED!

    The Vermont AFL-CIO

Upon adoption, we released a public statement and the full resolution
immediately. By far it is the most radical statement in support of Black
Lives Matter and police reform and against racism to ever come out of
an AFL-CIO state labor council, and we managed to produce this while
also holding our United! coalition together. Rapidly, the statement circulated through social media.[8] As anticipated, there was a backlash. Within
days, if not hours, AFSCME Council 93 issued a letter to us slamming the
organizing moratorium and demanded an immediate rescinding of the
policy or threatening to retract all their dues. Their problem was the call
for a moratorium on organizing new police units. Interestingly, they did
not take issue with the other key elements.[9]

Backlash and Again Teetering on the Brink

I was not surprised by a backlash from AFSCME, but the ferocity of it was
more than I had expected (but insofar as it did not immediately rescind
dues, it was still within the bounds of what I considered an acceptable
risk that we could mitigate). Here, being an AFSCME member and union
rep myself, I asked the Vermont AFL-CIO Executive Board to not make
any collective or individual replies and to allow me a chance to navigate
an acceptable resolution. In short, I knew that discussions with AFSCME
on these matters would be delicate, and one wrong move would carry
defeat.[10]

   My starting point here was the knowledge that there was no way the
majority of the executive board and presidential advisory committee

would retract the policy. The fact that this was a compromise that fell short of ejecting law enforcement marked this as the limit of restraint the majority would be willing to show. Further, if any elected leadership were to get in the business of issuing and then rescinding political statements based on blowback (be it from the relative right or relative left), such a body would see their credibility crumble. This was not in the cards. But, if we were to avoid implosion, responding with righteousness or arrogance would also be a fool's move. In short, I knew I would have to talk with the Council 93 executive director, Mark Bernard, and that I would have to acknowledge the difficult position we had put him in (93 being a dues-paying affiliate to an organization that had taken a hard critical stance concerning law enforcement, while having cops in its ranks). And I would have to find a way to incentivize AFSCME into looking the other way, staying all in with the Vermont AFL-CIO, and moving on with no change in position from my leadership.

When we talked, Bernard, out of the gate, said point-blank that all he had to do was make one phone call to AFSCME International president Lee Saunders and dues would be cut off. And knowing the players and the political realities of the labor movement, I knew that this was not hyperbole; it was a fact. Mark further made the reasoned argument that once one goes down the road of singling out one job class as unworthy of union representation, it's a slippery slope to others. For example, if police are barred for political or philosophical reasons, then are corrections officers next? What about border guards? Perhaps even machinists working in factories that produce military equipment? What about truck drivers that transport such military equipment or longshoremen that unload goods we take issue with? Pushing the envelope, could one argue that the slow-burn crisis of climate change should precipitate a reevaluation of union representation of workers whose jobs, in part or in whole, rely on the petroleum or coal extraction industries? In short, it was argued that our moratorium was in contradiction to our own Ten-Point Program for Union Power, which supported the right of all workers to form a union, and that us singling out police in the resolution ultimately gave ammunition to those anti-union forces that would love nothing more than to whittle away at the general right of a worker to form a union. While I saw the reason in his argument, I personally did not agree when looking at the very specific historic moment concerning policing and racism in the US.

No matter, this conflict was not going to be resolved through changing minds, but rather by finding a unifying point beyond the issue at hand.

Here I suggested that perhaps there was a path forward that could be built around areas of common interest. I also expressed that I fully understood the difficult situation he was in given the makeup of AFSCME in Massachusetts, New Hampshire, and Maine. But I also suggested that perhaps we could find a path forward, one that would not compel any policy shift, if we instead focused on areas of common interest. Specifically, I proposed that if AFSCME looked the other way, I would be inclined to assign five part-time Vermont AFL-CIO organizers for a period of months to do door-to-door work building membership within AFSCME Local 1674, the Howard Center, and further that I would put those organizers under the direction of Council 93.

Local 1674, located in Chittenden County, Vermont, is a private-sector social services and mental health agency. Organized in the 1980s, it has never been a majority union (other than on the day they won their recognition vote) and has forever been a source of frustration for AFSCME. With a bargaining unit size of seven hundred plus, it should be AFSCME's most important local in Vermont, but with no fair share dues agreement in the contract, and with embarrassingly low membership rates, for decades it has been more of a drain on AFSCME than an asset. In fact, low watermarks have seen membership well under 10 percent (or sixty total members). As recently as 2018, its membership stood at 16 percent. With membership dangerously low, they have never represented a true strike threat during negotiations, and so their bargaining power, if one was to make a clear-eyed assessment, has always been low. But with a newly elected leadership headed by local president Dan Peyser, there were plenty of signs of life.[11] Under their new leadership, smart shop-floor organizing was on the rise, their steward system was increasingly effective, and every quarter over two years saw modest membership growth. So there was a base to build from. And, by their CBA, if they reached a membership rate of 45 percent and were able to hold it for three months, they would trigger a contract reopener to bargain over fair share dues. And if fair share were to be achieved, this local, overnight, would produce more resources that could be used to support new organizing than any other AFSCME local in Vermont—resources that would be seen by both AFSCME and, through per caps, the Vermont AFL-CIO. But more than dues money, making a serious effort toward majority union membership would mean that the local would be building their own internal power that could manifest at the bargaining table and beyond. So my offer of putting resources toward such an effort, as part of an agreement to resolve our difference over police in the labor movement, resonated. I made the case that this could be a desirable outcome by further stating that come two years from now, the average Council 93 member inclined to support law enforcement would be more inclined to remember that we had brought in hundreds of new members in Vermont as opposed to the Vermont AFL-CIO's stance on police matters. Executive Director Bernard seemed to ponder on that. And some weeks later, meeting him in New Hampshire on other AFSCME business, we closed on this very deal with a handshake. I reported the agreement back to the Vermont AFL-CIO leadership, and the leadership supported the terms. Hence, we moved forward (and not back).

While it was nip and tuck for a time, and while our stance on policing and Black Lives Matter did precipitate a near crisis of unity, in the end we pushed as far as we could go while keeping members, affiliates, and internationals within the fold. One step further would have spelled the end of our leftist experiment. One step back and our United! coalition would have fractured. Resolving the conflict with AFSCME in the manner in which we did allowed us to stay true to our own internal democratic process and our collective principles and only committed us to further building an important section of our local labor movement in the Howard Center (which, ironically, was one of our most left locals and a vocal critic of the system of policing generally).

As of May 2022, the Howard Center Local 1674 organizing effort is ongoing. But as a result of such efforts (and other actions of the local), for the first time membership stands at over 250 dues-paying workers, the membership rate has more than doubled since 2018 (at over 42 percent), and a trajectory now exists whereby one can see a time when they will become a majority union on the not-so-distant horizon. Thus, near defeat (concerning a breakdown in solidarity post–BLM statement) was turned into a measurable victory.[12]

Through Risk, Alliances Emerge

More broadly, our policy statement on policing had measurable impacts both on law enforcement reform and in our long-term strategic interest in developing a partnership with Black community organizations. First, the Vermont General Assembly banned police use of chokeholds in non-life-and-death situations, and the City of Burlington cut the police department budget by 30 percent (both in 2020). More long term, the City of Burlington has begun to rely more on community service officers and park rangers (neither having law enforcement powers and neither being armed and both being represented by AFSCME). While more than the lion's share of credit for these reforms needs to go to the thousands of protesters and Black activists who organized around these issues unflinchingly for months, the fact that a major labor organization of over ten thousand members also stated support for such changes lent a degree of mass momentum to these efforts. So in our small way, and not without risk, we did our part and chose to be on the right side of history.

But the most important result of the Vermont AFL-CIO taking this public position on Black Lives Matter and police was the eventual opening of dialogue between ourselves and the major Black activist organization in our largest city of Burlington. With some credibility established on Black community concerns, months later we organized a sit-down between ourselves and the Black Perspective. The conversation was intended as a starting point: a way for our organizations to get to know each other, better understand each other's issues, and explore future collaboration. At this meeting, the Black Perspective told us about their continuing concerns around racism, institutional discrimination, opportunity limits, and police brutality. Executive Vice President Tristin Adie, Dwight Brown, Executive Director Liz Medina, and I did a lot of listening. We also talked in general terms about possibilities for partnership and about possible job placement programs through our Building Trades and encouraged the Black Perspective to work with us, as needed, on antifascist organizing and in general as part of an emerging popular front. We argued, as we have done from the start, that labor, social movements, and community organizations are stronger when we work together, and not in silos. All told, this was a good first meeting.

Building from this conversation, we went on to jointly organize a well-attended panel discussion for union members concerning race (and racism) at work, which included speakers from the Black Perspective and Migrant Justice and Black AFL-CIO leaders Dwight Brown (AFSCME) and Omar Fernandez (APWU). In addition, one member of the Black

Perspective went on to engage us in discussions about the possibility of helping her unionize her workplace (something we then spent some months exploring with her and her coworkers). We also jointly took part in the 2021 May Day demonstration in Montpelier, and we were honored to invite the Black Perspective to our 2021 convention at Jay Peak, Northeast Kingdom, where Black Perspective leader Madey Madey spoke to our rank and file about the ongoing need to combat racism in Vermont and in society in general.

These joint activities may seem modest, but relationship-building between unions and community organizations from social movements should not be viewed as something one can achieve overnight. Building trust and knowledge of each other takes time. But this is time well spent, as we will only be able to mount a challenge to the powers of the oppressive and exploitive status quo when we all come to the fight together, on the same side, as the many against the few. And so while we have only just begun this task of forming a deeper alliance with Black community leaders outside the labor movement, none of this may have been possible had we not taken risks, acted with reason, and been on the right side of history in the aftermath of the George Floyd murder.

CHAPTER VIII

Aftermath: Residual Challenges, New Elections, and Structure Building

**To reach a port, we must sail—sail, not
tie at anchor—sail, not drift.**
—Franklin Delano Roosevelt

AFT Locals and Firefighters Pull Their Dues

Even while United! was rapidly making moves to implement our Ten-Point Program for Union Power, and even as we were taking on risk by stretching the parameters of progressive unionism within the AFL-CIO, we still had to deal with the political realities sparked by our 2019 election win and its backlash. Immediately following United! coming to power, AFT-Vermont and the firefighters filed a complaint with the national AFL-CIO essentially stating that the elections were not free and fair and that the results should be nullified.[1] In addition, in a case of taking their ball and going home, a number of AFT locals who supported Riemer, including the 2,080-member Local 5221 (which was headed by Deb Snell, who was president of this local and president of AFT-Vermont), pulled their per cap dues from the Vermont AFL-CIO.[2] Initially, AFT seemed to indicate that the pulling of their dues was a transitory act pending national AFL-CIO findings and remedies relating to the complaint, but as time would tell, this vindictive act would remain in effect even after those issues were resolved. It was also reported to United!, through friendly contacts within the AFT, that these actions were taken by AFT leadership (both the AFT-Vermont Executive Board and AFT local leaderships) and did not come from the rank and file, nor were the rank and file consulted on these matters (let alone afforded a vote).

United! was not surprised that AFT and the firefighters took a sour-grapes approach to their election loss (as the walkout of fourteen of their

Vermont AFL-CIO executive director Liz Medina speaking at the 2021 convention, Northeast Kingdom, Vermont.

delegates at the 2019 convention when facing defeat had foreshadowed as much), but we were all shocked that many AFT locals, following Snell's lead, would pull their dues. Such an action was never considered or even discussed by AFSCME, the Trades, or the many other United! partners in the event that we were on the losing end of the election. And frankly, at different times during the 2019 campaign, events could very well have broken a different way and Riemer could have won. While United! had confidence that it would rise to the challenge and manifest a victory, when the possibility of defeat was broached as a topic, the only thought was to have United! constitute itself as an internal opposition, using what seats it had won on the executive board and rank-and-file pressure to push the Vermont AFL-CIO in a more progressive direction. But to pull dues, that as a concept was so far beyond the pale and so against the grain of labor solidarity that no one had remotely fathomed this as a possibility. Yet this is exactly what Snell and her die-hard supporters did in the aftermath of their failure, and it was a financial reality we would have to mitigate.

On September 16, 2019, the very day we won our election, the new executive board assigned District Vice President Liz Medina to reach out to Riemer and seek to assure her and AFT that we looked forward to working with them in solidarity. Medina was given this task because of her past friendly relationship with Riemer. We further assigned other leaders to do likewise with other pro-Riemer affiliates such as the firefighters and USW Local 4. Unfortunately, with AFT, this olive branch bore no fruit, and Medina reported back that her conversation with Riemer was curt (at best). After AFT-Vermont submitted their complaint to the national AFL-CIO, we again reached out, this time offering to appoint members of their choosing to advisory committees in order that they would have a regular voice during our deliberations. To our offers we received no positive replies.

I did eventually open a dialogue with Alison Lathrop, the new president of AFT Local 3180 (Vermont state college faculty). Over a period of months, through such discussions, trust was built and they would again pay their per caps (and they also sent a member, Liz Filskov, to our 2020 convention). Local 3180, with about 650 members, was the second-largest local in AFT-Vermont. Thus, with AFT Local 3180 and Local 3203 (AFT-Vermont's third-largest local, representing over 630 professors at UVM), we retained the solidarity of AFT locals representing over 1,200 members despite the efforts of a few to irreparably damage this relationship.

The economics of AFT locals withdrawing dues presented some challenges to the Vermont AFL-CIO, and it certainly hampered our ability to commit more resources to organizing. Thankfully, this was not an existential threat. Even so, at every opportunity we sought to dampen any hard feelings through amplifying the voice of these locals as they faced various workplace challenges, and, despite our deep frustrations, never taking the low road with them in any of our public statements. For the remainder of 2019 and throughout 2020, I personally maintained some positive back-channel dialogue through AFT-Vermont Executive Board member Jason Winston (who was politically sympathetic to the new direction of United!).[3] We also sought to develop a direct means of communication with their rank and file by seeking to have our staff and AFT district vice presidents offer to attend AFT local meetings. Despite our efforts, as of May 1, 2022, the per cap issue, and that which underlies it, continues to persist.

United! Fires Its Political Director and Sweeps New Election

The 2019 election complaint filed by AFT-Vermont and the firefighters to the national AFL-CIO sparked a monthslong investigation by the national AFL-CIO into the 2019 convention. And through the course of that investigatory process, although United! was cleared of alleged wrongdoing, a number of disturbing facts were uncovered regarding the outgoing administration and our political director (Dennis Labounty of USW Local 4, our one full-time staffer). Labounty, who was a sincere and likable man who believed in labor, had served as our political director for approaching twenty years. He was hired by former Vermont AFL-CIO president Ron Pickering of the United Steelworkers and subscribed to the old model of labor whereby polite lobbying and making friends with powerful Democrats was understood as the path to successful power building.[4] And for about five months of every year, 99 percent of his job seemed to consist of him being in the statehouse every day to monitor bills, provide testimony where appropriate, and maintain relationships with lawmakers. He also ran (and lost twice) for Vermont state represent-ative as a Democrat.[5]

Even with this long history, things didn't look good. Under Labounty's watch, proper recordkeeping did not occur, thus calling into question the validity of membership totals and resulting delegate strength enjoyed by affiliates (an issue that Damion Gilbert first flagged at the elections committee meeting). This failure also allowed for two delegates (repre-senting a combined five members, not enough to change the major election outcomes) to be seated whose unions were not current on their dues (thus they should not have been seated). But most disturbingly, the entire convention was run under the wrong constitution!

As such, other than the positions of president (myself), executive vice president (Tristin Adie), and secretary-treasurer (Danielle Bombardier), none of the other executive board positions even existed under the consti-tution that was in effect. Rather than geographically based district vice president positions, our bylaws actually called for election of officers based on economic sectors and international size. Further, the posi-tions of member-at-large (Tim LaBombard) and volunteer-in-politics (Omar Fernandez) no longer existed! The national AFL-CIO told me that a mistake of this magnitude had never been seen before in any other state labor council in the country, ever, during the long history of the AFL-CIO.

The error originated in the 2017 convention on the watch of Dennis Labounty and the former president. There, a set of constitutional amend-ments were passed by the delegates that would have reverted the structure of our leadership board and election process back to an older version of the constitution (the one that we were told was the governing document for the 2019 convention). However, for state constitutional amendments to go into effect, they must be sent to the national AFL-CIO in Washington, DC, for approval. However, Labounty never sent them off, they were never approved, they never took effect, and he never followed up on the matter with the sitting president. And as a major aspect of his job (as our only full-time staff) was to organize the convention, when he provided the constitution that he asserted was in effect for 2019 to the president, the delegates, and the candidates for office, he sent out the version that had never been cleared by the national AFL-CIO. Once discovered, the national AFL-CIO ordered that beyond the positions of president, executive vice president, and secretary-treasurer, all other officers lacked official standing, and that the elections for executive board seats would have to be rerun (and that that election would be facilitated directly by them).

This put us in a difficult position regarding Labounty. While his views of the labor movement and how we build power were not in line with those of United!, given his long tenure with the Vermont State Labor Council (and prior to the findings of the national AFL-CIO), I was inclined to keep him on for the remainder of his career (likely another five years). But because of his unprecedented mistake resulting in the nullification of eleven officer positions and the need to rerun elections, I and the executive board felt we had no choice but to fire him, which we did on July 9, 2020.[6]

The national AFL-CIO special election was slated for August 15, 2020. Due to the COVID-19 pandemic, it would be held remotely. Under the constitution actually in effect, all but one of the executive board seats would be elected from caucuses representing job types or internationals. United! seemed secure in these races, with the exceptions being our two AFT seats (should Snell and her allies seek to challenge United! again) and the VP-at-large seat that would be voted on by all the smaller locals (whose combined international membership in Vermont was under one thousand) who did not automatically secure representation on the executive board through another VP position. In this race, United! put Ron Schneiderman of UFCW Local 1459 forward as our candidate. In response, as a kind of October surprise in August, USW Local 4 and the firefighters put forward (get this) Dennis Labounty as their candidate against

Schneiderman—the very man whose dire mistakes led to the need for this special election!

As we did in the 2019 election, United! rapidly moved to secure support for as many affiliates as possible for our candidates, highlighting our ten-point program and our achievements since 2019 as our campaign message. And for the VP-at-large race, supporting Schneiderman, we expanded our 2019 base by bringing OPEIU Local 6 (representing three-hundred-plus nurses at the Rutland Regional Medical Center) into the United! camp. Local 6, our largest local not affiliated with an international with a thousand or more members in Vermont, had not sent delegates to the last convention. Their support now represented a significant increase to the United! base.[7]

On Election Day, it was clear that the Schneiderman-Labounty contest would be the only one in question. Other than our allies from Local 3203, AFT failed to send delegates. Further, a motion from Labounty to utilize weighted voting in the elections failed to reach the 20 percent delegate support to go into effect.[8] In the end, United!'s Schneiderman beat Labounty and United! swept every single race, and so our new executive board would consist of myself (AFSCME) as president, Tristin Adie (AFGE) as executive vice president, Danielle Bombardier (IBEW) as secretary-treasurer, Ron Schneiderman (UFCW) as vice-president-at-large, Dwight Brown (AFSCME) as AFSCME vice president, Helen Scott (AFT) and David Feurzeig (AFT) as AFT vice presidents, Tim LaBombard (IBEW) as Building Trades vice president, Mike Ross (AFGE) as federal workers vice president, Brian Ritz (IBEW) as IBEW vice president, and Omar Fernandez (APWU) as postal workers vice president. United! now occupied every single seat in the Vermont AFL-CIO leadership.

The Labounty Arbitration and the Old Guard

Following United!'s election win over Labounty, we found ourselves heading toward arbitration over his July 2020 termination (as was provided for in his employment contract). Representing us was labor attorney Tim Belcher. Belcher, who was on the list of Vermont attorneys recommended by the AFL-CIO and who also served as chief counsel for VSEA, took the case pro bono.[9] Together we spent days preparing for the arbitration, and we both felt confident heading into the October 14, 2020, hearing. But then, twenty-four hours before, the Vermont State Employees' Association, which for some time had been aware that Belcher was representing us on this matter, ordered him to remove himself from the case or suffer adverse actions. VSEA, of course, was his employer, so he had little choice but to comply.[10] That left me, with twenty-four hours to prep, to handle the case myself.

VSEA's actions concerning Belcher clearly were intentional and aimed at helping Labounty while passive-aggressively hurting United! VSEA's executive director, Steve Howard, liked Labounty, his noncon-frontational approach to lobbying, and his loyalty to the Democratic Party.[11] Further, if United! was allowed to make progress implementing its ten-point program, and if such progress was viewed as an example of how a left approach to unionism could work (and be more effective than the old guard model), this could incite reform movements within VSEA (and NEA, for that matter). Thus, it was in Howard's perceived self-interest to keep United! distracted and to take small, under-the-radar jabs at the Vermont AFL-CIO as opportunities presented themselves.[12] Forcing our attorney to remove himself from this arbitration case twenty-four hours before a hearing achieved these purposes, and if we lost the case as a result and were forced to bring Labounty back as staff, VSEA's leadership would find a grateful ally in our political director. And frankly, the fact that this happened the day before the hearing was a smart move from a reac-tionary point of view. Point being, if they had done this weeks before, it would have been easier for us to adjust, and perhaps contract with another skilled labor lawyer. But now, I would be compelled to pull an all-nighter preparing for a task I had not anticipated having to carry out alone. But this was not my first rodeo.

Reviewing Labounty's witness list (which was a who's who of the old guard and labor figures unfriendly to United!), exhibits, and argument outlines, it was clear that he would be seeking to put the blame for the wrong constitution being used on the former president (as if he had no responsibility).[13] He would also be making a political argument that his termination was ideologically driven, as he himself was not part of the progressive wing of the labor movement.

He further would seek to red-bait United! and me by attacking our solidarity actions with Migrant Justice, our critical stance regarding ICE deportations (as our executive vice president, Tristin Adie, had spoken at a rally that, in part, called for ICE to be shut down), our unwillingness to prioritize good relations with the Democratic Party, and my personal endorsement (signed as a district vice president of the Vermont AFL-CIO) of left-leaning Emily Kornheiser in the primary against an incumbent liberal Democrat for state rep out of Brattleboro in 2018.[14] None of these political arguments had any bearing on the situation surrounding the termination, but the fact that he was intending to use them made clear that any future engagement between him and United! would not be tenable.

For our part, we had a summary of the national AFL-CIO investigation findings, which pointed to Labounty as the responsible party for multiple (serious) missteps in organizing the convention, and a bench of labor leaders (from within United! and without) ready to testify that the failures of the past Vermont AFL-CIO administration rested on Labounty's shoulders.[15] Despite only having twenty-four hours to prepare to be the one making our case, I felt confident.

After a day of arguments, testimony, and cross-examination, I came out of day one feeling that we were in a very strong position. It also looked like it would take another two days to conclude the hearing. I fully expected that we would prevail. However, having done union work and argued grievances for years, I also knew that anything could happen. Therefore, from a position of strength, I negotiated a resolution with Labounty's attorney whereby we would mutually agree to change the termination to a resignation, and in return for Labounty dropping his right to continue with the arbitration process, we would pay him a nominal amount as a severance package.[16] While I expected that we would win the arbitration, in this case I felt that one in the hand is worth two in the bush. The matter was therefore resolved, and Labounty would be gone for good. His friends in VSEA's leadership must have been disappointed.

With the Labounty issue resolved for good, we had enough resources freed up to create a new organizing-centered executive director position. And in January 2021, we hired Liz Medina to serve in this role. Medina, thirty-five, who previously was a district vice president coming from the United! slate, was a member of the UAW Local 2322. This was her first paid union position. She brought with her a firm commitment to organizing, support for social justice unionism, and the clear understanding that if organized labor is to grow its power it also must become more militant and rank-and-file driven. She was the perfect fit for this staff role.[17]

Enter Liz Medina as Executive Director and a New Strategic Direction

Bringing on Medina as our top staffer allowed us to double down on the new priority being placed on organizing. First, understanding that the principles of the current executive board may not always be shared by future boards, but wanting to lock in our new direction, we negotiated a union contract with Medina (through the UAW) that stipulated that she could not be compelled to be at the statehouse any more than two days a week (thus allowing her to commit a majority of her time to organizing far removed from lobbying). Second, through her own initiative, she also set up a web portal whereby nonunionized workers could reach out to us if they had an interest in forming a union at their shop. Such leads are now followed up on by Medina, who calls the worker in question in order to get a sense of the issues they are facing, the size of the potential bargaining unit, and the general lay of the land. In turn, with this basic intake complete (if workers in the shop are not already inclined toward a union to affiliate with), the lead is then passed on to a jurisdiction committee, who determines which affiliate would be most appropriate to hand it off to based on job type and industry.

After having this system in place now for a year, we have received dozens of leads that are now in various stages of pursuit. Recognizing that workers on the shop floor, when armed with knowledge and support, are the best organizers, Medina has also arranged for free (remote) organizer trainings in which such workers can learn the basics of how they can advance their efforts of unionizing. As of May 2022, this new approach to gaining new shops is still in the earlier phases, although the organizing of Soteria House (now with AFSCME), along with the previously mentioned UFCW organizing drive concerning a dairy processor in the Northeast Kingdom, were a direct result of this intake and training program.[18]

Medina's trainings of the yet-to-be-organized were not limited to being online. On April 22 and 23, 2022, partnering with the AFSCME Local 1369 shop Rabble-Rouser, she also put together an in-person training for the unorganized on the basics of how to form a union. This free two-day class was held in downtown Montpelier. Working with the Local 1369 president, Ryan Geary, the intent was to build on the recent union affiliation of Rabble-Rouser, a twenty-employee worker cooperative café in the capital city, to encourage more area service and retail organizing in the area. This training was just a first step, and efforts to spark organizing in this sector by the Vermont AFL-CIO are ongoing.[19]

Another Medina-inspired organizing effort occurred in May 2022, when we partnered with the Maine AFL-CIO to provide our members a free six-week online training facilitated by renowned union organizer Jane McAlevey. This training, which in past years was offered by and for union members in Maine alone, was geared toward the all-important internal organizing, as union members were provided the tools needed to build more rank-and-file power on the shop floor. More than thirty Vermont union leaders and activists registered for the course.[20]

Again in 2022, this time in June, Medina represented us at the Labor Notes Conference in Chicago, where she, with central labor council leaders from western Massachusetts and Virginia, served on a panel discussion and workshop aimed at making progressive reforms in state labor councils and central labor councils.[21] Attending the workshop, which was filled to the max, were members and leaders from ten central labor councils from all parts of the US. Sharing the experience of United! and seeking to export our model to other bodies within the AFL-CIO is something that must have efforts like this attached to it if we are to build an organized progressive base beyond Vermont.[22]

While Medina's efforts at trainings marked a significant shift in focus for the Vermont AFL-CIO, her most important work was in supporting United!'s strategic plan whereby we sought to build a system of local rank-and-file contacts in each and every union shop on each shift throughout Vermont. From as early as 2019, United! recognized that good politics alone would never change the balance of power in Vermont (let alone beyond). To do this, we did not just need the right people in leadership, we needed the great mass of members to be informed and engaged; we needed to build and support a natural leadership on each shop floor. We also needed to cause a cultural change within the Vermont labor movement such that our membership base felt a real connection to the Vermont AFL-CIO as a whole and came to view it as an extension of their desires and ability to impact the larger social and political issues that they had a stake in molding. We also needed to circumvent the problem of gatekeepers (often a local president or business agent) when it came to two-way communications between the statewide executive board and the members. And finally, if we could build a comprehensive system of local union contacts throughout the state, as the system matured we viewed this not only as a way for the executive board to communicate to the base, but also as a way to have the base communicate with us, and as a means for rank-and-file leaders to communicate laterally to other shops (be that for getting advice, to make solidarity requests, or for any other reason).[23] Medina, prior to becoming executive director, shared this understanding with United! when she served on the executive board. And as our top staff, she continued to.

But given the meager lists that were inherited from the previous administration, we had little to build on. In fact, we did not even have a comprehensive account of all our union shops. At best we had incomplete (and old) data on affiliated locals alone, and nothing on what shops those locals actually represented. For example, for USW Local 4 all we had was the name and contact info for their president and the address of their union hall. Same went for AFSCME Local 1343. However, USW Local 4 represented about thirty-five shops in Vermont, and AFSCME 1343 a dozen shops in Chittenden and Franklin Counties. Thus, step one would be to build a database that actually accounted for all our shops. Liz diligently went to work on this and began to recruit local union contacts in those shops as they were identified.

Medina engaged in this process by meeting with those limited contacts we did have and gaining invites to local meetings, where she would talk about this effort and why and how it carried long-term importance to the labor movement. And of course, she would also inform members about the other efforts we were involved in, as well as asking them what challenges they were facing and how we could better support their efforts. Liz took part in dozens of these meetings. Speaking personally, it was inspiring to show up to a number of different AFSCME meetings all across Vermont (acting in my role as a union rep) just to find Liz there as well talking about this project and asking members about their struggles. And Liz did not stop there. She also made a point to do informal shop visits and sought to identify contacts through mass emails and social media efforts. With all of her visits, she would also bring dozens of United!'s Little Green Book, which she would hand out to members.

United! understood building the local union contact system as the single most important legacy we could leave the Vermont AFL-CIO. Where we may win victories here and there on specific issues, victories alone do not increase capacity, alter the long-term culture of member engagement, or improve our sustained ability to mobilize. But creating such a system would. Thus, from 2021 forward, this project was put on the agenda for every monthly executive board meeting. In this way we intended to keep this a priority and to measure our progress along the way.

As of June 2022, this effort was still underway, but already we had recruited hundreds of local union contacts throughout Vermont. However, given the scope of the project we were still a year or more out from realizing a more mature formation. And further, identifying and recruiting leaders to serve in this role was no more than building the foundation on which a system would rest. The crucial part would be working toward a cultural shift whereby those contacts would view themselves as a central aspect of the labor movement as such. And here, we have only begun with this education. In the long run, it will be crucial that these leaders be regularly asked to do union-building tasks aiming to keep their members informed and engaged in activities supporting our broader political agenda. And for our part, we will need to consistently strike a balance in asks, one that does not overask (and risk burnout) or underask (and risk devaluing and disengagement). But I am confident that this model will find success in the years to come.[24]

The 2021 Elections: Affirmation of United!'s Growing Support

On September 18 and 19, 2021, we again held our annual convention. This one would be in the Northeast Kingdom (at Jay Peak) and would be our first in-person convention since the start of the COVID-19 pandemic. It was also an election year. And given the constitutional amendments that were passed in 2020 (which were approved by the national AFL-CIO), the elections would be for nineteen executive board seats (up from eleven in 2020). Thus United!, in the months preceding the vote, put forward a slate of seventeen candidates for office, with myself heading the ticket for president. However, this time my running mate for executive vice president would be Dwight Brown from Local 1343.[25] The campaign theme was distilled to "Working Class Unity—Union Power."

Like in 2019, United! approached the election as a public effort. We passed the hat among United! supporters in order to raise money for a number of lawn signs and campaign posters (which were put up in key communities including Burlington, Montpelier, Barre, Bennington, St. Johnsbury, and Newport). I also wrote an op-ed that was published in a number of Vermont media outlets calling for union members to again support United! in the elections, highlighting our success in implementing our Ten-Point Program for Union Power (aka the Little Green Book).[26]

As before, United! chose to make the election and the campaign a public effort as we viewed this as an opportunity to raise working-class issues throughout Vermont. And we also believed that who is elected to the leadership of the state labor council will have direct relevance not only to the Vermont AFL-CIO, but also to working people as a whole. Thus, we wanted to use the campaign to talk about issues impacting the many, such as one's right to unionize, the need to expand the social safety net, and why the defense (and expansion) of our democracy must rest with the working class as a whole.

Come September 18, we had over one hundred registered delegates, alternates, and rank-and-file members at the convention (once again making this one of the best-attended conventions in decades). And on day one, instead of having a dozen politicians from the Democratic and Republican parties talk at us (as was typical prior to United! coming into power), we organized workshops on social justice unionism and on building for strike actions. We also had speakers present from allied organizations and movements such as the Black Perspective, Migrant Justice, Vermonters for Justice in Palestine, Democratic Socialists of America, the Vermont Progressive Party, and Chief Don Stevens of the Nulhegan Abenaki Tribe. Also addressing our convention was APWU International president Mark Dimondstein (who provided a letter that was read from the podium thanking us for leading the way toward a new progressive unionism) and Association of Flight Attendants president Sara Nelson (who provided a video greeting stating her support for our efforts to revitalize labor).

Nominations for officer positions took part at the end of the first day. We did this here, instead of just before elections on day two, in order to allow for candidates to debate and engage with the rank and file that afternoon and night, prior to the vote, so that members could be better informed before they cast their vote. And further, upon nomination, each candidate was afforded time to address the room and say why they were running and where they stood on the issues. (United! candidates all identified themselves as part of the slate.) However, as it turned out, every United! candidate ran unopposed (myself and Dwight Brown included).

On the one hand, United! having earned the support of the rank and file to the extent that opposing candidates were not nominated from the floor was a good feeling. However, I was also disappointed that the elections would not be contested. I and United! all felt that it is through opposition that elections become more meaningful, and the members having to weigh where candidates stand concerning the issues and their vision for the future of the labor movement is an important deliberative process. Frankly, it would have been good for our internal democracy if we would have had a night of informal debate. But with our three main opposition groups choosing to not be present (AFT Local 5221, USW Local 4, and firefighters), and with the measurable progress United! was able to point to over the last two years, this was not to be.[27]

On day two of the convention, on September 19, United! was affirmed as the unopposed winners in all of its races (with Dwight Brown becoming the first Black person to hold the office of executive vice president in Vermont AFL-CIO history), and Damion Gilbert of Local 1343 (a United! supporter) was elected chair of the rank-and-file presidential advisory committee.[28] With the closing of this convention, United!, now winning three consecutive elections since 2019, would be assured no less than two more years of being in power.

CHAPTER IX

Exporting the Revolution within Labor: United! in VSEA and NEA

> Every act of rebellion expresses a nostalgia for
> innocence and an appeal to the essence of being.
> —Albert Camus, *The Rebel*

Resisting the Pressure to Stay in Your Lane

From the moment United! took office in 2019, we felt pressure from lobbyists and Democratic lawmakers, liberal advocacy groups, and even moderates from within other unions every time we veered from the path of mainstream liberal advocacy and engagement. And veer we did!

Never did United! refrain from calling a spade a spade because it made the establishment uneasy. I would venture to say that even our enemies would readily agree with this statement. But the pressure, at times, was intense, and as president I initially felt it more than others (later, Liz Medina, our executive director, would bear much of this burden herself through her work in the statehouse). Experiencing this, I could see how a reform-minded president, if not steadfast in their principle and will, could, over time, be beaten back into lanes defined as acceptable by the status quo.[1] And if not guided and held accountable by a majority progressive slate of leaders behind them (in addition to a well-defined leftist platform), it would be easy for many to be driven back into becoming the problem they had initially hoped to solve. But those pressures will always exist under our current capitalist system of power, punishment, and reward. This will be a factor we must always wrestle with. But when it comes to those moderate or reactionary forces in labor that would rather serve the interests of the masters, these are problems we can and must seek to mitigate in the here and now as a core aspect of building our movement.

School Workers Action Committee (NEA) leader Tev Kelman speaking at a
demonstration to defend public pensions, Montpelier, Vermont, 2021.

In United!'s experience, the VSEA and NEA leadership at times
sought to undercut us. They certainly felt more comfortable cozying up to
politicians than they did us. Examples of their lacking solidarity include
when they softly walked away from support for the AFSCME 1343 picket
in summer 2020. Likewise, when we were calling for reasonable police
reform (also in summer 2020), VSEA's executive director, Steve Howard,
arranged for his union to provide testimony in the statehouse in favor of
police use of chokeholds against the public. And again in 2020, it seemed
apparent that VSEA and NEA leadership were providing support to our
terminated political director, Dennis Labounty. All told, United! did not
feel these acts could go without a response. But rather than engaging in
a frontal counterattack, we instead made the decision to counter these
challenges asymmetrically, through the exporting of our United! revolution within labor.

Create Two, Three, Many United! Slates

United! clearly understood that in the long run our ability to make foundational change in Vermont did not rest with the AFL-CIO alone. Rather,
it would take a unified labor movement, along with allies, to make a run at
the entrenched powers that be. But such a unity could not be a reflection of

a kind of lowest common denominator like politics. Rather, any labor unity aimed at systematic change would have to be built on a working-class-left agenda that held the democratic empowerment of members as nonnegotiable. And where such a principled unity was impossible due to the objective political conditions, those conditions would have to be changed.

Thus, United! sought to actively pursue relationship-building and coordination between ourselves and the more radical caucuses taking form within NEA and VSEA. We resolved to provide moral, ideological, and material support to leftists within these other unions so that they themselves could more effectively struggle for the kind of progressive change needed in NEA and VSEA (the kind that once realized would serve as the foundation on which real labor unity could be built). And while NEA and VSEA had shown themselves to be incapable of altering the balance of power within the AFL-CIO (largely because their natural allies, establishment figures from the old guard, were far removed from the rank and file), United!'s connections within NEA and VSEA were rooted in their base, among regular members. Therefore, we understood that the most impactful way of pushing back against NEA and VSEA leadership was to support internal movements aiming to transform these unions from within.

While the Vermont NEA already had a radical caucus taking form for a period of time (School Workers Action Committee), VSEA really just had a collection of radical or disenfranchised members who consistently felt alienated with the moderate, reactionary, and risk-averse leadership at the top. So here United! quietly reached out to those connections that we had in order to help encourage the formation of a United! caucus within their union. We helped encourage such discussions and were happy to offer them use of our Zoom account. United! officers, including myself, also met with them on occasion to share our reflections and lessons learned from our 2019 election victory. As a result, Vermont State Workers United! was organized as a progressive caucus aiming to challenge internal VSEA elections in September 2020. And with my recommendation, the caucus chose Agency of Transportation (AOT) worker Jerold Kinney as their candidate for president.[2] His primary opponent would be VSEA's well-known (but unprincipled) first vice president, Aimee Towne.

In late summer 2020, Kinney, with the active support of the caucus, campaigned hard. Running on a platform that mirrored that of Vermont AFL-CIO United!, Jerold focused on building support among state highway

garages with fellow caucus members spreading the word in other departments.[3] Throughout the election season, I personally served as Kinney's
unofficial campaign advisor, even helping him gain a spot on a local radio
program (WDEV's *Equal Time*) to talk about the race and his caucus. On
Election Day (September 7, 2020), in a three-way race, Kinney came in
second with nearly 30 percent of the vote (with Towne the victor). While
Jerold fell short of the win, there was no secret that United! was providing
moral support for him and his caucus, and winning on 30 percent of the
ballots among their own members certainly gave VSEA's old-guard leadership reason to consider the price should they choose to fuck with us
again. And reaching the near 30 percent level of support in a caucus's first
run at office also serves as a strong starting point for future elections and
internal reform efforts. So even without the victory, United! was pleased
with this outcome.

Within the Vermont NEA, the School Workers Action Committee also
challenged their old guard in a run for president in March 2021. And once
again United! gave moral support to their candidate, Tev Kelman.[4] Like
United!, School Workers Action Committee sought to better empower the
membership and asserted that the NEA should be more active on broad
social and economic issues, such as pushing for single-payer health care.
During the COVID-19 pandemic, they were at the forefront of school-
based union members pushing for safe working conditions. In fact, it
was through such organizing independent of NEA leadership that they
were able to build a more robust database of NEA members favorable
to reform and increased activism. Using such contacts, Kelman came
close to unseating the moderate incumbent, Don Tinney, with it being
announced on April 6, 2021, that he had lost but finished with a strong 45
percent of the vote.[5]

Defending Public Pensions from Below

A high point of the three caucuses working together came in the winter
and spring of 2021. During this legislative session, the state treasurer,
Beth Pearce (a Democrat), publicly called for massive changes to the
pensions enjoyed by state workers and teachers.[6] Citing underfunding,
she called for workers to pay in much more, for the benefits to be reduced,
and for workers to labor more years into their old age before being eligible
to collect. Almost immediately the Democratic Party leadership in the

general assembly, led by Speaker Jill Krowinski, came out in support of these massive attacks on public workers. In the House, hearings began as the first step in carrying out these attacks. Both the VSEA and NEA leadership condemned the attacks, rightly pointing out that workers paid in every penny that was asked of them, but both Democratic and Republican administrations willfully lowballed state contributions at such an irresponsible level so as to cause the pension funds to face economic challenges in the moment. Instead of placing the burden of this failure on the backs of workers, VSEA and NEA called for alternative approaches to addressing the problem, such as a wealth tax or using the influx of federal money (received as part of the COVID recovery effort) to bolster the funds. But initially these calls fell on deaf ears, even if they were being said to Democratic Party politicians who the VSEA and NEA leadership had time and again endorsed (a sin not shared with the AFL-CIO under the leadership of United!).

Politicians only started listening to workers when rank-and-file teachers began organizing informational picket lines across the state. And on March 30, two hundred VSEA and NEA members (with a number of AFL-CIO folks present in support) picketed in front of the statehouse.

Independent of VSEA and NEA leadership, the radical caucuses in these unions planned a mass demonstration in Montpelier for April 3, 2021. Vermont State Workers United! and the Schools Workers Action Committee rallied their members for what increasingly seemed to be destined to become a large and angry action. In solidarity we, the Vermont AFL-CIO, called on our members to also turn out in support (recognizing that an attack on one is an attack on all). But even as momentum clearly favored the action, VSEA leadership (headed by Towne), instead of mobilizing to support this demonstration being organized by their own members, called for a different action on the same day, at the same time, forty miles away in Burlington.

This disrespectful act by VSEA leadership was intended to undermine and isolate progressive leaders from within the caucus by diminishing the size of the statehouse demonstration, and to allow VSEA leadership to distance themselves from members who rightly intended on denouncing Democratic Party figures in no uncertain terms from the statehouse steps. However, VSEA's attempt to undermine the action failed, and it was clear for all to see that the demonstration would be big (and would include as speakers Jerold Kinney from Vermont State Workers United!, former VSEA first vice president Michelle Salvador, Tev Kelman and Dana Decker from School Workers Action Committee, myself from Vermont AFL-CIO United!, and others).

Then, with the mass protest looming, twenty-four hours before it was to begin, the Democratic Party folded under public pressure, stated that no major pension changes would be pursued in 2021, and announced that instead the issue would be punted to a summer study committee that would include union members. This was a huge defensive win, but one that was temporary in nature unless the pressure could be kept up. It was achieved largely by the direct-action planning of members through organizing through the two progressive caucuses. But recognizing that the same attacks would likely resurrect themselves in 2022, the mass demonstration went forward as planned on April 3, 2022 (even as VSEA leadership cancelled their competing action).[7]

More than five hundred workers attended the demonstration in Montpelier. Speaking from the podium, Kelman said:

> We are here to celebrate the power of working people, the power of thousands of rank-and-file members of NEA and VSEA, along with our allies in the communities, who called, who picketed, who testified, who organized for power within our unions, and yesterday we won a real victory for the working people of Vermont.... And while we did not start this fight, we are here today to say we will finish it!

Jerold Kinney of VSEA addressed the crowd by saying, "I am here to tell the governor and legislature to get your hands out of my pocket. This is my money, not yours! ... I'm done being nice!"

Michelle Salvador bellowed from the steps of the statehouse:

> There are only two sides here. On the one side ... is wealthy billionaires who want to gut your pension. And on the other side is public workers.... This is not Democrats versus Republicans, it is antigovernment versus us.... The plan is to reduce government and shrink taxes [for the rich], but to do that it requires that they devalue public sector workers by reducing our compensation.... Shame on you! Our pensions are not a gift, they are an agreement, they are deferred wages they are trying to take from us.

As president of the Vermont AFL-CIO, I spoke to the five hundred assembled workers last. With my words I sought to condemn the Democratic Party, who had launched this attack (with the support of the Republicans), warn workers to be wary of those from within our ranks who would have us forget this ugly history when the next election rolled around, and ask how many more times we would allow for Democrats to betray us before we collectively say enough is enough. I also warned that although we had won on this day, the war was far from over. Here I asked:

> What are you willing to do to defend your pensions? When they come back next year, what will you do? You should write, you should speak, you should pay attention. But you need to be willing to do more than that. They do not do what we ask them to because it is right. They do it only when they fear us! And if you decide, the rank and file, that the time has come to strike to defend your retirements, we will stand with you! Some will tell you that you do not have the right to strike. Well, I got news for you, brothers and sisters. Nobody had the right to strike until we came together and stood firm and struck in the 1930s for our rights! The teachers in West Virginia did not have the right to strike. The teachers' union in Chicago who just threatened a strike vote for safe conditions to return to work during COVID did not have that legal right, yet they were unafraid to take that vote.... And always remember that it is only through your solidarity, through your actions, through your labor that you have power, and when we stand together we are the most powerful force in Vermont! Which side are you on?!

As I walked off center stage, hundreds of workers chanted back, "Which side are you on?! Which side are you on?! Which side are you on?!"[8]

The April 3, 2021, demonstration to defend public pensions was a good day, and a vivid example of how progressive rank-and-file caucuses, even when not in power, can play a serious role in building union power and effectively fighting in defense of working-class interests.[9]

CHAPTER X

Building International Solidarity: Rojava, Palestine, and Cuba

> There are only two roads, victory for the working
> class, freedom, or victory for the fascists, which means
> tyranny. Both combatants know what's in store for
> the loser. We are ready to end fascism once and for
> all, even in spite of the republican government.
> —Buenaventura Durruti

Solidarity with the Revolution in Rojava

Even as United! endeavored to transform the Vermont AFL-CIO and to achieve social and political impact within the Green Mountain State, we also recognized that the struggle against the forces of capital is international by nature. We viewed our own struggle as a continuation of a worldwide fight of the many against the few for a reordering of society whereby economic equity and a more direct democracy would become the foundations on which a more just community is built. And while United! was under no illusions concerning our ability to significantly impact those struggles in faraway places, we also believed it to be our responsibility to reach out our hand in friendship and solidarity where we could and where our political objectives dovetailed with those of others.

Internationally, from 2019 to the present, the most far-reaching revolution unfolding was that in Rojava, Syria. Here the Autonomous Administration of North and East Syria, along with their armed forces, known as the YPG and YPJ, had liberated large sections of Syria from ISIS control and had taken steps to implement a direct participatory democracy, autonomous of the Assad regime, in traditionally Kurdish majority areas.[1]

The scope of their revolution, the equitable economic order they sought to build, and the radical secular democracy they envisioned

Vermont AFL-CIO Executive Board member Katie Harris arriving in Havana, Cuba, for 2022 May Day celebrations.

(one not so different than the empowered town meeting system of self-government we supported at home) was on par with the far-reaching social uprisings witnessed during the Paris Commune of 1871 and that which was advanced by the CNT and FAI during the Spanish Civil War of 1936–39.

If Rojava had been in Europe (or North America), as opposed to the Middle East, their revolution, and the day-to-day advances and setbacks, would be on the front page of every newspaper on a regular basis. But Western bias relegated them to backwater status, hardly worth mentioning even when facing invasion from Turkey (a NATO member). But for United!, the aspirations of the Rojava Revolution were something that could not be understated, let alone ignored. Thus, we felt the need to publicly state our solidarity.

Prior to United! entering office in 2019, Rojava was already gaining the attention of labor in Vermont. In fact, in 2018 the Green Mountain Labor Council (a regional affiliate of the Vermont AFL-CIO) adopted a resolution in support of Rojava and went so far as to encourage Americans to volunteer with the YPG and YPJ.[2] In turn, the labor council offered to provide three months of free housing, food, and a union job to any and all returning volunteers who chose to reside in Vermont. And in response to this commitment, one returning American, Alex McDougal, who served as a heavy machine gunner during the retaking of Raqqa, took us up on this offer. It was my personal honor to put him up at my off-grid cabin in the mountains while IBEW Local 300 president Tim LaBombard got him a union job installing solar panels. In turn, Alex attended a number of union events, including our 2018 political conference at the Old Socialist Labor Party Hall in Barre. So by the time United! was in charge of the Vermont AFL-CIO, the issue of Rojava was already on our radar.

Come June 2021, with United! occupying every statewide officer position, the Vermont AFL-CIO, through a vote of the executive board, became the only state labor council in the country to sign on to a statement from the Emergency Committee for Rojava that, among other things, called for the United States to provide Rojava with economic and medical aid, to conduct targeted sanctions against Turkey (who had occupied northern Rojava), and to recognize the autonomous Rojava government.[3]

Further, on September 19, 2021, at our annual convention, our members overwhelmingly passed a resolution stating that the Vermont AFL-CIO recognizes the government of Rojava, that we stand in solidarity with the revolution, and that we encourage Vermonters and American workers to volunteer with the YPG and YPJ in their armed struggle aimed at the establishment of a direct participatory democracy.[4]

Free Palestine

Beyond lending moral support for revolutionary movements, United! also sought to uphold basic anti-imperialism concerning the right of self-determination of an oppressed people. Thus, on June 16, 2021, our executive board also voted to endorse the Labor for Palestine statement calling for the end of Israeli occupation of Palestinian lands and for the US to stop enabling Israeli aggression though military and economic aid that is used, in part, to keep Palestinians subjugated. Signing on to this statement was the right thing to do given a recent uptick in Israeli violence at that time (and increased resistance by the Palestinian people, including a general strike against the decades-long occupation). And as with the Rojava statement, we were once again the only state labor council to sign on.

Let Cuba Live

In July of the same year, we were approached by the director of Labor against Racism and War, Yasemin Zahra, who asked if we would endorse an open letter to President Joe Biden demanding an end to the embargo on socialist Cuba.[5] The letter was to be published as a full-page ad in the *New York Times* on July 23, 2021. I have always admired the great achievements of the Cuban Revolution when it comes to providing free universal health care, free higher education, guaranteed housing, and basic nutrition to its people. I also hold in high regard the fact that Cuba was the only country in the world to send troops to Angola (back in the day) to fight with arms against an invading apartheid South African state. So it was with enthusiasm that I brought the solidarity request back to our executive board, which in turn voted to sign on to the statement. Once again, we were the only AFL-CIO state labor council to publicly support this effort.[6]

Building on this statement of solidarity with the Cuban people, Labor against Racism and War asked the Vermont AFL-CIO if we wished to recommend a member or leader to take part in a youth delegation to Cuba for the 2022 May Day celebrations in Havana. This was an invitation-only event. Without hesitation, as president, I recommended Katie Harris who, at thirty, was the youngest member of our executive board. Harris attended, meeting Ulises Guilarte de Nacimiento, general secretary of the Federation of Cuban Workers (and other Cuban labor leaders and officials) in the process. And in 2022, Harris, representing United!, may well have been the highest-ranking US union official in Cuba for May Day.[7]

War in Ukraine

In spring 2022, Vladimir Putin's Russia invaded Ukraine. From the start, I recognized that Putin was motivated by imperialism, driven by the desire to rebuild an empire lost. But I had serious concerns about the growing fascist presence in Ukraine. And even though it was plain that Putin was overstating the fascist threat to serve his own propaganda needs, it was also wildly inaccurate to depict the concerns about fascism and Nazism as nonexistent or fabricated. The fact is that since 2014, Ukraine willfully and officially incorporated the Nazi Azov Battalion (now Azov Regiment) into its armed forces and continued to provide arms and resources to these Nazis up to and during the invasion.[8] This marked the first time since the fall of the Franco regime in Spain in 1975 that actual fascists, as an organized unit, were formally part of a state military. Thus, to me, until and unless this reality was reversed I could not, in good conscience, support the arming of Ukraine by the US and NATO (even if Ukraine was suffering an unjustified invasion inspired by empire). And the existence of the Azov Battalion was not my only concern.

Ukraine, in the buildup to the war, dedicated hundreds of statues, memorials, plaques, and street names to Stepan Bandera and other World War II–era Nazi collaborators who played a direct role in the murdering of thousands of Ukrainian Jews and other ethnic minorities in the 1940s. Further, in recent years numerous armed fascist groups, such as the so-called National Militia, were operating in the country, dishing out their version of vigilante justice and attacking Roma communities. The preponderance of all this evidence, for me, could not be mitigated by the president, Volodymyr Zelenskyy, being Jewish. In short, there was too much smoke to will myself into believing that there could be no fire.

Among United!, I was not alone in my concerns. Executive Director Liz Medina, being an unapologetic antifascist herself, likewise was troubled by the notion of US arms potentially flowing to overtly Nazi formations in the name of combating Russia. She urged me to steer the Vermont AFL-CIO away from supporting Western involvement in the conflict.

In the end, I made the decision to not place the war in Ukraine on any executive board agendas. And while my fellow board members could have requested that it be added, they did not. And given the massive pro-Ukraine propaganda campaign being embraced by liberals and conservatives alike, and given that the corporate media was willfully ignoring or actively seeking to diminish the Nazi problem within Ukraine, I was content to allow the Vermont AFL-CIO to steer clear of staking out a definitive position on the matter—especially so because I did not know how a vote would go if it came up.[9] However, remaining in total silence on a major issue of the day is also not ideal for an organization that seeks to lead.

So, on March 21, 2022, I unilaterally released on op-ed on the war that acknowledged the right of the Ukrainian people to defend themselves against Russian imperialism but also called for the US and NATO to demand that the Ukrainian government, as a condition of receiving weapons, forcefully dissolve the Azov Battalion and commit to the West that no guns would be handed over to Nazi or fascist formations as part of the defense of their country.[10] The op-ed was published in a number of Vermont media outlets as well as by *CounterPunch*.[11]

For me, antifascism must be a core component of any progressive political program. There cannot be exceptions to this, and there can never be a time or circumstance when one can be justified in saying that "in this instance maybe it is okay to arm Nazis." While I often reject the notion that politics should be an all-sum game, when it comes to fascism, I feel that is the place where we must draw the line.

So Ukraine, since 2014 under three different presidents, could have chosen differently, or they, at any time, could have decided to revoke the Azov Battalion's standing within the armed forces. They did not. And until and unless they do, I cannot and will not support Western arms going to those who glorify the Holocaust.

In summation, by my count the enemy of my enemy is not my friend when they would replace their present tragedy with one that can lead to gas chambers for others. The Vermont AFL-CIO would therefore stay out of any political discourse that urged increased US or NATO involvement in Ukraine.

Ukraine aside, what should be plain at this point is that the Vermont AFL-CIO, through the leadership of United!, sought to be internationalist in outlook. We recognized that the fight for a more equitable and democratic world cannot start and stop at our borders. Given our progressive politics, this should not come as a surprise. What is surprising is that the national AFL-CIO did not attack us for voicing these positions (as they did when it came to Black Lives Matter and police reform, or concerning the general strike in the event of a fascist coup in the US). The national AFL-CIO, after all, claims exclusive jurisdiction on all political matters that are national or international in scope. As recently as October 2021, they exercised this asserted jurisdictional right when they inserted themselves into a San Francisco Central Labor Council debate, effectively forcing this CLC into dropping consideration of an antioccupation resolution concerning the Palestinian people.[12] Why the national AFL-CIO has not come after us on these matters, I can only speculate. But it certainly was not because we kept our positions a secret. Recall that our position on the revolution in Rojava was widely broadcast by ourselves and our allies (with the 2021 convention resolution being warned of well in advance). Our position against the continuing occupation of Palestine likewise became a matter of public record. And our demand that the Biden administration end the embargo on Cuba was published in the *New York Times*.

At the end of the day, it is the opinion of United! that state labor councils and CLCs should not be made to remain silent on national and international issues where the national AFL-CIO fails to provide leadership. Rather, we believe that it is through the voicing of opinion of the base, the more local labor bodies, that the national AFL-CIO can be made aware of the political inclinations of the base. As such, not only should the national AFL-CIO allow for such expressions of views (and the wider debate that may follow), but they should encourage such democratic expression. With this in mind, it is no accident that the Vermont AFL-CIO Executive Board, on April 14, 2022, advanced a resolution to the national AFL-CIO that, if passed at the June national convention, would set us down that path to allow for exactly that. But until such a time when national AFL-CIO policies change in order to allow for more bottom-up democracy, it will be important for state labor councils such as ours to be unafraid to take positions on those issues that working people across the globe are forced to wrestle with. Silence or acquiescence to injustice is not an option.

CHAPTER XI

Preparing for the Trump Coup: The General Strike Vote and Antifascism

> The sad truth of the matter is that most evil is done by people who never made up their minds to be or do either evil or good.
> —Hannah Arendt

Trump and the Disaster of the 2016 Election

In 2016, Americans unsurprisingly rejected establishment candidate Hillary Clinton for president. Clinton, like her husband, former president Bill Clinton, represented all that is wrong with the Democratic Party. From free trade to mandatory minimum prison sentences, to cozy relationships with the capitalist class, to repeated support for imperialist military ventures, the Clintons were and remain the figureheads of an oppressive status quo. Republican Donald Trump, on the other hand, in addition to being an insane pathological liar with fascist tendencies, presented himself as the outsider who as a starting point recognized the rigged nature of the system (even if it was billionaires like him who orchestrated much of the rigging). Trump also used race baiting and a right-wing nationalism to divide Americans and appeal to some of our worst impulses, but he did this while also saying that he would oppose free trade (repeal NAFTA) and would give voice to the blue-collar workers who the Democratic Party time and again had taken for granted and failed to deliver for. When pitted against Clinton, Trump's overtures to those who felt voiceless, combined with his quiet supporters among the ruling class (with all their resources), was enough for him to win the Electoral College (even if he lost the popular vote) and to become president of the United States in 2016.

But let's be clear: Trump, from the moment he took office, posed a danger to those vestiges of democracy remaining in the US. And even as he paid lip service to working people (mingled with a far-right xenophobia),

Vermont newspapers warning of a possible general strike, November 24, 2020.

he also was rabidly anti-union, as was shown in his National Labor Relations Board appointments (which led to procorporate rulings against workers and unions), his picks for the Supreme Court (which resulted in the overturning of mandatory union dues in the public sector), and in his administration's rule-making in areas that impacted unions (like when he sought to outlaw voluntary dues deductions nationally for homecare provider unions). And in April 2017, just three months into his presidency, he unveiled his true leanings when he failed to meaningfully condemn the violent Unite the Right clashes in Charlottesville, Virginia. In fact, Trump did the opposite, telling the American people that there were some very good people marching with the Nazis, Klansmen, neo-Confederates, right-wing militia members, and white supremacists on those days that saw an antifascist counterprotester murdered.

For the next three years, Trump's consistent attacks on democratic institutions escalated, as did his daily lies (which were enough to make Goebbels blush). And frankly, no swamp was drained. He became the swamp, one increasingly mired in fascist leanings and Russian manipulation, as well as sexism and racism. No worker was given real voice or power unless one came to falsely see themselves as represented by a white nationalist future in which "the other" would finally or again have their agency devalued and repressed by a conformity of discrimination and authoritarianism. But when massive Black Lives Matter protests broke out across the nation (sparked by repeated police murders of Black men), Trump uncritically supported law enforcement, condemned the protesters, and threatened to use the military to put down the protests throughout the country (going so far as to deploy Homeland Security personnel to Portland, Oregon, to detain demonstrators). He also was keen to refer to BLM and Antifa protesters as terrorists—all this while also calling the press the "enemy of the people."

The chaos and reactionary conflict Trump sought to inflame, while garnering cultlike support from his followers, also carried with it a backlash reflected in political poll after political poll (which throughout his time in office saw him lacking anything close to majority support among the American people). With the rise of the COVID-19 pandemic (which he declared was a hoax), it appeared that he would be beaten in the 2020 election if a more or less free and fair election were allowed to take place.

The 2020 Election and the Threat of a Fascist Coup

As his electoral defeat become more and more likely, so too did his undemocratic rhetoric. In one presidential debate with Joe Biden, he went so far as telling the far-right Proud Boys, an armed reactionary organization, to "stand by." He also floated the notion that the election should be postponed until after the pandemic, while additionally stating that the only way he could lose any election to Biden would be through massive fraud, and he refused to commit to a peaceful transfer of power postelection should he not be crowned the winner.

With these escalations in place, by the late summer and early fall Vermont's own US senator Bernie Sanders (himself a onetime presidential candidate) began to sound the alarm that a coup could be in the making.[1] We, the Vermont AFL-CIO, took Bernie's concerns seriously and began to give thought to what our response would be if Biden won but Trump refused to leave office. And here it was clear that our power as workers rested in our labor.

A general strike is when a city, state, or whole country is essentially shut down when labor of all kinds—carpenters, garbage collectors, electricians, office workers, transportation workers, service workers—all stop work at a coordinated time and refuse to go back to it. This is sometimes called a sympathy strike or a political strike, because workers are striking in sympathy with other workers or to advance or defend a political objective, and is often combined with direct action, marches, rallies and commandeering of land and resources to people. A general strike can fundamentally shut down a neighborhood, city, or whole counties, and on the broadest of scales, whole nations can be paralyzed by general strikes. General strikes—like the 1834 Philadelphia general strike—have been instrumental in passing what we view as basic labor laws today, like the ten-hour (and then eight-hour) workday, to name but one. The general strike is one of labor's most dramatic tools in fighting fascism, and it has a long history of doing so from at least the nineteenth century to the present day. They have proved critical not just in the Spanish Civil War but also in other revolutionary movements across the globe. They have been made illegal by the American government since the passage of the Taft-Hartley Act in 1947. But legal or not, if Trump chose to seek an end to democracy, what choice would we, as labor, have but to use all the effective weapons at our disposal?

It was within the paradigm of these disconcerting political realities that our Vermont AFL-CIO Executive Board concluded that our upcoming convention, slated for November 21, 2020, just weeks after the election, decided that the overarching theme of the gathering would be "democracy." Specifically, our United! leadership was unanimous in our decision to prepare a resolution for our members to consider that, if passed, would authorize us, as the elected leadership, to call for a general strike in Vermont if Trump lost the election but there was not a transfer of power on January 20, 2021.

But let me be very clear. When United! took power in 2019, we inherited a state labor council that was in disarray. Contact sheets for local officers were wildly out of date. Many affiliated union members did not even know that they were part of something called the AFL-CIO. In short, we were handed nearly zero infrastructure, and prior to 2019 we certainly did not have the ear of our members (let alone moral authority). While we made real progress addressing these weaknesses in the year we were in office, in no way did we have the ability to realistically call for and carry out a general strike under any normal circumstances. To do so in most instances would be a fool's game destined for failure. But facing down a potential fascist coup in the United States is certainly not a "normal circumstance."

Our calculation was this: On January 21, 2016, in the wake of the Trump election victory, twenty thousand Vermonters demonstrated in our state capital as part of the Women's March. While twenty thousand may not seem like a lot to folks in New York City or San Francisco, in Vermont terms, this was massive. Mind you, Montpelier, our capital, has a total population of only 7,800. Our state as a whole has a population of just over six hundred thousand. And that demonstration of twenty thousand was the largest political action in the Green Mountains in modern times. Point being, Vermonters were fired up and ready to take action when Trump won an election. If he lost this election, but sought to bring down democracy as a result, it was thought that the next rally could look like one hundred thousand (one out of six Vermonters). Further, we anticipated, under this scenario, spontaneous actions and resistance to break out across Vermont. Thus, if the Vermont AFL-CIO got out in front of this early, and if from the start we set up some basic infrastructure and provided ideological and tactical leadership, it was thought that the sheer momentum of history would make a general strike achievable. And if we did it in Vermont, our thought was that it could rapidly spread to other states.

But look, if we controlled the unfolding of history, and if conflict was unavoidable, we would have chosen 2024 as the year when a crisis in US democracy emerged (thus allowing us five years to build a compensative system of rank-and-file contacts in all our unionized workplaces). But history is not concerned with the trifling plans of men and women. History unfolds how it does, and the test of a people, of a labor movement, is met and judged based on how it rises to meet those challenges set before it, and even more so those of such weight that we wished we never had to tackle. And if a darkness were to threaten our republic, we knew that organized labor had an obligation to do everything in our power to resist said darkness. For us, that included taking steps to prepare for a general strike.

In the buildup to our November convention, a number of AFL-CIO central labor councils (such as those in Seattle, western Massachusetts, Rochester, and Troy) began to also pass resolutions flagging a general strike as a step labor must prepare to take if a coup was carried out by Trump and his cronies. But still, the national AFL-CIO, under President Richard Trumka, remained publicly silent on the tactic, although I did take part in one conference call with Trumka (and other state labor leaders) concerning the possibility of Trump taking antidemocratic steps postelection. During this call, I point-blank asked Trumka if he planned to call for or prepare for a general strike in the event of a coup. To this he did not give me a straight answer, instead electing to say no more than "All options are on the table." For me, given the magnitude of what appeared to be on the horizon, that answer was not good enough.

Thus, with national AFL-CIO leadership on the issue lacking, on October 25, 2020, just nine days before the presidential election, and twenty-seven days before our convention, we publicly released a statement making it widely know that we would hold a general strike authorization vote on November 21. At this point, the United! leadership was committed to doing what we felt we had to do in the face of right-wing threats.

Attacks from the National AFL-CIO

The response from the national AFL-CIO was swift. Within hours, the eastern regional director, David Driscoll-Knight (a top Trumka lieutenant and, by my estimation, a man of little vision beyond a blind loyalty to his union bosses), called me and implored me, in every way possible through confused logic and threat, to call off the vote.

At first, he argued that only the national AFL-CIO had the authority to call for a general strike (which as far as I could tell they had no intent to do), and then, when I stated very plainly that we were asking our members to authorize us to call for a general strike in Vermont alone (i.e., clearly within our jurisdiction), he changed tack and proceeded to argue that *no* AFL-CIO body had the authority to call for any strike, and that the power to strike was only vested in the affiliated internationals, alone, as separate entities within the AFL-CIO. Driscoll-Knight also informed me that there would be consequences for the Vermont State Labor Council if we did not support Trumka's party line. Here I clearly saw that he was threatening to place us under trusteeship, along with the forcible removal of all elected United! officers and the cutting of our national AFL-CIO funding (which amounted to a $30,000-a-year solidarity grant).

I was not impressed, and I was firm with Driscoll-Knight. I asserted that if democracy was to face its own demise, the Vermont AFL-CIO would not be complicit in its death. No, we would do everything in our power to resist such an attack, and the misguided and treacherous inaction of Richard Trumka would play no role in our decision-making on such a grave issue. Absurdly, Driscoll-Knight then tried to convince me that the most important thing the Vermont AFL-CIO should be doing now to defend our republic would be to set up informational tables in parts of the state to explain to the public how democracy works and why it is important, or some such thing. I laughed at this suggestion. I mean, the national AFL-CIO plan was to ask labor councils to conduct strategic tabling?! Jesus H. Christ, if that was the Trumka plan, coupled with some lawyering in coordination with the national Democratic Party, *we were fucking doomed*—or at least it was clear that the organization of real resistance would have to come from state labor councils, central labor councils, and locals.

So, I left that call with Driscoll-Knight more committed than ever to carrying out a general strike authorization vote, doing the basic ground-work necessary to make a mass work stoppage possible, and preparing for what could be a very dark time ahead.

Preparations for Conflict

I know that all of United! took the looming threat seriously. On a personal level, I also understood that a national conflict centered on a coup would carry danger to all Americans not only in a broad way, but also on a very personal level. I figured that if the coup came to fruition, and we were able to utilize the general strike as one means of resistance, then I, as Vermont AFL-CIO president, would be a target of repression. While I was not so concerned about myself, I did have concerns for my family.

At the time, I had two children: Freya, eleven, and William, seven.[2] And if the shit went down I would need to know they were out of harm's way (as much as possible) so that I could better focus on strike activity and whatever else came next (as a coup would inevitably lead to a violent conflict involving arms). Thus, I reached out to an old and trusted friend of mine in Montreal, David Battistuzzi, and asked if he could make arrangements for my kids (with their mom) to cross the border should a conflict intensify. Years before, Battistuzzi and I were members of the Northeastern Federation of Anarcho-Communists. Presently, he was a union member with CSN. He also maintained various left political connections in Quebec. He agreed that should the need arise my family could stay with him and his wife, Gaëlle Deblonde, in Canada. He further broached the subject with members of the Quebec Parliament from the leftist/separatist Solidaire Party. The aim was to have members of Parliament, as needed, meet my family at the border to seek to help them gain permission to cross as political refugees. Given that the border was locked down due to the COVID-19 pandemic, securing such assistance before the fact seemed important to me. So it was a load off my mind when Battistuzzi reported back that he had made contact and they were agreeable. So, from fall 2020 until the inauguration of Biden on January 20, 2021, my kids maintained packed backpacks, ready to go, should conflict intensify, although come what may I was absolutely committed to remaining in Vermont.

Prior to our strike authorization vote, we also came to the clear understanding that effective resistance to a coup must also include working with allied organizations both in Vermont and more broadly within the labor movement nationally. Thus, the Vermont AFL-CIO engaged in the Vermont-based Defend Democracy coalition, which included such organizations as Rights & Democracy, VPIRG, and others to plan out postelection steps should the crisis take form.[3] Coming out of this, we backed a rally in our state capital the night after the election that stated our common intent to defend democratic processes come what may in the coming weeks and months.[4] Nationally, we engaged within the Labor Action to Defend Democracy coalition to advance the support for strike activity across the United States should such a step be warranted.

Trump Defeated at the Polls, Coup Threat Intensifies, and Alliance Building

Then, on Election Day 2020, and confirmed in the days to come as the vote count concluded, it came to pass that Republican Donald Trump lost the presidential election to Democrat Joe Biden. Trump finished seven million behind Biden in the popular vote and was slated to lose the Electoral College vote 232–306. There were zero credible assertions of anything approaching widespread voter fraud. But as we expected, Trump did not concede. Rather, he claimed victory and immediately set about taking steps that could serve his interest in retaining power despite the loss. Just as we foresaw, a crisis in democracy was emerging over the near horizon. And still, the national AFL-CIO under Richard Trumka did not appear to have a plan if the situation escalated, and so the Vermont AFL-CIO's intent to make our own preparations were more pressing than ever.

Knowing that the acute danger of the moment would likely grow ever more perilous with each passing day, as state labor council president I did not wait until our convention and consideration of the general strike resolution to take preparatory action. Rather, I rapidly opened up lines of communication with our allies from the Vermont Progressive Party on the Burlington City Council (who represented the largest bloc on the council), as well as with influential Montpelier city councilor Conor Casey (a Democrat) and Bennington town manager Stuart Hurd. All of these communities had unionized public workforces, all of which carried a political bent that could make them focal points for a successful mass work stoppage. My thought was to sow the seeds of a politically supported general strike in these three strategic locations, and that success there would help us build momentum in other sections of the state. Bennington, being in the south, carried the symbolic power of being the birthplace of the Green Mountain Boys and headquarters for the 1770–75 rebellion against the Royal New York Colony, which claimed the territories that would become Vermont. Montpelier (in central Vermont) was important on many levels as the state capital. Burlington, in the north, was economically the most crucial as our largest city (with a population of forty thousand).

With the Bennington town manager, Hurd, I explained that the Vermont AFL-CIO would likely pass a general strike authorization resolution in the weeks to come and told him that I wanted to know if the town government would support us in this action if there was a coup. Here the city workers were organized into AFSCME Local 490, under local president Dan Cornell, and Bennington College workers by SEIU Local 200 (who signed a solidarity charter with us), and of course there were many other unions in town, including the postal and school workers. Hurd expressed to me that he was sympathetic and that he thought the select board would be as well. He agreed to bring the issue to the select board if events unfolded in such a way that a strike became probable.

In Montpelier, I asked Councilor Casey (who, in his previous election, was one of the few Democrats we had endorsed) if we could count on him to seek to rally support for a strike with the mayor (Progressive Anne Watson, who we had also endorsed in her previous election) and city council should it come to it. He assured me that he would. Montpelier, in addition to having thousands of unionized state workers (in the non-AFL-CIO-affiliated VSEA), had its public employees organized into AFL-CIO unions. And while NEA had many of the school workers in their ranks, AFSCME Local 1369 represented support staff.

For Burlington, with the help of Vermont Progressive Party executive director Josh Wronski, I organized a virtual meeting with the Progressive Party caucus on city council. Here the ask was to line up the city squarely behind a mass strike, with city government support, if the coup came. With AFSCME Local 1343 representing 250 city workers, IBEW Local 300 representing workers at the publicly owned power plant, and dozens of other major shops in the city (like at UVM, the schools, and so on), labor had the power to shut down the city if it so chose. But to the councilors I expressed that our intent would be to approach such a strike rationally, and in such a way that essential public services (like water, electricity, fire department, the hospital) would be retained. But what I wanted from city government was a commitment that the strikers would be supported and that jobs would not be at risk. And further, if, through the actions of the Progressive Party, the call for the work stoppage was amplified, I saw a very real path whereby the strike could reach down into every workplace in every corner of the city. The Progressive Party caucus, in this meeting, in no uncertain terms shared the deep concerns about the precariousness of democracy within the US at this dangerous moment and expressed to me their deep commitment to partnering with us on this general strike effort. Also, I invited them to our convention as guests (an invitation that was accepted by city council president Max Tracy, Brian Pine, and Zoraya Hightower). All told, the Progressives agreed to be at the ready to support the Vermont AFL-CIO should that time come and to seek to have the city support us. This support from the democratic socialist–oriented Progressives, whom we had endorsed in the previous successful election, was more than welcomed.

As our November 21 convention drew near, we received a letter from national AFL-CIO president Richard Trumka just days before, again demanding that we call off the strike authorization vote. The letter argued that such a vote ran counter to internal bylaws that forbid a state labor council from forcing an affiliate to strike or holding a strike authorization vote. The letter also insinuated that if we did not acquiesce to his demands he would take punitive steps against us and would further investigate whether every aspect of our convention was done according to national and state bylaws. Our Vermont AFL-CIO Executive Board reviewed the letter and determined that the bylaws he cited were clearly in reference to traditional economic strikes aimed against an employer, and further the fact that our prepared resolution simply empowered leadership to "call for" a general strike, and in and of itself did not force affiliates to heed such a call. In no event did any AFL-CIO bylaws anticipate the possibility of a political strike in reaction to a fascist coup. Thus, we viewed the letter as nothing more than a pile of threats aimed at us for daring to take a divergent political line, one both more militant and more effective than what he was prepared to do. And while we fully acknowledged that Trumka's power to retaliate was real, collectively we judged our obligation as Vermont's foremost labor leaders to resist the demise of democracy as paramount over any desire we may harbor to remain in office ruling over a rump labor movement at the sharp end of a sword wielded by would-be dictators.

The 2020 Convention and General Strike Vote

On November 21, 2020, we convened our convention (which was held remotely due to the COVID-19 pandemic). With seventy-two registered delegates and alternates, and with additional rank-and-file members present along with invited guests (from the Vermont Progressive Party, Democratic Socialists of America, social justice allies, and a delegation of union workers from the UK who had requested and been granted observer status), over one hundred were in attendance. Thus, once again our convention was one of the largest and most attended in decades. There were three major agenda items: (1) the general strike authorization resolution, (2) a workshop on building rank-and-file networks of shop-floor

leaders throughout Vermont, and (3) a series of Vermont AFL-CIO constitutional amendments aimed at democratizing our state labor council.

The agenda was all linked to the idea that we must first defend the
democracy we have (the general strike) while we also worked toward building our internal capacity in order to achieve more collective power (the
rank-and-file networks) so that we could more effectively fight to expand
the democratic rights of workers throughout the Green Mountains. We
wanted to achieve this while also further democratizing our own labor
federation so that we could better become that which we sought to uphold
externally.

I opened the convention, with a YPG flag behind me, by addressing
the members directly, challenging them to weigh the dangers facing our
democracy against how they felt we should act to counter this threat and
urging them to gauge such a decision according to how history would
remember us.[5] In brief, I sought to appeal to our common historic belief
in democracy as Vermonters, ask that we put aside any partisan divisions,
and do what together we believed to be right regardless of the dangers.
And with the tone set, we rapidly moved to the pressing business at hand.

In addition to reinforcing our commitment to building an internal
system of local rank-and-file contacts in every unionized shop in Vermont,
over two-thirds of the delegates present approved Vermont AFL-CIO
constitutional changes that would further democratize the federation.
These changes increased the minimum delegates each local was afforded
to conventions from two to five, doubled the additional delegate allotment
per five hundred members within locals, increased the elected executive
board from eleven to nineteen, and increased the threshold required to
move from a participatory democratic process at conventions to weighted
voting from a 20 percent delegate vote to a 30 percent delegate vote.

Concerning the former, in our platform we sought to go further.
United! actually supports moving to a one-member-one-vote system
when it comes to electing officers. However, the national AFL-CIO, who
must approve all state constitutional changes before they go into effect,
informed us previously that they would not allow for a state labor council
to allow all their members to vote in union elections.[6] Rather, they require
that elections of officers be done only by the delegates at a convention.
And here, once (or if) a motion is made for weighted voting, if the requisite
number of delegates support such a motion, then delegates get to place a

vote equal to the number of members they represent. Thus, if a local with a thousand members sends one delegate to a convention, and if weighted voting is in force, that one delegate can place the equivalent of a thousand votes. From a democratic process point of view, United! opposed this system, because it encourages locals to have minimum participation at conventions. In essence, it incentivizes less participation as opposed to more. Regardless, the national AFL-CIO previously expressed to us that the maximum change they would approve would be a raising of the bar to 30 percent. And hence our constitutional amendment on that issue was crafted to reach that maximum level.

At our convention, delegates also voted to eliminate all anticommunist language (a holdover from the Red Scare and Cold War) and replace it with language barring fascists and racists from holding office in the Vermont AFL-CIO. We also adopted an essentially socialist (and anticapitalist) preamble, as follows:

> We, the working class, produce all of the goods and services in our society; we also constitute the overwhelming majority of people. However, instead of fully directing and enjoying the fruits of our labor, we have allowed the lion's share of our wealth to be given to the few who compose the wealthy capitalist class. Throughout the history of capitalism, these few have waged class war so that they may hoard what they have never earned, as well as that which they have stolen. The capitalist class, i.e., the wealthy and elite— which claims ownership over our industry, commerce, finance, and land—has kept the spoils of this war by means of combination, governmental intervention, and the sowing of division among us.
>
> The costs of their class war are great. Far too many have been, and continue to be, deprived, malnourished, or even starved. Others have been, and continue to be, brutalized and even killed through willful negligence or violence. Our very planet is being destroyed. To save ourselves, the working class must organize itself beyond individual unions. All workers must band together to build a more just society. Instead of working for the profit and wealth of the few, we will work for the wealth and health of all. Instead of unnecessary weapons, mismanaged funds, unnecessary poverty, and unjustly imprisoned masses, there will be bread and roses for all our people.

Namely, ample social benefits and common expressions of our vast, diverse cultural heritage will be enjoyed by all workers. Instead of spreading hate, we will spread love of all our people.

We, the representatives of the various trade and labor Unions in these Green Mountains, do hereby form the Vermont State Labor Council, AFL-CIO, for the purpose of organizing and concentrating the efforts of the working class for our mutual protection, education, and advancement. We would work toward establishing a more just society based on economic equity and a more direct democracy, and to that end we adopt the following.[7]

In the end, perhaps somewhat surprisingly, all of these constitutional amendments were approved by the national AFL-CIO and remain in effect today.

When the convention turned toward the general strike authorization vote, our members and seated delegates took over an hour in debating and amending the resolution.[8] From the start, it was apparent that our membership took the threat posed by the electorally defeated Trump administration seriously. And likewise, our members also understood that what we chose to do or not do if a fascist coup was to become manifest in our country was the central question of the day.

As the debate unfolded, it was of interest that one delegate from OPEIU, George Noel, the business agent for Local 6, took the floor to state that he was in general agreement with what the resolution sought to prepare for but questioned if the convention had the authority to adopt such a resolution in light of the national AFL-CIO's opposition to it. Brother Noel referenced and discussed the letter sent by Trumka ordering us against engaging in this issue.[9] What is of note here is that Noel had the Trumka letter. We did not send it to him (nor did he serve in our leadership). In other words, Trumka targeted Noel (and others?) with a direct communication regarding the letter, likely because he is a union staffer, a business agent, and often staff persons within labor are more likely to heed the directives from up above (not saying George is of that type, just meaning that in general this is sometimes the case).

In response, myself and other executive board members, such as Dwight Brown (AFSCME), responded to this question essentially by saying the executive committee had received the letter, fully reviewed it, and concluded that Trumka's interpretation of the governing bylaws were wrong and politically motivated. Brown went even further and stated something to the effect of "Look, calling for a general strike if there is a coup in this country is actually the *least* we should do" and that whenever democracy comes into crisis in the United States organized labor has a moral and political responsibility to take steps to defend said democracy.

After robust discussion, the question was eventually called. First I asked for an unofficial indicative vote from *all* persons at the convention (delegates, alternates, rank-and-file members without standing, allies, and guests). Here, 92 percent of those present voted to authorize the executive board to call for a general strike in Vermont should the coup unfold. Then I called for an official vote of just the seated delegates, and 87 percent of them also voted for the general strike authorization. The matter was settled. The following, in part, was the resolution as it was adopted:

> THEREFORE BE IT RESOLVED that the Vermont AFL-CIO is empowered by the delegates at the 2020 state convention to call for a general strike of all working people in our state in the event that Donald Trump refuses to concede the office of President of the United States.
>
> BE IT FURTHER RESOLVED that the Vermont AFL-CIO will work with allies in the antiracist, environmental justice, feminist, LGBTQ+, immigrant rights, and disability rights movements to protect our democracy, the Constitution, the law, and our nation's democratic traditions.
>
> BE IT FURTHER RESOLVED that the Vermont AFL-CIO will call on city and county governments to pledge to protect protesters defending democracy, and commit to not using police action or curfews to curtail these activities, and to use all available resources to stand up against any effort by the Trump administration to steal the presidential election.
>
> BE IT FURTHER RESOLVED that the Vermont AFL-CIO commits itself to the long-term goal of winning genuine democracy through the abolition of the Electoral College and two-party system, through the collective action of our affiliates and allied organizations.[10]

Taking Steps toward the General Strike

In the weeks and months following the general strike resolution, our executive board monitored the emerging political situation in Washington closely. As we expected, Trump continued to not concede, and his henchmen went about filing frivolous motions to the courts proclaiming widespread voter fraud without one ounce of proof (all motions being dismissed). More dangerously, Trump personally asked the Georgia secretary of state (a state Biden won) to produce twenty thousand more Trump votes to switch the outcome (votes that did not exist) and actively pressured Republican legislatures in states that voted for the Democrat to not certify the election results and instead to send alternative, pro-Trump delegates to the Electoral College. Fortunately, a critical mass of local and state election officials retained a basic level of integrity to stifle these efforts, but the efforts themselves showed that Trump was looking for a way to pull off a coup with a veneer of legalistic legitimacy.

Here in Vermont, at first with the assistance of State Representative Brian Cina (of the Progressive Party and a member of DSA), I opened up a channel of communications with the Vermont National Guard. I was concerned that Trump might seek to use the military to stay in power (as some of his advisors were pushing him to do), and I felt it was important that we seek to know early on where our Vermont military stood.

While some on the left, for ideological reasons, are apt to paint the armed forces with a uniform brush as all equally reactionary, I knew that many of our union members had served prior to attaining their current jobs. I also had the experience, in 2005, of being embedded with the Vermont National Guard in the New Orleans area in the aftermath of Hurricane Katrina. At the time I was working as a freelance journalist (and was a member of the National Writers Union UAW Local 1981) and was in Louisiana filing stories for the *Vermont Guardian* and various leftist publications.[11] One night, after shadowing Vermont National Guard units as they patrolled a residential neighborhood, the servicemen present told me their stories from the Iraq war zone. Revealing in those stories was a clear distinction between the perceived views and actions of their units as opposed to the regular army. Where the army was more apt to take an aggressive approach, the guard, while always ready to use force to defend themselves, favored a more passive approach to the occupation and conflict (or so they reported). Some even reported that they opposed the war, and one stated he would not go back even if ordered. I bring this up here only to highlight that there are very real differences between the different branches of the US military, and in the lead-up to a potential fascist coup it behooves those planning a resistance to understand, to the best of their abilities, where the various branches will fall if the shit were to go down.[12]

Initially, I sought to open dialogue with Adjutant General Gregory Knight as early as October 2020. The general's willingness to engage was minimal. However, the line of communication remained open, and as political tension mounted, come January 2021, a Captain Mikel Arcovitch was assigned to liaison with us. The captain and I exchanged phone calls and emails. I expressed that the Vermont AFL-CIO were prepared to engage in a general strike to defend democracy and said that we wanted to know if the Vermont National Guard would stand with us (or at least aside) even if Trump nationalized the guard and sought to use them as an extension of his power. While I never did get the clear commitment I was looking for, not unsymbolically, on January 6, the same day as the right-wing insurrection in DC, I received the following as part of an email from Captain Arcovitch:

> The Vermont National Guard serves the Governor of Vermont, and are sworn to uphold the Constitutions of Vermont and the United States. I can't speak to hypothetical situations, but can tell you we have received no such requests at this time.

From November 2020 through January 2021, we also sought to provide clear updates to our members about the unstable political situation, reaffirm our commitment to and need for defending democracy, and keep our lines of communications with allies and political figures open. During this period, we also refrained from our attacks on the Democratic Party. While United! clearly viewed the Democrats as part of the broad problem when it came to the rights and empowerment of working-class people, we were also cognizant of the fact that under coup conditions in which the party to their right was leading the reactionary charge, we felt it wise to leave open the possibility of working with them (while retaining our full scope of decision-making authority) on the tactical level if the need were to arise. Further, we felt it was important to acutely focus on the extremist elements on the far right as our immediate common enemy.[13] With that focus in place, we also actively engaged with the media in order to seek to popularize the notion that a mass general strike was on the table and the right thing to do if there was not a transfer of power on January 20, 2021.

The January 6 Insurrection: Democracy Hangs in the Balance

The closest we got to seeing the acute need to mobilize for the strike was on January 6, 2021. On that day that will live in infamy, armed right-wing forces, encouraged by Donald Trump, stormed the US Capitol and forcibly stopped (or rather delayed) the official certification of the Biden win. This violent fascist insurrection sought to shut down the certification, thus making the certification miss its constitutional deadline. If this were to be achieved, the awarding of the presidency could have been thrown to Congress, and here, as a result of the way by which voting is awarded per state, the advantage would have rested with the Republicans. And with that, Trump could have had a path to retain power even after losing an election by every conceivable way of gauging such. But the insurrection failed, and after a long delay, once security was reestablished within the Capitol, Congress reconvened, and they and Vice President Mike Pence finished the Electoral College vote count and announced Democrat Joe Biden the winner.[14]

While January 6 was the most dangerous moment in the postelection period, the defeat of the insurrection was not the end of the threat. There were still those in the Trump camp urging him to declare martial law as a means to stay in the White House, and paramilitary groups on the far right continued to saber-rattle for some weeks. In fact, on January 17, 2021, all fifty state capitals were on high alert after the FBI received intel that armed pro-Trump partisans would descend on capital cities throughout the nation, Montpelier being no exception.

In response, I asked our executive board to endorse a prodemocracy counterrally called for by a number of local activists on the same day and at the same time. However, despite my argument that it was important to show that we were not afraid to confront fascists be they armed or not, a majority of our leadership declined. They felt that embracing such a conflict, especially when all Vermont political parties (Progressive, Democrat, and Republican) seemed united in condemning the January 6 insurrection, would be unnecessarily provocative.[15] Thus, my motion to back the counterprotest was defeated. Even so, as an individual I did go to Montpelier on that day, and I am not reticent to state that strapped to my side was a loaded .357 Smith & Wesson revolver (with a twelve-gauge laid across the back seat of my Jeep). And further, I made sure that a few trusted people were also there, also packing heat (just in case).

As it turned out, an armed counterpresence was not needed. While one hundred Vermonters showed up (to city hall) to express their support for democracy, and while there was an unprecedented police presence in our capital on that day, the *only* right-winger to heed the fascist call was a single unarmed Canadian who found himself (for whatever reason) on this side of the border and apparently felt it his duty to show his blind support for Trump. Thus, no further insurrections took form that day in Montpelier or in any other state capital.

From January 18 through the swearing-in of Biden on January 20, it seemed that the far right had played their hand and lost (this time). While there was always a small chance a final Hail Mary would be thrown, the wind was out of the sails of the fascist aspirations. And on January 20, the transfer of power finally took place (even if Trump never did concede defeat).

Throughout the period of November 21, 2020 (the day we passed the general strike resolution), through January 20, 2021 (the day Biden took office), we did not hear from the national AFL-CIO, nor did Richard Trumka take any punitive measures against us. In fact, it was complete radio silence.

While I do not have firsthand inside information about the deliberations of the national AFL-CIO inner circle during this time, I would nevertheless speculate that Trumka, like the rest of us, saw that the threat of a coup was increasingly real. And in that time of danger, it did not serve his interest to mount (what would become) a public fight against the *only* AFL-CIO state labor council that not only foresaw the dangerous actions Trump would take to retain power (and the violence used on January 6 to advance his fascist aims), but also took the meaningful step of preparing for a general strike should historical developments demand. And frankly, as a coup became more and more of a present threat, perhaps even he recognized that we were right. But regardless of his motivation, it was not until months after Biden assumed the presidency that Trumka would make good on the threats he had issued in fall 2020. And further, even though the Vermont AFL-CIO did not end up having to pull the trigger on

the general strike, every person in our United! leadership held their head high knowing that when it mattered, when democracy came under threat from a fascist takeover, we prepared to do the right thing, come what may.

The Vermont AFL-CIO's Antifascism

With or without being in the White House, Trump, through four years of undermining democracy and human dignity while giving voice to a new nationalism and xenophobia, had created the conditions within which fascism can flourish. As such, it is not enough for a labor movement to be prepared to call for mass work stoppage if there is a coup. Rather, the rise of fascism must be combated on many lesser levels, and the preparation for conflict must be anticipated by labor long before disaster strikes. Thus, the Vermont AFL-CIO did not rest on its laurels after January 20, 2021. Rather, we have since gone further by also chartering an antifascist union motorcycle club, the Green Mountain Riders, who are specifically tasked with the role of acting as an auxiliary force to our appointed sergeant-at-arms in order to provide security at union events, or in reaction to fascist threats.[16] And at our 2021 Vermont AFL-CIO Convention our members, by an overwhelming vote of our delegates, adopted a policy position whereby we became the first state labor council in the nation to oppose any new gun control measures. We did this explicitly to allow us to maintain and increase our ability to defend ourselves against a rising fascist movement that is already armed (and which no gun control law will ever realistically reverse).[17]

Later, in June 2022, I and Executive Director Liz Medina attended the national AFL-CIO convention in Philadelphia as delegates (with me representing the Vermont state labor council and Medina representing one of our CLCs).[18] One resolution we came with (submitted by the Vermont AFL-CIO) called on the national AFL-CIO to take steps to organize a nationwide general strike should there be a second coup attempt in the aftermath of the 2024 presidential election. Part of that resolution called for the formation of an AFL-CIO antifascist task force geared toward studying the problem of rising fascism and providing action steps to state labor councils aimed at combating fascists on the state and local level. The national AFL-CIO Executive Council undemocratically refused to allow our resolution to come to the delegates for open debate and a vote. However, Medina at one point spoke from the floor articulately demanding action on the rising fascism and introduced the proposal for the creation of the antifascist task force as an amendment to a resolution against racism. To this, Medina received applause. We had coordinated the night before with APWU president Mark Dimondstein and Association of Flight Attendants president Sara Nelson, and Nelson stood by ready to second the motion. However, presiding officer Fred Redmond (the national secretary-treasurer) ruled that amendments were out of order but offered to forward the request to the national AFL-CIO's Racial Justice Commission for consideration. Director Medina agreed to this.

In short, United! and the Vermont AFL-CIO takes antifascism seriously, and we understand that when fascists again seek to take power, we would be fools to rely on the state alone to defend us from such a menace. Rather, it will only be the working class, as the great majority and as led by the labor movement, that will possess the numbers, means, and motivation to confront those forces that would plunge our republic into darkness. And finally, let it never be forgotten that in late 2020 and early 2021, the United States was only one presidential order and one reactionary general away from seeing our politics devolve into shooting in the streets.[19]

Labor cannot lose sight of this.

In brief, if we are to defend our democracy and in fact build more democracy, and if we are to effectively resist domestic fascist threats, we must prepare now for whatever the future may hold. And here we must never forget the lessons that history teaches us, not least of which being the experience of workers in Spain during the Civil War of 1936–39. *¡No pasarán!*[20]

CHAPTER XII

War against the Old Guard

Well I stand up next to a mountain
And I chop it down with the edge of my hand
—Jimi Hendrix, "Voodoo Child (Slight Return)"

When They Finally Came for Us

On March 3, 2021, the attack from Richard Trumka and the national AFL-CIO finally came. Yet again, this unprincipled witch hunt started with another phone call from Eastern Regional Director David Driscoll-Knight. I recall it came while I was in Newport, just south of the Quebec border, visiting our shops from Local 2413 (Northeast Kingdom). Driscoll-Knight told me that Trumka was opening a formal investigation into our passage of the general strike resolution and to see if we had committed any procedural violations at or leading up to our 2021 convention. This time I raised my voice to Driscoll-Knight, made it emphatically clear that we were proud of our decisions when a crisis in democracy was afoot, and informed him that we would not suffer such retaliation in private or without fighting back. He asked me if we intended to go to the press. I told him that we would do what we had to do. The call rapidly ended.

From that point on (as long as Trumka remained national AFL-CIO president), after having to deal with the snake in the grass Driscoll-Knight on the issue of Black Lives Matter and police reform and more recently on the general strike, I would no longer allow the normalization of national AFL-CIO staff conducting direct communications with me as the standard. Instead, I would often direct national AFL-CIO staff to reach out to my staff (our executive director, Liz Medina). I decided this because I held an elected position, and therefore I needed Richard Trumka to know that I would be willing to talk directly with him and other

nationally elected leaders, but I would not invite the perception that he or anyone else could hide behind their staff. Thus, I sought to set right the perception of power.

Quickly after the phone call with Driscoll-Knight, we did indeed get the letter of investigation from Trumka. And by March 14, 2021, the Vermont AFL-CIO put up on our public social media the full video of our general strike debate and vote as it unfolded at our convention. (The video quickly gained over 3,800 views.) We weren't inclined to apologize for not being cowards, and we intended to signal that if a fight must be had, we were prepared to do so in front of the entire labor movement.[1]

The Fight Must Be Public Even If We Can't Win

On March 22, 2021, I convened our executive board to meet and discuss the new threat and formally decide on our collective response. The United!

leadership was not surprised about the retaliation, but they were pissed. It was clear that the logical aim in conducting the investigation was to justify the forced removal of all of us from our officer positions and to place the Vermont State Labor Council into trusteeship, with Trumka and the national AFL-CIO taking dictatorial control over organized labor in Vermont. Given that all the "facts" were already known (as we had been forthright with the national AFL-CIO and the media in the months prior), Trumka could have unilaterally issued a written reprimand at any time. But if he was to usurp the local democracy of our labor council, he would have to go through this motion. Thus, we were under no illusion about what was happening here.

The executive board unanimously agreed that we should fight this attack on union democracy in the public arena and that we would not shy away from open criticisms of Trumka and the undemocratic nature of the national AFL-CIO. We also committed to keeping our rank and file informed and educated on the matter in order to keep our base united. In brief, our intent was to make the assault as costly as possible for Trumka and the old guard. We would make them pay a price.

Further, it was agreed that we would seek to use this challenge to go on the offensive, in that we would reach out to the more progressive state labor councils, central labor councils, internationals, and locals throughout the country not only to ask for their support but also to suggest the creation of a national progressive caucus within the AFL-CIO. Here we would use the Trumka attack on us to illustrate why the national AFL-CIO was in desperate need of internal democratic reform, articulate the leftist program of the Vermont AFL-CIO as a starting point from which we could build a national platform, and aim to utilize such a caucus to both better put the labor movement on combative footing and have impact on the 2022 (internal) national elections should a progressive such as Sara Nelson throw her hat into the presidential ring.[2] In short, we wanted to explore making United! into a national force. Executive Vice President Tristin Adie was appointed to head our caucus-building efforts, and I, as president, would be lead in public messaging via the media.

Soon after that executive board meeting, I made a call to my uncle, Patrick Brown.[3] Pat served as the general counsel of the New York State Building Trades AFL-CIO for many years and had a clear understanding of the power dynamics at play. I wanted to get his advice as a person who would understand the inside game. Pat also was sympathetic to our politics and our plight. On the call, he compared our position to that of the Scots concerning the Battle of Falkirk. Like at Falkirk, he saw this as a fight we had to engage in but which we could not win. And I too knew we could not win …

Our mere ten to eleven thousand members were a drop in the bucket next to the millions that are the AFL-CIO.[4] I also soberly understood that we lacked the resources, both money and staff, required to overcome the massive odds against us. And it was no secret that Trumka had powerful friends within the internationals and the Democratic Party that could be brought to bear against us. But I also recognized that we had a historic obligation to make this a fight. If the national could attack and disman-tle a state labor council for daring to defend democracy, if this were not resisted in plain view to the best of our abilities, it would bring about a chilling effect among AFL-CIO unions across the nation and could set back labor militancy for years to come. So even if defeat was woven into our fate, we had no choice but to engage in the battle. And for me to lead the fight as effectively as possible, I had to will myself to believe (even if against all logic) that we could in fact win. So this is what I did, even if deep down I knew better.

Richard Trumka and the Betrayal of Reform

National AFL-CIO president Richard Trumka serving in the role of villain (a role he willfully chose) was both unfortunate and serves as a cautionary tale of how a labor leader can be changed by the trappings and prestige of office. Trumka, it will be recalled, started off as a leader in the United Mine Workers of America, where, at times, he was unafraid to confront the bosses. He then came to national union office in 1996 when he ran for and won the position of AFL-CIO secretary-treasurer as part of the reform-oriented New Voices slate under newly elected president John Sweeney. At first, New Voices seemingly put a priority on provid-ing national resources to grassroots organizing and engagement with central labor councils and state labor councils. But by the time Trumka was elected president in 2009 (two years after I was first elected to an executive board position within the Vermont AFL-CIO), and increas-ingly in every year since, the AFL-CIO more and more cut back on their organizing efforts and fell into the failed pattern of putting the election of Democrats, and suit-and-tie lobbying, above all else. By 2021, in fact, Trumka's track record was such that the only times he seemed to take risks was when confronting the rank and file about an internal racism that had to be addressed and overcome. But here, in 2008, the focus was never meaningfully to join the Black community in their four-hundred-year struggle for real liberation, but rather to cajole white workers to vote for Democrat Barack Obama for president.[5]

By the time of the telling of this story, few would even remember that Trumka began as a reformer. Fewer still, on the wider left, would see him as anything more than an old-guard union boss more comfortable in the company of Senate Majority Leader Chuck Schumer or Speaker Nancy Pelosi than with rank-and-file union members. And as this story unfolded, he represented all that was wrong with organized labor; he was our enemy.

The Gathering of Allies

Early on, I reached out to Mark Dimondstein, international president of APWU and a member of the national AFL-CIO Executive Board. Dimondstein was one of the few truly progressive national leaders within the upper ranks of the AFL-CIO. He was also supportive of the reform efforts being taken by United! and agreed we did the right thing by preparing for a general strike. Mark offered United! his full support and pledged to work with fellow progressive Sara Nelson (also part of the national leadership) to circulate a letter among national executive board members supporting United! and calling for Trumka to put an end to his retaliation against us. Likewise, our executive director, Liz Medina, made contact with Sister Nelson, who, like Dimondstein, offered her full support. Thus, we would not be totally isolated concerning the inside game. But we also knew that an inside game alone was not enough.

Externally I reached out to a friend, labor writer Steve Early (and former CWA organizer), explaining the situation and asking if he would write an article on our plight. Come April 2021, he did just that, and it was favorable to our cause, painting it as a kind of David-versus-Goliath battle with progressive reformers pitted against an increasingly conservative old guard. The article made its rounds, being published in many forums including *In These Times* and *CounterPunch*. That first article led to numerous media inquiries (just as we'd hoped), and I began to do the rounds of interviews for a growing audience. At first, my language toward Trumka was somewhat reserved. Initially, I even implied that he may have been acting on incorrect information from his staff. But with each passing interview, my charges against him became more and more harsh and combative. This was by design. My thought here was to at first provide him with a face-saving out, but then to escalate my rhetoric as he failed to set a new course or do the right thing. So in the four months between March and June 2021, when the investigation was still active, I eventually came to the place where I had no qualms publicly calling into question Trumka's commitment to democracy itself (both defending it in our republic and practicing it within the labor movement).

Parallel to the media campaign, Tristin Adie continued to seek allies within AFL-CIO affiliates. But here we were up against a culture of inaction and the realities of capacity. And frankly, our efforts to spark the formation of a national progressive caucus was bearing little fruit. The Chicago Teachers Union and UTLA, while sharing similar politics with United!, seemed to be exclusively focused on their own local struggles and were unwilling to expand their sphere of action. Other state labor councils, even those that were sympathetic to our cause, were reluctant to stick their neck out in fear that they too would suffer retribution from Trumka and his leadership. In fact, the president of the Virginia AFL-CIO went so far as to say they were with us but thought we were wrong to take this public, and instead should be filing appeals through internal channels. Of course, United! rejected such a notion, as we felt that would play directly into the hands of Trumka (who would be able to pull the strings within such internal processes). Even so, our request for solidarity did not fall totally on deaf ears. A number of labor bodies and allied organizations, such as Rochester Central Labor Council AFL-CIO (New York), Southeastern North Carolina Central Labor Council AFL-CIO, Asian Pacific American Labor Alliance Philadelphia Chapter, Asian Pacific American Labor Alliance Maryland Chapter, Jobs and Equal Rights for All, the *Organizer* newspaper (San Francisco), the Liberty Tree Foundation, Solidarity Info Service (California), and US Labor against Racism and War, did offer public support, but their numbers were too few to be anything remotely close to decisive; in fact, on their own their limited scope lent an appearance of weakness. Thus, we would have to look elsewhere to increase the pressure on Trumka.

One place where it was thought we could find support was among the old-school radicals from the New Left. Recall that some figures of that era, such as Jeff Jones of the Weather Underground, took note of our previous militant position concerning Black Lives Matter and police reform. So perhaps they could be mustered to stand with us now. And in the five decades from their time on the radical fringe, many from the New Left had assumed places of influence and respectability in the fields they had remained active in (and as fighters from a past time, they held a degree of moral authority within progressive circles). Thus, in May 2021, I reached out to the current AFSCME Local 1343 president, Ron Jacobs (a firm United! supporter), and asked him if he would coordinate an effort to produce an open letter to Trumka on our situation, calling for all retaliation to end, and to have it signed by (old) New Left leaders and allies.

Ron was the perfect person for this task, as he, in addition to being a union member working at the Burlington library, was the author of a number of books on the New Left, including *The Way the Wind Blew* and *Daydream Sunset*, and was well connected in those circles. Jacobs readily agreed. Through his efforts on May 19, 2021, signed by twenty-seven notable New Left figures such as Jeff Jones (Weathermen) and Roxanne Dunbar-Ortiz (Cell 16), the letter was sent to Trumka and also made public through social media and a few allied leftist publications such as *Enough Is Enough*.[6] In part it read:

> We, as organizers and members of various movements and organizations in the New Left of the 1960s and 1970s (and their allies)—who organized for economic and social justice and against racism and war—wholly support the direction the AFL-CIO Vermont Leadership Council and other progressive unions are taking in support of those same goals in 2021. We call on the AFL-CIO national leadership to back off from its threats and intimidation of these labor organizers and join in developing a national movement for economic and social justice now.

Also in May 2021, we were approached by Australian Trotskyists who had been informed about our conflict with Trumka through leftist media. They supported our fight, felt we took the right position when the Trump coup was still a threat, and offered their solidarity (which we readily accepted). In turn, they crafted another open letter to Trumka in support of us and, come May 30, 2021, sent it to Washington, DC (and circulated it through social media). This letter simply and succinctly asserted:

> Richard Trumka, AFL-CIO President:
>
> We defend the right of the Vermont AFL-CIO to have passed a motion authorising a General Strike if the 2020 election results had been overturned in a coup. This motion voted on by the rank-and-file delegates at the Vermont AFL-CIO 2020 Convention was in the proud tradition of labor fighting together against the threat of fascism and dictatorship. We defend the right of workers and the organised labor movement to strike together to defend their democratic rights.
>
> We therefore stand in solidarity with the Vermont AFL-CIO and demand that you immediately drop the vindictive and retaliatory "misconduct" investigation into the Vermont AFL-CIO.

The letter was signed by nine proworker organizations from different parts of the world, the Liaison Committee for the Fourth International and its national groups: Consistent Democrats (United Kingdom), Frente Comunista dos Trabalhdores (Brazil), Tendencia Militant Bolchevique (Argentina), Socialist Workers League (United States), Socialist Fight (UK), Trotskyist Platform (Australia), United Front Committee for a Labor Party (US), Workers Power (US), and Jews against Fascism (Australia). It was additionally signed by a number of individual labor leaders from the US and elsewhere.[7]

Then, on June 11, 2021, United Electrical Workers Local 203 (Vermont) issued a public statement in our support, as did the Central Vermont Chapter of the Democratic Socialists of America on June 26, 2021. Point being, it must have been becoming clear to Trumka that the longer he kept his retaliatory investigation open against us, the more we would find support from the left.

Winning the War of Public Media

On June 10, 2021, we were yet again afforded an opportunity to push back against Trumka's attacks, this time by Trumka himself. Here the national AFL-CIO invited me to take part in the Northeast regional meeting of state labor council leaders (something they had to do, since I was Vermont AFL-CIO president). The meeting was to be held remotely due to the continuing COVID-19 pandemic. All state presidents were invited to provide videos (up to 120 seconds long) welcoming other delegations to the meeting. Of course, I jumped on this and made a two-minute recording slamming Trumka for coming after us in the wake of the general strike vote. Further, on behalf of United!, I called for not only a robust and ongoing defense of our democracy, but also for internal reform, making the AFL-CIO more democratic (and committed to social justice unionism). I figured that Trumka's staff would be forced to make the difficult decision to play the video or not. If they did, it would give voice to an internal leftist opposition in full view of the top union leaders of the Northeast. If they didn't, which by our mind would be the better outcome, the Vermont AFL-CIO could circulate the video through our own social media and we could bill it as "The video Trumka will not allow you to see." Thus, we were laying a trap for Trumka, the parameters of which were of his own making. So lo and behold, Trumka's lieutenants, in their shallow wisdom, did not show the video (surprise surprise), and we went forward with our plan. In short time, we had over 2,500 views. They played right into our hands.[8]

As the spring grew old and a young summer matured, I was afforded a larger and larger audience through the media to air Vermont AFL-CIO's grievances. From the *In These Times*–associated podcast *Working People* (May 2021), to the *America's Work Force* podcast (June 2021), to a number of Pacifica-related interviews with Steve Zeltzer (throughout), culminating in the nationally syndicated (250,000-plus viewers and listeners) *Economic Update with Richard D. Wolff* (recorded in June 2021 and aired in July 2021), the Vermont AFL-CIO's principled stance on the general strike during the coup threat versus Trumka's reactionary and retaliatory attacks directed at us was gaining increasing national attention.

During these interviews, I also freely pointed out Trumka's hypocrisy insofar as he politically gave support to the winter/spring general strike in Myanmar (Burma) against that country's military coup while seeking to punish the one state labor council in the US that itself took steps to strike in the event of a Trump coup. And while the national AFL-CIO consistently did not make any detailed statement in public against the actions being taken against us, just being forced to say "no comment" and having to decide to not return the calls of various media inquiries certainly reminded them that the fight they were picking was not invisible.

As our audience grew, I also chose to couple Trumka's attack with the national AFL-CIO's failure to see through passage of the PRO Act (which increasingly seemed doomed to failure as a result of key Democrats not supporting it, and others unwilling to abolish the filibuster).[9] Here I charged Trumka and the national AFL-CIO with lacking the muscle to see this bill through due to their decades-long failed political strategy of putting all our eggs in the basket of lobbying and a Democratic Party that (although in control of the White House, the House of Representatives, and the Senate) ultimately did not give a fuck about working-class people in this country or the unions who they count on for endorsements. I argued that instead of sinking tens of millions of dollars into electing Democrats and lobbying, we should be alternatively embedding organizers in *every* state and creating the kind of bottom-up pressure, like we saw during the Great Depression, whereby politicians would ignore us at their own peril (and at the peril of the capitalist order).

I also argued that in order to build mass solidarity and see effective mobilizations, we would have to build a true rank-and-file democracy within the AFL-CIO so that we could achieve a natural buy-in from our members and have them feel more ownership over our social and political priorities. In this way, on behalf of United!, I sought to turn Trumka's attack into a broader debate about the future of organized labor itself. And here the goal was to create as much stress and tension as possible for Trumka and his backers and (like in United!'s 2019 successful campaign for office) paint a stark dichotomy between ourselves (as the progressive force for change) and Trumka's national AFL-CIO (which represented a conservative, visionless appendage to the Democrats). They had to be made to feel pressure and had to understand that their escalations would be met in kind by us through any effective means at our disposal.

But even while I advanced such messaging, it is of note that I did so by also stressing that myself and United! had confidence that the AFL-CIO as such could be made into that vehicle for change that our times demanded. Thus, we did not attack the AFL-CIO as a body, but rather the Trumka administration (and those who came before it), who feared foundational change and sought to keep grassroots members disempowered and without agency.

To put it simply, our thought was and remains that with millions of members working in every sector, it would be destructive and counterserving to abandon the AFL-CIO. In United!'s mind, the road to change starts with transforming the AFL-CIO from within, from the bottom up, and not with any external and quixotic fantasy of a different, better, or recreated wheel. And while the struggle for internal change is hard, it's the toll we must pay if we are to ever ride the labor movement to comprehensive victories.

Contemplating a Government in Exile

Even as we were actively seeking to cause as many problems and as much stress to Trumka as we could gin up, these were also hard times for the Vermont AFL-CIO. Every day we waited for the other shoe to drop and for Trumka's attacks to escalate. Anticipating a national AFL-CIO takeover through trusteeship, I began to float to our executive board the concept that should we be removed from office that we be prepared to declare a kind of government in exile and seek to retain a continuity in leadership regardless of our status in the eyes of the national AFL-CIO. And in case such an event came to pass, United! took a few basic steps to make this possible, including securing our member contact lists in locations outside the reach of Trumka's people. The thought here was that regardless of what the undemocratic national bylaws had to say, an elected leadership morally and politically could only be removed from power by another election by the rank and file. And given United!'s broad base of support among dozens of affiliated locals, we would be able to exercise leadership with or without the national AFL-CIO's support and recognition. Further, we would be able to leverage our position as a "government in exile" to nationally agitate for internal democratic reforms within the AFL-CIO so as to make such undemocratic power grabs less likely in the future. But again, these were difficult probabilities to deal with. Even so, on a personal level, it did make me smile to think that on any given day from March through June 2021 Trumka could leave a meeting with President Joe Biden in the White House and then have to give thought and discussion to the problems he was facing with the Vermont AFL-CIO.

Come late spring and early summer, the assigned national AFL-CIO investigator interviewed maybe a dozen of our leaders. Within limits, we agreed to take part in these interviews in order to make clear that United! and the actions around the general strike had deep support within our many affiliates and that the leadership, be they from AFSCME or the Building Trades, spoke with one voice on these matters. No one offered any apologies or demonstrated any hesitation regarding pride for our past actions. When my turn came at the end of the rotation, I was firm with the investigator, making clear that we had taken the correct action in November and would do it again if similar circumstances were to arise. I ended the interview inviting them to find fault with our decisions, and I dared them to put us under trusteeship so that my next interviews could be with the *New York Times* and *Boston Globe*.

Our Victory

Then, on June 29, 2021, word came down: *we won*; Trumka had had enough and the national AFL-CIO was backing down.

In a letter full of inaccuracies and half truths, Trumka informed us that his investigation found no violation on our part concerning convention procedure (other than allowing the general strike authorization vote to go forward) and that he had decided to take no punitive action against us (we would not be removed from office and our solidarity grant funding would be maintained for the year) other than sending us this sternly worded letter (although he did threaten that future violations would cause him to pull the trigger on trusteeship). The letter was clearly crafted for public consumption more so than for us, and it claimed, in essence, that we were a weak state labor council with a decreasing membership (not true), pointed out that we were the smallest state labor council in the country, and accused us of fomenting internal labor conflicts with non-AFL-CIO unions such as VSEA and NEA.[10] He also highlighted the fact that a number of AFT locals chose not to pay us their affiliation dues.

What the letter got willfully wrong was that we in fact were one of the only state labor councils in the US that was actually growing (gaining over a thousand members over the previous year), that our membership totals (11,500 at that time)[11] were modest due to the fact that we are the second-least populated state in the country (just over six hundred thousand residents), and that our limited conflicts with non-AFL-CIO unions entailed us giving moral support to progressive rank-and-file caucuses within those bodies (and in opposition to their more conservative leadership). Not surprisingly, the jab he took at us concerning some AFT locals failed to articulate that these were locals who lost to United! in the 2019 elections and thus were subject to political realities more complex than one line in a letter could do justice.[12] The letter also sought to imply that

Trumka, unlike what we had been saying in public, did have a plan to deal with a coup, but (bizarrely) that plan seemed to dictate taking no action.

From the letter: "In the lead-up to the presidential election, the Executive Council debated the labor movement's appropriate response in the event then-president Trump refused to concede defeat. The Executive Council made the strategic decision to not immediately call for a general strike in such a situation, in order to avoid providing Trump a reason to invoke martial law."

Despite Trumka's assertions in the letter, underlying all was the unmistakable fact that we had won an unqalified victory, cutting down a mountain that at the start had looked unmovable. It was almost like Trumka, in engaging in the fight with the Vermont AFL-CIO, picked up a scorpion and then did not know what to do with it once he had it in hand. But we knew what to do, and in the end we fought hard and came out unscathed and on top.

All told, when it came to the question of a general strike if a defense of our republic's democracy came under threat, when it came to building real internal union democracy, and when the choice was to build union power from below or instead hitch our wagons to an unreliable (at best) or hostile (at worst) Democratic Party, the Vermont AFL-CIO was on the right side of history while Trumka chose the wrong road.[13] But even as we rightly celebrated the victory of the Vermont AFL-CIO, we also recognized that our victory was not complete. Where we sought to use our trials and tribulations to our advantage and play offense, we have to acknowledge that thus far we've failed to build that national AFL-CIO progressive caucus that we set out to achieve. And without a broad coordination among progressive elements within labor all aiming toward common objectives, the conservative elements within the national AFL-CIO, those whose leadership controls the resources and broad direction, shall remain in power and stubbornly refuse the internal political reckoning that is long overdue.

But as I write these words, it is also true that Donald Trump is out of office and United! carries on in our task of building the Vermont AFL-CIO into the most progressive and bold state labor council in the United States of America. Our work is far from over, and our victories far from complete. Ultimately, our struggle is tied to the rank-and-file fight in all parts of the United States (and beyond), and a more final victory will only be realized when internal movements like United! or the social justice unionism we see with key locals like CTU and UTLA replicate themselves at all levels of the labor movement. Even so, the Vermont AFL-CIO has done our part and will do more in the years to come (of this I have no doubt). This book, covering our experiences from 2017 to 2022, gives voice to our story. I only hope that this story may be of use to union members likewise struggling for progressive change in Texas, Tennessee, Pennsylvania, Kansas, or Montana. In the end, we will win or lose together, as the labor movement we need to become.

Afterword

A lot of people won't get no supper tonight
A lot of people won't get no justice tonight
The battle is gettin' hotter
In this iration
Armagideon time
—The Clash, "Armagideon Time" (written by Willie Williams)

Vermont AFL-CIO Progress from Late June 2022 through September 2023

The chapters you have just read were all written prior to June 26, 2022. Since that time, much has transpired within the Vermont AFL-CIO. Many of these campaigns, developments, victories, new alliances, betrayals, and defeats that have unfolded could, in and of themselves, constitute a new chapter. But even if I committed to making such a detailed update, by the time I finished, undoubtedly there would be even more to report on. Such is the reality of a healthy, growing, and assertive labor movement. So, not wanting to play the role of Sisyphus, I will simply try to outline, in brief, some of the more major developments that haven taken place from late June 2022 through September 2023 in this afterword.

First, our membership continues to grow. Since summer 2022, LIUNA, UFCW, AFSCME, and AFT have all organized new shops and increased their membership, with AFT organizing another significant bargaining unit of 350-plus at the Central Vermont Medical Center and one of 2,000-plus workers at the UVM Medical Center. Further, SEIU unionized hundreds more, resident doctors, also at the UVMMC. SEIU, with active aid and support from the Vermont AFL-CIO, further unionized the South Burlington Starbucks and Burlington Ben & Jerry's. For all of these new

United! leaders at the 2023 Vermont AFL-CIO Convention. From left to right, David Feurzeig, Paul Montague, and Katie Harris.

bargaining units, SEIU has committed to signing a solidarity charter with us. And in August 2023, the nearly six-thousand-member Vermont State Employees' Association became a direct affiliate of the AFL-CIO. While United!, in 2019, inherited a Vermont AFL-CIO with ten thousand total members, we now count twenty thousand members within our ranks.[1] Thus, during United!'s four years in power, AFL-CIO union membership in Vermont has doubled. *Doubled.*

Further, reflecting our continuing commitment to organizing (and our growing resources), in January 2023 we created a new staff organizer position, and in summer 2023 we took steps to build out our on-call organizer resource, now with a salting program aimed to better assist affiliates in unionizing additional shops. And of course, we have continued to provide training opportunities both for stewards and for workers looking to form a union, one of the highlights being a Burlington training in January 2023 provided by Labor Notes that was attended by fifty stewards from many locals and internationals.

Seeking to foster an engaged and a more active membership (with the ability to exercise power on the local level), in January 2023 we began to hold monthly meetings in Burlington for rank-and-file members, shop-floor leaders from all unions, and even nonunion workers interested in organizing. We have termed these "workers' circles." The intent is to encourage worker-to-worker communication, in a geographic area, in order to share experiences and ideas and to build a tangible sense of interunion, working-class solidarity. After seeing success in Burlington, in summer 2023 we launched additional workers' circles in Montpelier and Rutland. In the long term, it is our hope that this effort can be further extended to other municipalities and that organizing in this way will help us identify and recruit additional local union contacts across the state and increase union-to-union and worker-to-worker mutual support and political engagement.

But even while the Vermont AFL-CIO clearly understands long-term (bottom-up) structure building to be the central task of realizing a broader political power, we have also not shied away from lending our support to more immediate mobilizations and worker actions. In October 2022, we did not hesitate in backing a public demonstration in support of UA/AFT UVM part-time faculty seeking to secure a fair contract (which they eventually did), as well as rallies in solidarity with workers unionizing with SEIU at Starbucks (2022) and Ben & Jerry's (2023) and in support of the Teamsters' UPS contract campaign (2023).[2] We also played a lead role in building solidarity with the UAW Goddard College support staff strike in spring 2023, not only building interlocal support for their three-week long picket lines (and for a rally they held at the statehouse in Montpelier), but also putting public pressure on the bosses to agree to fair terms for a next contract. In the end, the UAW won their strike, not only getting the raises they needed to see, but also securing a collective bargaining agreement with *no* management rights clause! And on May Day 2023, we celebrated all our victories with a two-hundred-member rally in Burlington, where union leaders and allies (such as Migrant Justice) spoke on their victories (and on where we need to continue to struggle going forward).

Concerning politics, in the lead-up to the 2022 Vermont general election, by way of a democratic decision-making process at our convention, the Vermont AFL-CIO took a strong public stand in support of the right of women to have an abortion. Coming in the wake of the horrific US Supreme Court decision overturning *Roe v. Wade*, we were proud to spend PAC money on radio ads calling on working-class Vermonters to vote in favor of a state constitutional amendment that would solidify a woman's right to choose. Our Women's Caucus (now called the Vermont AFL-CIO Women's & Gender Equity Caucus) also phone-banked in support of this effort, and our then executive vice president, Katie Harris, recorded a video backing the amendment that was widely circulated over social media. Further, Katie and I attended abortion rights rallies in Montpelier and Burlington where, on behalf of the Vermont AFL-CIO, we both spoke and condemned right-wing attacks on women's rights. And on Election Day in November 2022, the Vermont constitutional amendment unequivocally in support of the right to have an abortion was ratified by an overwhelming 76.8 percent of the vote—*with a majority supporting its passage in every single municipality in the state!*

Legislatively, on Town Meeting Day of March 2023, we were proud to back successful local ballot initiatives that created instant runoff voting for the office of mayor in the City of Burlington and just-cause eviction measures that would lend protection to renters in Winooski and Essex. Further, in June 2023, the Vermont AFL-CIO was the lead in seeing yet another responsible contractor ordinance pass, this time by the Barre City Council. Thus, since United! came into power (in 2019), working with our Building Trades, RCOs have become local law in three cities (Barre, Montpelier, and Burlington). While these wins are significant, our most ambitious legislative effort, the Vermont PRO Act, at the time of writing, is still underway. The omnibus bill, when passed, shall establish card check union recognition for all public sector workers, outlaw captive audience meetings during union drives (public and private sector), and provide the right to form a union for farmworkers and domestic workers. This bill was introduced in the Vermont House and Senate in winter 2023, and (with huge support from Vermont state senator Kesha Ram Hinsdale, Democrat/Progressive) in March 2023 it passed the Senate by a two-thirds majority. Come 2024, it will be one of our major priorities to see it through the Vermont House.

With elections, in 2022 we continued to endorse the entire democratic socialist Progressive Party slate for statehouse, as well as Progressive David Zuckerman for lieutenant governor. In this general election we only made exceptions for eight Democratic Party candidates (true labor champions). Eight Dem endorsements marks the *least* number of Democrats backed by the Vermont AFL-CIO in our entire history. Of the seventeen total candidates (Progressive and Democrat) we gave our support to, fifteen (including Zuckerman) won at the polls in November 2022. Further, on Town Meeting Day 2023, all three of the city council candidates in Barre (Teddy Waszazak, Emel Cambel, and Samn Stockwell) won, and in Burlington our candidate for City Council Central District (Melo Grant, Progressive) also won.[3]

Concerning the national labor movement, the Vermont State Labor Council, from summer 2022 to the present, has not backed down from our dedication to speaking the truth, demanding justice for the working class, and calling out those who willfully unmask themselves as our collective enemy through their deeds and aspirations. Thus, in late November through December 1 (2022), we vocally opposed Congress taking any action concerning rail workers that did not result in them gaining a minimum of five paid sick days. We further articulated that no matter how it may be spun after the fact, any political party that actively took rail workers' right to strike away from them (for this contract cycle) and imposed conditions that did not include paid sick days would be committing an act of treason against the labor movement. While this fight played out in Congress, with President Joe Biden playing the role of strikebreaker, we remained in communications with Senator Bernie Sanders's office. While Bernie fought the good fight defending rail workers, in the end he was only one of very few prolabor voices in Washington. So, a bad deal was forced on rail workers, and their legal right to strike was taken away through the actions of the Democratic Party (and with the support of the Republican Party). After this betrayal, the Vermont AFL-CIO was quick to call out the lies and anti-union animus of the Democrats even while other aspects of organized labor seemed to contort themselves in almost unbelievable ways in order to excuse, obfuscate, and play down the clear and unambiguous anti-union actions of this capitalist party. So later, when Rail Workers United (a more radical caucus within the national rail unions) asked the Vermont AFL-CIO to endorse their call for the nationalization of the railroads, we immediately recognized the justice of their request, and on April 2, 2023, by a vote of our executive board, we did exactly that.[4]

The above represents a brief outline of some of the major activities of the Vermont AFL-CIO from the end of June 2022 through much of 2023.[5] But there is one final update that remains to be given. Today, September 10, 2023, here in the Northeast Kingdom, less than twenty-four hours ago, at our largest annual convention in living memory, our membership elected my successor, Katie Harris, to the office of president of the Vermont State Labor Council AFL-CIO.[6] Katie, like myself in 2019, ran as the United! candidate for president (and she had my full support). Harris, who just today was sworn into office, will now serve as the second United! president within the Vermont AFL-CIO, and, at thirty-one, she shall be the youngest state labor council president in the United States of America. Katie, a member of DSA, will not serve alone. Once again, the majority of the new executive board (fifteen of the twenty-four seats), including Executive Vice President Ellen Kaye (UVM Staff United/AFT),[7] also comes out of United![8] This marks the fourth consecutive internal election in which United! prevailed and the first time in the history of the Vermont AFL-CIO when the three ranking officers (president, executive vice president, and secretary-treasurer), the executive committee, are all women.[9] Having our members once again place United! in power is a vote of confidence in all we have achieved since 2019. Thus, it is with assurance that our progressive struggle will continue that I hand the reins of United! and the Vermont AFL-CIO to President Harris and the thousands of rank-and-file union members who will make even greater victories possible in the not-so-distant future.

A Conclusion: The Legacy of the Vermont AFL-CIO

To conclude this tale, the story of the Vermont AFL-CIO from 2017 to 2023 is a set of experiences with direct relevance to AFL-CIO state labor councils across the US and all union members or workers who seek to build labor organizations that are unafraid of taking on our class enemies, wherever they may be found. The chapters you have now read show how we were able to use smart and effective tactics to win sweeping victories in internal union elections and, further, how to do so as a movement guided by a commonly held progressive platform. But winning elections, of course, is not a goal in and of itself. With that in mind, after taking office United! found creative ways to implement our vision and respond to emerging political realities without imploding our federation nor selling out our core progressive values. As such, at times we sought to strike a difficult balance between principle and pragmatism—always a calculated move, rarely without risk. In brief, we strove toward expanding political discourse, moving to the left in the process, without alienating our base. Any group of workers who likewise take control of their union as United! did will also be tasked with similar challenges. I hope that the illustrations of the situations we faced, and how we navigated them, can serve in some small way as a guide to those who come after us.

We also worked hard (and continue to work hard) not only in finding our collective political voice but also in building up the capacity of our state fed, to redirect resources toward organizing and to begin the process of internal change in a way that democratizes the labor movement and better allows us to mobilize, inspire, and involve our members. This involved efforts to change both our structure and our culture. To the extent that any federation, state labor council, or union is successful in this regard, coupled with new organizing, will likely determine their long-term ability to grow power. I do not pretend that we did it all right, that we somehow have a monopoly on knowing the best path forward, but I do know that the status quo, as it has repeatedly reaped a harvest of failure, must not be an option.

Also not an option, in the long run, is for state labor councils, central labor councils, locals, and individual union groups to go it alone. There can be no shift in social and political power on the scale that foundational change requires if we only seek to change within our individual silos. Thus, United! made efforts to support similar progressive caucuses in the two large non-AFL-CIO unions in Vermont (NEA and, at the time, VSEA). We also sought to organize a national progressive caucus within the AFL-CIO (though, to date, without success). Further, in 2022 United! sent two resolutions to the national AFL-CIO for consideration at their convention in Philadelphia. One called for preparations to defend democracy through a general strike, and the other sought to allow all 12.5 million members to directly elect national officers (whereas currently about five hundred delegates undemocratically make such selections with little or no accountability to the rank and file). To support these resolutions, I and Executive Director Liz Medina attended the convention as delegates. And even though the national AFL-CIO Executive Council undemocratically refused to allow the resolutions to reach the delegates for a full debate and vote, Medina and I were able to speak to the suppression of the resolutions from the floor, highlight the irony of how an undemocratic and rigged process could stifle a vote on union democracy, and call for change within the AFL-CIO.

Through their suppression, they put a soapbox right under our feet, and as a result we had very promising conversations with a number of state labor council presidents, officers, and delegates. I recount this to highlight that United! full well knows that radical change within the labor movement will not and cannot happen without a blooming of a more radical approach spreading well beyond any one location.[10] And toward that goal United! continues to work.

When democracy came into crisis in our republic, we here in Vermont prepared to do what would have to be done. Given the existential threat we as a nation faced, we summoned the courage to do right regardless of the bureaucratic consequences that the national AFL-CIO president sought to corral us with. While we as a people escaped the fascist coup threat of 2020–21 with vestiges of our democracy still intact, we must be clear in the knowledge that democracy remains precarious in the United States. We could very well face a new, more sophisticated coup threat in 2024, or at any point beyond. And the enemy will have learned lessons from 2020–21, and they will be more prepared, more effective. Even as we wait for the second try at a palace coup, we must not understate the slow-motion coup against democracy that is already underway. From the right-wing Supreme Court diminishing our rights while expanding those of corporations, to draconian voting restrictions being passed in so many Republican-controlled states, to extreme gerrymandering of electoral maps, to reactionary state governments empowering themselves to send alternative (false) delegates to the Electoral College in the event that the voters don't choose the right candidate at the polls, democracy is already in peril. Presently the right wing in our country (politicians controlled by corporate interests) has the power to define the domestic agenda even though they represent only a minority of the population. A second coup attempt in Washington, following a future presidential election, could be the death blow to the dream that our better natures have of "America." But when that blow comes, will the national AFL-CIO and the labor movement as a whole be ready? Our enemies have learned from our recent past, but have we?

There should be no moral or political doubt that if we were to face a right-wing coup, organized labor must be prepared to organize a general strike. And with 12.5 million members (by far the largest labor organization in the US), the national AFL-CIO must be ready to take the lead. But if the national AFL-CIO is unwilling or unable to do so, it will be up to the state labor councils and the central labor councils to do what our high-ranking "leaders" will not.

With that, I will end this book with a call to state labor councils, central labor councils, and union members everywhere to get engaged, fight like hell, and seek to transform your labor bodies from within. Let us create a truly progressive, member-driven labor movement that is ready, willing, and able not only to defend democracy, but to go on the offensive in the struggle to build power, economic equity, and a more direct participatory democracy. The road will be long and hard, of this I have no doubt, but I also know that in the end we will win, *because we must win.*

United!
David Van Deusen, president of the Vermont AFL-CIO (2019–21 and 2021–23)
Northeast Kingdom, Vermont, September 10, 2023

Ten-Point Program for Union Power: The Little Green Book

The gods of the valley are not the gods of
the hills, and you shall understand it.
—Ethan Allen

Official Platform of the Vermont AFL-CIO
A New Path toward Progressive Change for Labor

Unanimously adopted as the official platform of the Vermont AFL-CIO by the elected executive board on October 6, 2019. Motion made by district vice president for Windsor County Ed Smith, OPEIU. Seconded by district vice president for Washington/Lamoille County Liz Medina, UAW. All in favor. Again confirmed by motion of the executive board on August 31, 2020. Motion made by Tim LaBombard, IBEW. Seconded by Omar Fernandez, APWU. All voted in favor.

Organized Labor has been the most powerful force for change in the history of the United States of America. From the eight-hour day/forty-hour work week, the establishment of the weekend, livable wages (in Union shops), to workplace safety standards, Labor has won these foundational victories through collective action and solidarity. However, for some decades Labor, nationally, has been on the decline. After endorsing Bill Clinton for president (1992), Clinton and the Democrats in Congress sent our manufacturing jobs to low-wage (super-exploited) nations through NAFTA and other free trade agreements (agreements which we opposed, and which we still oppose). And with these good manufacturing jobs, so went thousands of Union jobs.

Today in Vermont (2019), the ten-thousand-member strong AFL-CIO continues to be a major force within the Labor Movement,[1] but few would

David Van Deusen (center) with Vermont AFL-CIO members at the Old Socialist Party Labor Hall in Barre, Vermont, for our 2019 political summit.

rationally deny that we have largely stagnated. This stagnation comes as [former] President Trump [2016–20] and his increasingly far-right Republican Party have launched existential attacks on Labor. The most dire of these include the politically motivated Supreme Court ruling outlawing fair share dues in public sector Unions, the [Trump] administration's so-called rule change outlawing even voluntary dues through payroll deductions for most Unionized home health care providers, and the appointment of corporate stooges to the National Labor Relations Board.[2] This is not the time for Labor to stagnate ...

This wilting of Labor does not have to be. We can (and must) be a social and political power once again; one capable not only of defending against the attacks we now face from DC, but also of going on the offensive and delivering positive life-altering changes for working people. But we will not achieve our potential if we stay on the road more traveled. We cannot continue to do what we have always done and expect a different result. Nor can we be satisfied with candidates that run for Union office who support all the good things, but who neglect to tell us how we will get there. Instead we must be bold, we must experiment, and we must forge a way forward which not only transforms the Vermont AFL-CIO, but also delivers a powerful Labor Movement with the muscle needed to transform Vermont as a whole. And here, the Vermont we intend to deliver is one wherein working-class people not only possess the means to live a secure and dignified life, but one where we, as the great majority, wield the democratic power required to give social and political expression to the many. Such a transformative potential presupposes first a unity around an effective program, and second the development of our immediate political power.

Therefore, the Vermont AFL-CIO supports:

1. UNION DEMOCRACY: The fact is the next VT AFL-CIO election (as with all past elections) will not be as democratic as is desirable. The leadership of the VT AFL-CIO is elected by a limited number of delegates. The rank and file of our Unions have little to no direct say in who will be in these leadership positions. In many past elections, the rank and file are not even knowledgeable about who is running, what the issues are, and what is at stake concerning the direction of the Labor Movement. This is not acceptable. Therefore, the VT AFL-CIO shall:

    a. Petition the National AFL-CIO for a change to our Constitution whereby every member of a VT AFL-CIO Union will have a single and equal vote concerning the election of officers. Elections shall continue to be held every two years at our State Convention. However, now a concerted effort will be made to reach out to our ten thousand rank-and-file members in order to invite their participation and in order for them to become educated on the issues, the candidates, and ultimately place a vote in favor of those candidates they feel best represent the interests of the Labor Movement. By conducting elections in this way, we will also be able to build a stronger and more representative presence of our members at our Conventions;[3]

    b. Direct the VT AFL-CIO President, Executive Committee, Executive Board, and elected officers to operate transparently and to consult with the rank and file when contemplating action on an issue, as well as to report back to the rank and file after such bodies take action. This transparency shall be manifest through regular online and email updates which will be made available to members of affiliated Unions;[4]

c. Direct the VT AFL-CIO President, Executive Committee, Executive Board, and elected officers to act in accordance with the general will of the membership, even when such will comes into conflict with the private views of the leadership;[5]

d. Make a priority of rebuilding our local Central Labor Councils all across Vermont in order to provide a better means of giving an organized voice to our rank and file and to promote the development of personal relationships of solidarity among members from different area Unions. Here we declare that rank-and-file members of non-AFL-CIO Unions (such as the VSEA, NEA, UE, etc.) shall be invited to participate, just as they have for years through the Green Mountain Central Labor Council;[6]

e. Look into the feasibility of establishing a quarterly Labor newspaper in order to better facilitate discussion, debate, and education of Union members.

2. WORKING-CLASS UNITY: Like our grandparents who fought unapologetically with arms against Germany and Italy in World War II, we are antifascist. We oppose fascism, racism, sexism, and discrimination of all kinds wherever it raises its ugly head, and we support those that actively resist the attempts by the further-right to normalize discriminatory, racist, and fascist ideologies. We understand that Labor is strong when we stand in solidarity with each other; when we are united as one single working class regardless of the difference we may experience between each other. What matters to us is not one's race, ethnicity, religion, country of origin, gender, or orientation, but rather that you stand in solidarity with your Union brothers and sisters and with working people as a whole. We shall not be fooled by those that want to divide us into antagonistic camps. We know our strength comes from our unity, and from this unity follows true working-class power. An injury to one is an injury to all.[7]

3. OUR SOCIAL PROGRAM: Within the great majority of our contracts we have already won livable wages, adequate paid time off, affordable quality health care, and degrees of shop-floor democracy on the job for our members. In many cases, we secured these benefits for our members generations ago. And thus we will continue to place a priority on organizing new shops where we can seek to secure these

benefits for thousands of more working people without the need for recourse to state government. However, we also appreciate our responsibility to the larger working class who is not yet organized into a Union, and we shall continue to fight for the universal realization of these standards for all working people. As such, we support actions and legislation which guarantees all Vermonters:

a. $15 an hour livable wage (adjusted for inflation);[8]
b. Twelve weeks of paid family medical leave;
c. Single-payer health care;
d. Free college tuition for all public colleges and universities;
e. Affordable housing (housing costs suffered by a family should never require any more than one week of one's monthly pay);[9]
f. Affordable childcare for all;[10]
g. Access to healthy locally produced food;
h. Access to a defined benefit pension plan;[11]
i. The right to a card check recognition in order to make the process by which workers gain Union representation fairer;[12]
j. And furthermore that the creation of these new social programs will NOT be funded through any new regressive taxation schemes. Rather taxation must be progressive in nature, and we must demand that the wealthy & corporations pay their fair share.

We will fight to realize this agenda by working to build a Popular Front of fellow Labor organizations and allied groups from outside the Unions. Here we shall seek to increase levels of agitation within our communities, and we will also seek to support rank-and-file Union members as they advocate for these positions in their cities/towns/shops and in the Statehouse.[13]

4. POPULAR FRONT: As we take steps to realize a more equitable and democratic Vermont, we recognize that the Labor Movement, while constituting the key strategic element concerning social forces with a direct interest in creating fundamental change, is stronger when we work in partnership with other organizations and community groups where our interests overlap (or where our interests are not in contradiction to each other). After all, the forces that oppose us, while unable to muster the numbers that we have, are presently in possession of great resources and wealth. We counter this imbalance

by building bridges to other organizations whereby our constituency is further enlarged. Therefore, where non-Labor organizations, be they farmer or environmental groups, are ready and able to embrace our core working-class values, and where those organizations are ready and able to work with us on our program, we shall be ready to give them a seat at the table and to work to coordinate with them to create actions in support of a common, popular agenda. To further the development of this Popular Front members of the Executive Board of the VT AFL-CIO shall:[14]

a. Seek to meet with non-Labor organizations in order to discuss areas where we share common interests;

b. Seek to secure a commitment from those organizations concerning support for this program;

c. Bring issues and concerns emanating from these organizations (that are not articulated in this program but which are also not in conflict with this program) back to VT AFL-CIO Conventions in order for our membership to consider taking a stand on said issues;

d. Invite delegates of such organizations to VT AFL-CIO Conventions as non-voting participants.[15]

5. GREEN NEW DEAL: We recognize the threat of climate change and the environmental challenges which we face at this time in history. Adequately addressing these challenges will take a coordinated effort to, among other things, rebuild our aging infrastructure in such as way so as to minimize our carbon footprint. This will mean the construction of new renewable energy plants. This will also mean hardening our existing infrastructure, such as power lines, roads, bridges, culverts, etc., in such a way as to make them resilient in the face of an increasing number of extreme weather events. We also recognize the opportunities which such construction presents to a generation of workers. Therefore, the Vermont AFL-CIO supports a Green New Deal (in Vermont and nationally) insofar as such a program guarantees that:

a. Related construction projects involving public money (or tax breaks) shall be done via Project Labor Agreements (PLAs) that guarantee a prevailing wage,[16] safe working conditions, and that this work is done with Union labor;

b. Infrastructure built with public money must be publicly owned. Furthermore, any work required to maintain or service the facility once it is operational shall be done by Union labor;

c. Any new taxation levied to pay for such projects, or that are used to encourage a positive environmental change in society shall NOT be regressive in nature. The fact is that working-class people are already paying their fair share. The wealthy and corporations on the other hand have seen their taxes cut time and again. It is time for the richest 1 percent (that has 40 percent of our nation's total wealth) to be compelled to surrender aspects of that wealth in order to right the wrongs that their profits have necessitated on the rest of us;[17]

d. The Vermont AFL-CIO will work with climate justice organizations in order to realize a Green New Deal as long as such organizations share in our demand for economic justice (as articulated above) to be a nonnegotiable aspect of this social project.[18]

6. ELECTORAL POLITICS: The time of the VT AFL-CIO endorsing candidates simply because they are a Democrat is over. In the last election (2018) we endorsed the great majority of the Democrats who won. And in return, [in 2019] they FAILED to hold a single hearing on card check, FAILED to pass the livable wage, paid family medical leave, and free college tuition bills. Single-payer health care was not even manifest as a whisper in the Statehouse last year. In brief, our practice of making broad endorsements and often picking the least bad of two less-than-ideal options has again proven ineffective. At minimum, the VT AFL-CIO will only consider endorsing a candidate if they have a proven record of being a Labor champion. Here we shall require candidates who seek our endorsement to sign a pledge whereby they shall support us on our issues, as we define them, come hell or high water. Second, the VT AFL-CIO shall form a study committee, chaired by our Volunteer-in-Politics and composed of members from diverse affiliated Unions, who shall be tasked at looking at alternative approaches to electoral politics. These alternative approaches may include:

a. Implementing a moratorium on PAC contributions to political parties and candidates from political parties which refuse to be proactive on Labor issues;

b. Implementing a moratorium on endorsing candidates for the
    Vermont House and Senate from any party which refuses to be
    proactive on Labor issues;
c. Exploring an institutional relationship with the Vermont
    Progressive Party whereby Labor delegates to their executive
    board would hold sway over party policy on Labor issues;
d. Exploring an institutional relationship with another pro-Labor
    third party;
e. Exploring the formation of our own political party;
f. Consider taking a step back from electoral politics and instead
    putting all our resources into organizing new shops and thus
    growing our base of political power;
g. Any combination of the above, or a different approach as may be
    looked at by this committee.

This committee shall report its findings to the VT AFL-CIO COPE
Convention which shall be held in January 2020. At the COPE
Convention these electoral issues shall be discussed and debated
by Union members. A vote shall be held in regards to which approach
to take. The VT AFL-CIO Executive Board shall act in accordance with
this membership vote.[19]

We shall NOT rejoin the Working Vermont coalition (with VSEA
and NEA) until and unless these fellow Unions come to share our
views on electoral politics and on the values expressed in this program,
and further commit to engaging in a meaningful discussion as to how
to better involve the rank and file in such a coalition. However, we will
still seek to informally work with the VSEA and NEA on specific issues
of mutual interest (be they legislative or otherwise).

7. WORKING-CLASS DEMOCRACY: We have seen the Democratic
    and Republican parties time and again fail to sufficiently represent
    the interests of Organized Labor and working people generally in
    Montpelier (and in Washington, DC). Even when they have done
    right by us, it often is years after Vermonters demanded action.
    We have also witnessed the disproportionate influence wielded by
    corporate lobbyists in the Statehouse. In short, even though work-
    ing people constitute the great majority of Vermonters, our voice is
    often drowned out by big-moneyed interests. We therefore propose

a change in our Vermont Constitution whereby the people shall be empowered to circumvent the politicians in the Statehouse through a Town Meeting–based referendum system. We shall work to realize this Constitutional change through an effort to build public support for this expansion of democracy culminating in a statewide vote on this proposal in accordance with the procedures set forth in our present VT Constitution for amending this document.[20]

8.   PRIORITY ON ORGANIZING NEW SHOPS: Here it is not good enough to say "we support new organizing"; of course we do, just as we all do. Rather here we must dedicate more resources to this crucial aspect of our work. Thus the Vermont AFL-CIO shall:[21]

a.   Ask our Political Director[22] to spend the summers working with affiliated Unions aiding in their efforts to organize new workers. Specifically, affiliated Unions shall request such AFL-CIO assistance from the five-member Executive Committee. The Executive Committee shall weigh the request, typically authorizing the Political Director to provide such assistance for a defined amount of time;

b.   Forgo spending money on a lobbyist, and instead dedicate that money toward short-time organizers who shall be retained on a standby list. These organizers will be paid a livable wage of $15 an hour, and may be assigned for short periods of time to affiliated Unions who request assistance in organizing new shops. Organizers may be assigned to projects from one day to two weeks in order to provide concrete support to our affiliates;[23]

c.   Use our social media to publicize and build support for affiliated Unions which are engaged in new organizing drives.[24]

9.   WE ARE NOT AFRAID OF STRIKES: The Vermont AFL-CIO knows that when our members are united, when we stand together with our allies, our ability to withhold our labor is a powerful tool. We have seen the power of strikes in Vermont, most recently when the UVMMC nurses went to the picket line (2018) in order to secure a more equitable share of their employer's wealth. Nationally, in recent years, we have seen statewide teachers' strikes across the country (some wildcat strikes), which as with our nurses, have typically resulted in major wins for impacted workers. Historically we have

also witnessed general strikes impacting entire cities, states, and even nations. Governments have been brought down by the power of a strike. And while we do not advocate for any irresponsible use of this powerful tool, we do not fear its use either.[25] When strikes occur, the Vermont AFL-CIO shall:

a. Provide vocal and physical support for the strikers utilizing our social media, letters to the editor, op-eds, sending rank-and-file members of our Unions to the picket line, and providing monetary assistance whenever possible;[26]

b. Encourage affiliated Unions to proactively establish a strike fund. Furthermore, prior to the launch of a strike, when Unions are heading to the bargaining table, the Vermont AFL-CIO shall seek to coordinate Union-building proposals among our affiliated Unions. Here model language shall be provided to affiliated Unions which, among other things, establishes a common right for our members to NOT cross picket lines, allows for all our Unions to establish political PACs, grants our members seats on employer hiring committees, as well as on language for any other issue which our affiliated Unions express an interest in.[27] In addition, the VT AFL-CIO will seek to provide affiliated Unions a list of other contracts in which this language is already included, for use during fact finding. Point being, we are part of a Labor federation so as to receive support from other Unions and as a means to learn from each other. And here the VT AFL-CIO will manifest this role, as was intended by those that came before us.

10. BUILDING A MORE POWERFUL LABOR MOVEMENT: We understand that having progressive Labor members capture the leadership within the VT AFL-CIO (which we intend to do on September 15, 2019), in order to implement the above program, will be a historic victory for Vermont's Labor Movement. However, the AFL-CIO does not represent the majority of Vermont's Organized Labor. The NEA has fourteen thousand members in our schools. The VSEA represents seven thousand workers (largely employed by the State). The UE[28] represents hundreds more, as do a number of other nonaffiliated Unions such as SEIU[29] and the Barre Granite Cutters. These Unions are not part of the AFL-CIO. The VT AFL-CIO recognizes that the foundational social, economic, and political change we envision,

over the long run, will require a united Labor Movement (working with our allies) and a united working class in order to be victorious. Therefore progressive elements within the Vermont AFL-CIO shall seek to organize ourselves as a kind of internal Union political party whereby rank-and-file members of these other Unions (those that agree with this ten-point program) will be encouraged to join this party, and in turn run for office within their Unions. Here the Vermont AFL-CIO will provide encouragement and moral support for these candidates. And as we demonstrate success inside our Labor federation, we project that candidates supporting our program will also gain internal electoral success in their efforts to capture the leadership within their Unions. As this process unfolds, we shall seek to coordinate the efforts of all the Unions in our common effort to move our working-class agenda forward. But capturing the leadership positions of Labor is not an end in itself. For even with a progressive leadership in place, power will only be realized in its full potential through an active and engaged rank and file.[30] Here the Vermont AFL-CIO will seek to grow such rank-and-file participation not only through seeking to expand the internal democratic rights of Labor organizations, but also by facilitating workshops on member engagement at Conventions and (upon invitation by affiliated Unions) at Local meetings throughout the State. TOGETHER WE WILL WIN![31] CONCLUSION: The above represents the program of Vermont AFL-CIO. The Vermont AFL-CIO committed to carrying out this program in order to build a more powerful Labor Movement in Vermont. We further ask that Union members share this program with coworkers. It is not enough for a few of us to share a vision; our vision must be the united vision of Labor. In the end the Union is YOU and without an active and engaged rank and file we will not be able to make the changes our times demand. When we stand together, when we have that common vision and take those steps necessary to implement that vision, we are a powerful force. Our program is just the start, not the end. UNITED WE ARE UNION STRONG!

Electoral Policy: Building Power beyond Political Parties

I'm no longer accepting the things I cannot change....
I'm changing the things I cannot accept.
—Angela Davis

Vermont AFL-CIO 2019 Resolution on Elections and Parties
Overwhelmingly approved by rank and file through an indicative vote at December 2019 Vermont AFL-CIO Political Summit held at the Old Socialist Labor Party Hall in Barre, Vermont, and officially adopted by the executive board on December 7, 2019. Again confirmed by motion of the executive board on August 31, 2020.

WHEREAS: The Vermont AFL-CIO's true power is in our labor, solidarity, commitment to taking mass rank-and-file action, and organizational density;

WHEREAS: The Vermont AFL-CIO shall grow our power, the power of the working class, and achieve far-reaching social, economic, and political victories largely through self-organization;

WHEREAS: The Vermont AFL-CIO is beholden to no political party;

WHEREAS: There are presently three major political parties in Vermont (Progressive [democratic socialists], Democrat, and Republican);

WHEREAS: The Vermont AFL-CIO has no self-interest in propping up any political party which does not effectively fight for union rights and workers' rights;

WHEREAS: A political party needs to demonstrate a unified and unqualified support for organized labor in order to be viewed as a true friend of labor;

Vermont AFL-CIO executive director Liz Medina speaking at the Defend Democracy demonstration in Montpelier, Vermont, January 2021.

WHEREAS: The Vermont AFL-CIO strongly asserts that union members should never be asked, encouraged, or expected to support political candidates which do not support us on our issues;

WHEREAS: Too often and for too long organized labor has taken a short-sighted view and has backed political parties and candidates who rather than being labor champions are, at best, a lesser of two evils;

WHEREAS: This flawed political approach has led to a regression of union power;

WHEREAS: The Vermont AFL-CIO understands the need to build union and working-class power independent of political parties and candidates who do not stand with us;

WHEREAS: The Vermont AFL-CIO is taking the long view of building a more profound union and working-class power throughout the Green Mountains and beyond;

AND WHEREAS: Electoral politics is just one part of said objective and is far from any envisioned endpoint;

LET IT BE RESOLVED THAT: Politics as usual is over...

AND FURTHER: That the Executive Board of the Vermont AFL-CIO, taking into account the views and priorities of the rank and file, will provide every major political party in Vermont a set of clear legislative directives every biennium;

—These legislative directives shall seek to increase the rights, better the living standards, increase the social benefits, and further the democratic reach of union members and working-class people as a whole;

AND FURTHER: The Executive Board will inform the political parties that:

—Successful legislative action on said directives may result in the Vermont AFL-CIO supporting select candidates from their party in future election efforts;

—Such endorsements shall be reserved for the proven and unwavering allies of organized labor who sign an AFL-CIO pledge concerning our social, economic, and political priorities;

—Where the Vermont AFL-CIO chooses to make such endorsements, union resources shall be put to the impacted campaigns, and said campaigns shall be conducted in such a way so as to not only win the vote, but also to leave a stronger local labor movement in its wake;

—Failure to legislatively implement said directives, by all or part of a specific political party, shall carry the consequence of the Executive Board of the Vermont AFL-CIO, insofar as such action is within their defined powers, withholding any and all political endorsement of candidates for Vermont House and Vermont Senate whose primary affiliation is of said party;

—Such a moratorium, when triggered, will remain in effect for a period of not less than two years (and may be extended by a majority vote of the Executive Board);

AND FURTHER: Such a moratorium may only be overridden in extraordinary cases concerning specific incumbent candidates when said candidates are active members of the Vermont Workers Caucus, a like prolabor caucus, or are an active or retired union member in good standing, and if the candidate commits to signing a Vermont AFL-CIO pledge concerning our social, economic, and political priorities;

AND FURTHER: In other extraordinary cases, nonincumbent candidates, especially those running in a primary against an incumbent viewed as an adversary by organized labor, may also be exempted from this moratorium if said candidate has a platform and proven record of supporting labor on all our issues, and if they commit to signing a Vermont AFL-CIO pledge concerning our social, economic, and political priorities;

AND FINALLY: Such exemptions shall only be acted upon through a two-thirds majority vote of the Vermont AFL-CIO Executive Board;

This policy shall remain in force within the Vermont AFL-CIO, ad infinitum, until and unless it is amended or withdrawn by official act of the Executive Board, by an act of members/delegates at a duly held Vermont AFL-CIO Convention, or by being superseded or ruled to be in conflict with any part of the Constitution of the Vermont AFL-CIO or the Constitution of the National AFL-CIO.

President Van Deusen's General Strike Speech Opening the 2020 Convention

It will only be through our unity, through our solidarity,
through our collective action as a labor movement
and as a working class that the economic chains
that bind us will once and for all be shattered.
—David Van Deusen, president of the Vermont AFL-CIO (2019–23)

November 21, 2020
Vermont AFL-CIO President Addressing Vermont State Labor Council Convention

Union brothers and sisters, allies, working people, Vermonters:

There are times when the decisions we make, the actions, together, we agree to carry out or not, define us as a people, as a union, and as a labor movement. Today we may be standing on the precipice of one of those great historic moments.

No matter who you voted for in the US election, the results are in. Trump lost by any measure. And while I am not now nor ever have been an acolyte of the neoliberal policies of the national Democratic Party, I am a firm and unapologetic believer in democracy. And even while I see with clear eyes the great shortcomings of our democratic republic (from systemic racism, sexism, xenophobia, and economic elitism, to name but a few), I also know, as the Vermonter John Dewey once said, that "The only solution to the problems of democracy is more democracy."

So I do not come before you today to ask only that you steel yourself for the defense of this election and this outcome, nor do I suggest that our problems as a working class and as a labor movement will somehow dissipate because one man lost an election while another won; far from

Vermont AFL-CIO president David Van Deusen speaking to workers at the 2021 May Day demonstration in Montpelier, Vermont. From left to right: executive board member Dan Cornell, Executive Director Liz Medina, Executive Vice President Tristin Adie, President David Van Deusen, executive board member Rubin Serrano, and executive board member Traven Leyshon.

it. The fact is, no matter which wealthy elite sits in the White House, we, as labor, must unequivocally grasp that it will only be through our unity, through our solidarity, through our collective action as a labor movement and as a working class that the economic chains that bind us will once and for all be shattered. And toward that day we, together, endeavor.

But make no mistake: the Trump administration persists in its refusal to accept the election outcome and seeks, even now, to retain its hold on power. At this very moment machinations are being hatched which aim to send delegates to the Electoral College who choose to *not* represent the will of the people. Instead these plotters seek to give form to the will of the present administration alone and the billionaires that stand behind him. And if by hook or by crook this administration, which has told armed neofascists to "stand by," manages to maintain its hold on power, the vestiges of democracy which persist in this republic shall be extinguished for a generation if not more. We must not, cannot, and shall not allow this to happen.

And my friends, we are *not* weak. When united, when not divided by contrived notions of race, national origin, or gender, we are *strong*; UNION STRONG. After all, it is only through our labor that our state and our nation constitute themselves. As "Big Bill" Haywood once said, "All [working people] have to do is to put their hands in their pockets and they have got the capitalist class whipped."

So, my brothers and sisters, at this historic convention you will have a Vermont general strike authorization vote put before you in the event of a political coup in Washington. This resolution, which is recommended by your elected executive board, if passed, does not order you to strike. Rather it asks for your permission to allow your executive board to call for a strike and to do the hard work of organizing one if our democratic republic is threatened. Understand that if vested with this authority your leadership board will be judicious in exercising this power. It is only our intent to make this call if the democracy which we hold dear comes under a clear and imminent threat.

Over the last twenty years, it has been my absolute honor and privilege to walk on picket lines with many of you, shoulder to shoulder. I have organized with you. I have sat at the bargaining table, shared in your struggles, dreams, losses, victories, and maybe even a tipped a few jars of whiskey along the way. And I have never known you to back away from that which you know to be right.

So I ask you, as a union member and as a Vermonter, to consider the question of the collective defense of our democratic republic, and to not take this question lightly. I ask that you put aside any partisan leanings and that you ponder the resolution that will be considered later without fear of favor. I ask that you think simply about what is the right thing for us to do, together, should democracy come into existential crisis. And here let us reflect on the words of Hannah Arendt when she says, "The sad truth of the matter is that most evil is done by people who never made up their minds to be or do either evil or good." And brothers and sisters, it is my firm assertion that we are not those kind of people.

But defending the democracy we have now, alone, is not enough.

If we are to claim the mantle of "champions of democracy" we must live by that credo, and here we must seek to not only build a more direct participatory democracy here in Vermont, but also, through our unions, more economic democracy whereby working people have the security to not only live, but to live well!

If you work forty hours a week, you should not have to struggle to pay the bills. We don't just need livable wages, we need prevailing wages. We need health care as a human right, and not as a bargaining chip we have to defend in each round of bargaining. We need to know that our kids have a clear path to college and technical training without going into debt for the rest of their lives. In brief, we need free tuition for our state colleges (and we can't be closing down any campuses!). We also need to secure the tools required to unionize more shops, and for this we need card check. And we need to rebuild our COVID-shattered economy through a New Deal, a Green New Deal. And while we struggle through the pandemic, putting our lives on the line, we need adequate PPE, safer working conditions, and hazard pay. And most of all we need to come together, be internally organized, UNITED, and ready to support each other, each local, when we are compelled to bring the fight to the bosses to achieve our aspirations, and in order to see our UNITED program come into being.

And of course, we also need to practice what we preach.

So as we defend democracy, struggle to build a more participatory democracy, seek to enlarge our town meeting rights, and as we fight to expand our economic democracy, we must also reexamine our own bylaws and our own Vermont AFL-CIO constitution so as to make ourselves truly a democratic labor organization. And friends, it is your executive board's hope and expectation that today, at this 2020 Vermont State Labor Council Convention, that UNITED we will see through a number of democratic reforms which will vest more power and more authority with you, the rank and file.

In conclusion, I thank you for the honor of serving as your president. I ask that you and your families be safe and vigilant during this COVID-19 pandemic, and I thank you for standing UNITED in defense of the better ideals of the republic and for the kind of democratic change we know working people both desire and demand.

United!
David Van Deusen
President of the Vermont AFL-CIO

The Vermont General Strike Authorization Resolution

No more deluded by reaction
On tyrants only we'll make war
The soldiers too will take strike action
They'll break ranks and fight no more ...
—"The Internationale"

November 21, 2020
Vermont AFL-CIO Resolution: Protect Democracy
Adopted at the Vermont AFL-CIO Convention on November 21, 2020. Motion made by Jeffrey Wimette, IBEW. Seconded by Dwight Brown, AFSCME. Through an indicative vote, 92 percent of all rank-and-file members and allies present supported motion. Officially adopted by seated delegates with 87 percent in support.

WHEREAS, the Vermont AFL-CIO and our affiliates are committed to the defense of democratic rights and the institutions of democracy, regardless of the party affiliations of those in power;

WHEREAS, the Vermont AFL-CIO recognizes that democracy in the United States is hobbled by the archaic structure of the Electoral College and entrenchment of the two-party system;

WHEREAS, President Donald Trump and Vice President Mike Pence have refused to acknowledge the results of the election in multiple key states and continue to mount frivolous lawsuits and various political interventions in a baseless attempt to overturn the November 3rd results;

WHEREAS, President Trump has refused, on multiple occasions, to denounce the activities of white supremacist militias and organizations

United! leaders Tristin Adie (left) and Helen Scott (right) in front of Burlington City Hall supporting a protest for the rights of migrant workers.

that have stated desires to overthrow American democracy and instead has conveyed support for their actions;

WHEREAS, the Trump administration and Republican allies have conducted a concerted campaign to obstruct, sabotage, and reject a fair and complete count of presidential ballots by creating barriers to voting, targeted at people of color, immigrants, women, and young people. These tactics include intimidation of BIPOC voters at polling places and requirements to have two people sign a ballot that hurt women voters, as well as dismantling key infrastructure such as the US Postal Service;

WHEREAS, the Constitution requires voting results and Electoral College tallies to be completed and submitted to Congress by the first Monday after the second Wednesday in December, and the new 2021 Congress to validate the results, and voters should be determining the results, not courts;

WHEREAS, Trump has denied science, resulting in more than 250,000 Americans dying from COVID-19, and millions more facing deep economic pain due to ongoing impact from the virus, and can do irreparable harm during a lame-duck session;

WHEREAS, the extreme risk currently posed to the historic institutions of democracy in our nation may require more widespread and vigorous resistance than at any time in recent history;

WHEREAS, the labor movement and trade unions have played a proud and vital role in protecting democracy and opposing authoritarianism in many nations throughout the world;

WHEREAS, the most powerful tool of the labor movement in our history has been the power of the general strike;

THEREFORE BE IT RESOLVED that the Vermont AFL-CIO is empowered by the delegates at the 2020 state convention to call for a general strike of all working people in our state in the event that Donald Trump refuses to concede the office of president of the United States.

BE IT FURTHER RESOLVED that the Vermont AFL-CIO will work with allies in the antiracist, environmental justice, feminist, LGBTQ+, immigrant rights, and disability rights movements to protect our democracy, the Constitution, the law, and our nation's democratic traditions;

BE IT FURTHER RESOLVED that the Vermont AFL-CIO will call on city and county governments to pledge to protect protesters defending democracy, and commit to not using police action or curfews to curtail these activities, and to use all available resources to stand up against any effort by the Trump administration to steal the presidential election.

BE IT FURTHER RESOLVED that the Vermont AFL-CIO commits itself to the long-term goal of winning genuine democracy through the abolition of the Electoral College and two-party system, through the collective action of our affiliates and allied organizations.

Vice President Katie Harris's May Day 2023 Speech

We will not be fooled, we will not be silenced, and we will
not be defeated! We know that the only way to win this fight
is by organizing, by building rank-and-file power, and by
creating a militant labor movement. It is through our collective
power that we will create change, not through the whims
of politicians or the benevolence of corporate executives.
—Katie Harris, president of the Vermont AFL-CIO
(elected to office in September 2023)

May 1, 2023
Katie Harris Announcing Her Candidacy as United! Candidate for President at May Day Union Rally in Burlington, Vermont, before Two Hundred Workers

Comrades, on this May Day, we stand together in solidarity to celebrate the power of the working class and to recommit ourselves to the fight for our rights, our dignity, and our lives. Today, we raise our voices in defiance against the capitalist system that exploits us and enriches the ruling class.

The Vermont State Labor Council has put forward a ten-point program that demands a just and equitable society. We demand a living wage for all workers, universal health care, affordable housing, and a strong, unionized workforce. We demand an end to police violence, racism, sexism, and all forms of oppression. We demand a government that serves the people, not the wealthy elite.

But make no mistake: the ruling class and their political cronies don't give a damn about our demands. They want nothing more than to crush us, to exploit us, and to destroy our power. They want to pit us against

Katie Harris (center) speaking at sold-out Vermont Green Football Club game on Labor Night, 2023.

each other, to make us forget that, as a working class, there's a hell of a lot more of us than them.

We are the working class, and we are the backbone of society. Without us, the bosses would have nothing, the politicians would have no power, and the rich would have no wealth. And yet, they treat us like dirt, they pay us poverty wages, and they expect us to be grateful for it.

But we will not be fooled, we will not be silenced, and we will not be defeated! We know that the only way to win this fight is by organizing, by building rank-and-file power, and by creating a militant labor movement. It is through our collective power that we will create change, not through the whims of politicians or the benevolence of corporate executives.

As a union member at the Howard Center and the executive vice president of the Vermont State Labor Council, I stand with you in the fight against capitalism and for workers' rights. And I plan to continue that fight as I run for president of the Vermont State Labor Council this September as part of the United! slate. Together, we can build a powerful movement that can truly represent the needs and interests of working-class Vermonters.

So let's make this May Day a day of struggle, a day of defiance, a day of solidarity. Let's show the bosses and their political puppets that we will not be bought, we will not be divided, and we will not be crushed! We will fight with every ounce of our being, we will resist with every breath in our lungs, and we will win!

We will win for the working class, for the oppressed, for the marginalized, for the forgotten. We will win for our families, for our communities, for our future. Solidarity Forever!

United!
Katie Harris
Executive vice president of the Vermont AFL-CIO

Notes

PREFACE Working-Class Unity, Union Power!

1   The Green Mountain Anarchist Collective (GMAC) was the Vermont affiliate of the Northeast Federation of Anarcho Communists and was active from 2000 to 2009. The collective was founded by myself, Xavier Massot, and Rob Champeau, and over the years it included members such as Lady (of ARA and coauthor of *We Go Where They Go: The Story of Anti-Racist Action*), Wes Hamilton, Kristen Warner, Sean West Damon, Jonah McGreevy, Harris Bucklin, Heather Bryant, and many others. Those familiar with GMAC will note some similarities between our old platform, "Neither Washington nor Stowe: Common Sense for the Working Vermonter," and the Vermont AFL-CIO platform adopted after United! won elections. A strong similarity between the two is seen in mutual support for a town-meeting-based system of referendum government. Even so, when I was organizing with GMAC we were engaged with hundreds. Today (2022), as Vermont AFL-CIO president I am engaged with thousands. With that comes the ability to make real advances, but also the reality that the political program must be reflective of the members we represent. Thus, the Vermont AFL-CIO is certainly not as radical as the Green Mountain Anarchist Collective, but we are the furthest-left state labor council in the US, and further I still am guided by the basic notion of democracy whereby I seek to find ways for the Vermont AFL-CIO to become more internally democratic while supporting more democracy in society as a whole. These are facts that I take pride in. Those interested in reading more on the views and organizing work of the Green Mountain Anarchist Collective are encouraged to read my previous books, *On Anarchism: Dispatches from the People's Republic of Vermont*; *The Anarchist, Socialist, and Anti-Fascist Writings of David Van Deusen, 1995–2018*; and *The Black Bloc Papers*. The old GMAC platform, "Neither Washington nor Stowe," can be found at the following link: https://theanarchistlibrary.org/library/green-mountain-anarchist-collective-neither-washington-nor-stowe.

CHAPTER I Mass Labor Picket: Scott Walker and the Vermont Republican Party

1   With me that day were my children Freya, nine years old; William, five years old; and their mother, then wife, Angela Ogle.

2   The picket was endorsed by: Vermont State Labor Council AFL-CIO, Vermont Building Trades Council AFL-CIO, Green Mountain Central Labor Council AFL-CIO, AFSCME Local 490 (Bennington County), AFSCME Local 1201 (Rutland and Addison Counties), AFSCME Local 1343 (Chittenden and Franklin Counties),

AFSCME Local 1369 (Washington County), AFSCME Local 1674 (Howard Center), AFSCME Local 2413 (Northeast Kingdom), AFSCME Local 3797 (Windsor County), AFSCME Local 3977 (Lamoille County Mental Health), AFSCME Local 4802 (Vermont Home Healthcare), IBEW Local 300, Laborers' International Union of North America (Vermont), the Bricklayers and Allied Craftworkers Local 2 Vermont/New York, Iron Workers Local 7, Roofers and Waterproofers Local 241 Vermont/New York, USW Local 4, AFT-Vermont, United Academics at UVM (AFT), APWU-Vermont, UFCW Local 1459, Operating Engineers Local 98 Vermont/New Hampshire, Teamsters Local 597, Vermont State Employees' Association, VSEA Chittenden County Chapter, VSEA Central Vermont Chapter, VSEA Brattleboro Chapter, Staff Alliance at VSEA, Vermont-NEA, Burlington Education Association, Vermont National Staff Organization at NEA, UE Local 203, UE Local 255, Vermont Workers Center, Vermont Labor United, Vermont Women's March, National Association of Social Workers Vermont, Rights & Democracy, 350Vermont, Vermont Sierra Club, Vermonters for a New Economy, Green Mountain John Brown Gun Club, Black Lives Matter of Greater Burlington, Peace & Justice Center, LGBTQIA Alliance of Vermont, Vermont Progressive Party, Burlington Progressive Party, Burlington City Council Progressive Party Caucus, Young Progressives of Vermont, Vermont House of Representatives Progressive Party Caucus, Champlain Valley Democratic Socialists of America, Central Vermont Democratic Socialists of America, Vermont Liberty Union Party, Burlington Democratic Party, and Vermont Democratic Party.

CHAPTER II **Rock Bottom: The Near Death of Vermont Labor**
1   Starting with the rise of Bernie Sanders, first as mayor of Burlington, then as US representative, and later as US senator, the Vermont AFL-CIO did become comfortable not only endorsing him (as he proved himself to be a reliable ally of the unions and working people), but also typically finding one member of the Progressive Party to endorse in each general election for a statewide race. Anthony Pollina's run for governor in 2008 as the Progressive Party candidate serves as a good example. But these one-off endorsements did not fundamentally alter the fact that the AFL-CIO still carried forth the failed strategy of hitching their wagon to a Democratic Party that cared little for them.
2   Full disclosure: In 2011, I lent my support to Johnson's candidacy and effectively ran on the same reform slate with him as candidate for member-at-large. This came about for a number of reasons. Originally I had intended to run for president myself. But as a member of the tiny National Writers Union UAW Local 1981, the calculus at the time was that I needed the support of the relatively huge AFT to have a chance at winning. And in 2011, AFSCME and the Building Trades (who, ironically, would later become the core of our progressive United! slate) were inclined to lend their support to the old-guard slate (headed by Charbonneau). At first, Johnson, who claimed to support internal reform, did not reject my request for support, and he left that door open. But as the election drew near, he called me and said AFT would not support me because they were likely to run their own candidate. I asked him who that candidate was (full well knowing what the answer would be). After a pause, he said it was him. Given that Johnson was seeking to position himself to the left of Charbonneau, and given that he seemed open to reform, I backed him in return for him backing me for member-at-large. In the

end, our slate swept elections that year (with me beating a member of NALC to win my race), but with no uniting program or strategic vision, these wins amounted to nothing when measured against the need for making real change within the state labor council. And a few years later, Johnson would show his true colors when leaving office and becoming a right-wing collaborator. But in this failure I learned lessons that I would apply to our 2019 efforts.

3   The US Supreme Court's decision in *Janus v. AFSCME* was a politically motivated attempt to break public sector unions by effectively outlawing mandatory union dues in unionized shops.

4   In my opinion, NEA leadership naively assumed that (1) they could get the bill passed in its original form whereby NEA would have parity with nonunion seats on this commission, and (2) after achieving this they would be able to resist any future right-wing or neoliberal attempt to alter that balance against school workers. Point being, once you give away your right to collectively bargain, you are only one bad political step away from losing any leverage you have concerning the defining of this central workplace benefit. A foolish move in my estimation.

5   The collective weakness of the Vermont AFL-CIO, the one United! would inherit on taking office in 2019, was not a result of the old guard being bad people or intentionally selling out the labor movement. In fact, I believe they did the best they knew how to do and were capable of doing. But if they made any real assessments about the effectiveness of their politics, their assessments were wrong. And further, it is my opinion that they simply did not know what they could or should do differently, and they received next to no support from the national AFL-CIO as far as guidance goes. Besides, even if the national AFL-CIO was inclined to provide that guidance, it too would have sought to replicate the same failed policies they were themselves engaged in on the national scale—policies that by and large were already being used to ill effect by the Vermont leadership.

6   This dynamic became apparent in the years since VSEA made Democrat Steve Howard their executive director. Howard, who came to VSEA with zero union experience, was a former (losing) candidate for lieutenant governor and ran the union like a narrowly focused lobbying firm well within the bounds of polite nonconfrontational appendage to the Democratic Party. Further, rather than engage in any kind of systemic power building or assessment of how VSEA could alter the political framework from within which it operates, Howard saw to it that the union lined up behind nearly every political candidate with a "D" next to their name, even when those Democrats would turn around and screw VSEA members at key junctures (going on the attack against their pension benefits in 2021 being one such example).

7   Speaker Johnson (a Democrat), some years before becoming speaker, as a state representative penned a letter to then Democratic governor Peter Shumlin suggesting a number of ways that the state could reduce its budget by rolling back benefits to unionized VSEA state workers. This letter was repeatedly used by the state against the VSEA in bargaining as justifications for why the state was seeking concessions. Despite this, VSEA, insanely, would again endorse her in her next several elections to the statehouse. She finally lost her election, to a Republican, in fall 2020, thus removing this labor enemy from the equation.

8   Leyshon, a Trotskyist and member of Solidarity and former Teamster, was a longtime voice for internal reform. He was part of the reform slate with me in

2011, being elected then as secretary-treasurer. He would also go on to support our United! slate, ultimately being elected again as a district vice president for Washington and Orange Counties as a United! candidate in 2021.

9   It is now policy of AFSCME Council 93 to charge nonmembers a significant fee for service for union assistance.

10   Sanders would go on to win his US Senate election, and Zuckerman would win his race for lieutenant governor. In the contest for governor, Scott would come out on top.

CHAPTER III The United! Campaign: From Ashes Rise

1   Our Vermont AFL-CIO records indicate that Executive Director Riemer was and is a dues-paying member to AFT Local 8043, an AFL-CIO affiliate with exactly one member—Riemer. This gave the appearance that Riemer's local, or her membership in the local, was created in order to give her standing to run for Vermont AFL-CIO office.

2   "Card check" would have established automatic union recognition for any group of public sector workers in which a majority signed a union card. This would have allowed for unionization without going through drawn-out legal proceedings and formal elections through the Vermont Labor Relations Board.

3   Conor Casey and I have been friends for some years, going back to when he was political director of the Vermont State Employees' Association and I was an AFL-CIO district vice president for Washington County. Casey, a native of Ireland, was a diehard Democrat (and member of the Irish Labor Party). Despite our deep disagreements concerning electoral politics and the Democrats, we have always got on well and have enjoyed many good debates over a few pints.

4   Leyshon was a member of DSA and a member of the Trotskyist Solidarity organization.

5   Prior to her AFT and AFGE memberships, Adie was also a Verizon worker organized into CWA.

6   Some months later, Labounty would defect to the Riemer camp. This defection is covered in more detail later in this chapter.

7   See Appendix A.

8   Long after the 2019 election, Labounty was cleared, or at least not held liable, by a third-party investigation, but the same could not be said about his former treasurer, Caroline Gauthier. Ultimately, Local 1343 received $27,000 back from their insurance bond. Note that within AFSCME, top local officers are required to be bonded. In this way, the local is able to recoup financial losses, as a kind of insurance, in case of misappropriation of funds.

9   The volunteer-in-politics position was to be appointed by the new executive board but would serve as a voting member of the five-member executive committee. Thus Fernandez's victory relied on United!, as a whole, winning the election.

10   Demographically, as of July 1, 2019, Vermont was 94.2 percent white. BIPOC stands for Black, Indigenous, (and) People of Color.

11   The rest of the United! slate included Tim LaBombard (IBEW) for member-at-large, Omar Fernandez (APWU) for volunteer-in-politics (which would be an appointed by the next executive board), Ron Schneiderman (UFCW) for Windham County district vice president, Marty Gil (IATSE) for the third Chittenden County district vice president post, Dan Cornell (AFSCME) for Bennington County district vice

president, Eric Steele (AFSCME) for Rutland/Addison County district vice president, and Rubin Serrano (AFSCME) for Caledonia/Lamoille County district vice president.

12   If it went to weighted voting, delegates from the same local were also empowered to cast conflicting votes for opposing candidates with a weight proportional to the number of delegates divided by the total membership. As an example, if a local had five hundred members and five delegates, each delegate could vote how they saw fit, and each delegate vote would be weighted at one hundred votes. This would matter to United! as we sought to capture support from AFT Local 3203.

13   The only reason for her to include this in her platform was to seek to gain support from AFSCME Local 1674 delegates. Representing Howard Center workers, Local 1674 had been a minority union since after it won recognition in the 1980s. In 2019, 1674 had a marginally rising membership rate of about 17 percent. As of May 2022, they have climbed to 42 percent (in part through support relieved by the United!-led Vermont AFL-CIO). Riemer put much effort into turning this local against United! Previous to the campaign, in what she believed was a secret conversation, she even encouraged union officers to disaffiliate from AFSCME and, later, to seek affiliation with AFT. (Note: The suggestion of one AFL-CIO union to do this at the expense of another is a huge violation of AFL-CIO governing rules and solidarity.) Regardless, all of Riemer's machinations concerning 1674 would amount to nothing.

14   See Heather Riemer, Vermont Labor Solidarity Facebook post, August 22, 2019.

15   On August 30, the independent union representing AFT-Vermont staffers also issued a public endorsement for Riemer. But this union was not affiliated with the AFL-CIO and thus had no votes at the convention. And being that it would have been a shocking sign of no confidence had they not done so, this endorsement had no impact. Even so, the staff union endorsement came with the vocal backing of talented AFT organizer Kristin Warner, the former VSEA organizing director (and former member of GMAC). Kristin and I had history going back some years, sometimes as friends, long before (for a brief period) as something more than that, and sometimes as adversaries. Truth be told, her vote of confidence for Riemer over myself stung just a little bit. But again, none of this would have any impact on the outcome of the race.

16   The Donovan endorsement was issued on September 13. Donovan was a longtime prolabor state representative.

17   United! was kept informed about various directions being taken by the Riemer opposition through a pro-United! spy who had direct access to a number of these conversations.

18   See Deb Silmser Snell, Vermont Labor Solidarity Facebook post, September 3, 2019.

CHAPTER IV The 2019 Convention: United! Comes to Power

1   Riemer's nine locals included her local of one, AFT 8043.

2   The elections committee, in the end, did not rule on this motion and no attempt was made to circumvent the one-delegate-one-vote process.

3   The credentials committee never made a determination on this motion, as the question became moot when the AFT and their allies made no such moves.

4   In November 2023, Peyser and Gilbert would run against each other in a contested

election for AFSCME Council 93 Executive Board. Both sought to be the Vermont representative within the council's leadership. Peyser would win this election.

5   I will also note that I did have a private phone call with Labounty a couple weeks after he issued the Riemer endorsement. On the call, I told him I respected his free will to choose to support whichever Vermont AFL-CIO candidates he chose to but thought it was pretty crappy that he went and backed Riemer without first telling me. Karl candidly recognized this as an error in judgement and apologized. I accepted. He also told me that his decision to back Riemer largely came from being pissed at AFSCME for questioning his honesty via the investigation into 1343 expenditures while he was president. Here he expressed that after serving the union for so many years, he felt a deep sense of anger, and this influenced his decision concerning Riemer.

6   Again, knowing Labounty I never believed he was capable of embezzling money from his local. While we may not have shared all the same views concerning the labor movement, and even if Karl was backing my opponent, he was union through and through. If I doubted Karl's honesty, I would not have made that call, and in fact I would rather lose an election than make a transactional alliance with someone so low as to embezzle from their members' dues (as there are few acts lower than that). But I knew Karl to be a good man, even if his treasurer was guilty of nefarious acts (at worst) or shitty bookkeeping (at best). In the end, more than a year later, Karl was not found liable for any of the dubious spending uncovered by Local 1343.

7   These motions passed. United! brought these forth for tactical reasons. In brief, first we wanted our candidates to be able to state clearly that they were on the United! slate and to articulate the progressive vision for organized labor they sought to advance (and to call on members to vote for the entire United! slate). Second, we knew that United!, no matter what at this point, would win the great majority of the contests. Thus, before members voted for president, we wanted to be able to address the members and clearly state that they had already voted for change, for United! candidates, and the final decision they would make today would be whether a progressive, a United! candidate, would preside over the reform leadership they had just installed or whether they would have a person in the top leadership position who had opposed United! throughout the campaign. In brief, we figured that riding the momentum of United! victories prior to the vote for president could be enough to sway a delegate, and we wanted to leave no stone unturned.

8   Steve was a strong United! supporter and an all-around great and good-natured guy. Tragically, he passed away way too soon in 2023.

CHAPTER V **From Opposition to Governing**

1   In spring 2023, Vermont also gave serious support to another strike, that of UAW Local 2322, Goddard College support staff. Not only did UAW win the strike (and secure the raises they needed to see), but they also managed to secure a contract that continues to contain *no* management rights clause!

2   Smith was the district vice president for Windsor County.

3   We would also go on to print our platform, commonly referred to as the Little Green Book, in order to distribute to our rank-and-file members. The booklets, which fit in one's back pocket, have been printed in the thousands.

4   From the get-go, United! also sought to make progress in building a women's caucus within the Vermont AFL-CIO. Such efforts originally got off the ground in 2019 under the leadership of District Vice President Helen Scott. Coming out of this effort, it was recommended that larger Vermont AFL-CIO functions provide free childcare to members in order to make attendance by women (who culturally bear a disproportionate burden when it comes to caring responsibilities) both more likely and more inviting. Acting on this, we have facilitated such childcare at political summits and conventions ever since, employing unionized Head Start teachers (members of AFSCME Local 1369) to fill this need. However, progress in forming this caucus has come in fits and starts. The original efforts, although resulting in the childcare reform, faded as other issues such as the COVID-19 pandemic rose to the top. But in 2021 an organizing committee under the leadership of Vice President Katie Harris (AFSCME Local 1674), with support from Vice President Brittany Rhoads (AFSCME Local 3977) and Vice President Helen Scott (AFT Local 3203), again formed and the effort is again underway. Further, in May 2022 Committee Chair Katie Harris released a public statement on our behalf condemning the US Supreme Court's stated intent of overturning *Roe v. Wade* and sternly stating the Vermont AFL-CIO's unflinching support for women to retain the right to control their own bodies. Harris also called for the passage of a Vermont state constitutional amendment codifying a woman's right to an abortion, and called on union members and Vermonters to take part in upcoming demonstrations in support of abortion rights. And on June 24, 2022, when the Supreme Court officially overturned *Roe v. Wade*, VP Harris spoke at a demonstration in Burlington, again recommitting the Vermont AFL-CIO to fighting for a woman's right to control her own body. As president of the Vermont AFL-CIO, I did likewise at the rally being held at the same time in Montpelier. United! also hopes to form a BIPOC caucus as well in the foreseeable future.

5   Our organizers on staff would change over time, and at various points our organizers would include retired Teamster Dan Brush (a former Vermont AFL-CIO president), former candidate for Vermont governor James Ehlers, 1343's Damion Gilbert (who unfortunately we had to part ways with after he failed to carry out a mandated union task he had been assigned), and others. Never have these on-call organizers been full-time professional positions in nature. Rather, they have always been part-time and have been actual workers, retired union members, college students, or leftists in it to create real change.

6   To over 45 percent in 2023.

7   When asked about the impact of the Vermont AFL-CIO organizer and general outcome of the fight back campaign at UVM, District Vice President (and United! supporter from AFT Local 3203) Helen Scott reported: "From spring 2020 to spring 2021 hundreds of students, faculty, staff and community members collaborated to oppose cuts proposed by UVM management. They held a number of successful events and activities: car rallies, press conferences, petitions, panels, teach-ins, social media campaigns, articles and letters in local and national media outlets. This put UVM management on the defensive and pushed back against the worst of their attacks. The AFL on-call organizer [Dan Brush] provided very helpful assistance with this work during the time he was assigned to United Academics, providing organizational support and initiating specific projects—such as designing and distributing campaign buttons—which helped with community visibility."

8   In 2023, we also gained commitments from SEIU to sign solidarity charters for newly organized units at UVMMC, the South Burlington Starbucks, and the Burlington Ben & Jerry's ice cream shop.

9   As of 2023, AFSCME has also organized the Vermont Historical Society and the South Burlington Public Library.

10   In 2023, AFT-Vermont also organized another huge unit of two-thousand-plus within UVMMC as well as additional bargaining units of more modest size.

11   In 2021, we also organized a training for such workers interested in unionizing, which we provided for free.

12   As of December 2021, the Vermont AFL-CIO executive director is supporting workers in a half-dozen workplaces who are interested in forming a union (and who reached out to us through this new process). Here we are seeking to help them form basic organizing committees. However, as these efforts are still in their early phases, it would be premature to discuss them by name. Update: As of 2023, this tip line and our new commitment to lending support to active organizing drives was a contributing factor in AFSCME organizing Soteria House and the Vermont Historical Society and SEIU organizing both the South Burlington Starbucks and the Burlington Ben & Jerry's.

13   As of September 2023, this number has grown to twenty thousand AFL-CIO union members in Vermont!

14   Rampy would go on to be elected vice president of AFSCME Local 1674 in 2022.

15   RAD's founder and executive director was James Haslam. I have known James since 2002 through work on mutual projects by way of the Vermont Workers Center (which he used to be director of). I remember sitting in a tavern with him sometime in 2005. At the time I was a member of the militant Green Mountain Anarchist Collective (which itself was the NEFAC affiliate for Vermont). Over a beer I told James I would be president of the Vermont AFL-CIO in ten years. I don't know if he believed me or not, but in retrospect he should not have. Clearly I was wrong … it would take fourteen years.

16   It was a pleasure to again work with Nulhegan Abenaki chief Don Stevens, and just as the Vermont AFL-CIO 100 percent supported any and all changes in the Renew platform proposed by Chief Stevens to address the needs of their tribal citizens, Chief Stevens supported any and all changes we wanted to see to advance the interest of union workers. I and Chief Stevens already had trust and mutual respect. From 2010 to 2012, during a brief period when I was doing some work for the Sierra Club, we worked together in successfully establishing a tribal forest in the Northeast Kingdom. This land, which the tribe received ownership over in 2012, marked the first land held by the Nulhegan Abenaki Tribe in over two hundred years.

17   See David Van Deusen, "TCI Is No Friend of the Worker," *VTDigger*, December 29, 2019, https://vtdigger.org/2019/12/29/david-van-deusen-tci-is-no-friend-of-the-worker.

18   It is worth pointing out that conservative opposition to any carbon tax was not and is not contingent on the nature of the tax (regressive versus progressive). For the Vermont AFL-CIO, it was specifically the regressive nature of the tax, whereby working-class people would pay the same as the wealthy (thus workers would pay significantly more based on the percentage of their income), that caused us to reject it.

19   While the legislation would have shielded low-income Vermonters from the worst of its economic impact, the great majority of working families would have been left high and dry.

20   Publicly, we argued that the state should instead offer to fully pay for working-class households' transition to sustainable heat sources and that such a program should be paid for by wealth taxes and corporate taxes. And further, that in a time of 8.5 percent inflation, there could be no moral justification for forcing working people to pay more to heat their homes.

21   It is of note that in 2022 the Vermont Building and Construction Trades Council, a core United! partner, supported successful efforts within the Vermont General Assembly that required weatherization projects funded by state grants pay workers the prevailing wage. This energy-saving, climate-related bill had the very real and meaningful effect of increasing the hourly rate of impacted workers, including those at Capstone's weatherization program (already organized into AFSCME Local 1369), by as much as $10,000 a year. This example clearly highlights the important intersections of progressive environmental action with organized labor and the working class in general.

22   In 2022, with the endorsement of the Vermont AFL-CIO, Casey would be elected as state representative as a Democrat.

23   In 2022, with the endorsement of the Vermont AFL-CIO, Watson would be elected as state senator as a Democrat/Progressive.

24   In June 2023, we won this effort as well, making Barre the third city in Vermont to pass a responsible contractor ordinance. In this effort, the Vermont AFL-CIO was the lead, with the Building Trades in support. It is anticipated that our next target for passage will be the City of Rutland.

25   In 2019, Migrant Justice declined this offer to affiliate, stating that while they welcomed collaboration and mutual support, they were not ready to take this next step. It is my hope that as our relationship with them deepens, we can revisit this offer in future years.

26   The COVID-19 pandemic, from March 2020 through May 2022, would claim the lives of over one million Americans. To put that tragedy in perspective, the total number of American military personnel killed in World War II numbered 416,800 over a longer period.

27   Attending this press conference with the Vermont AFL-CIO were the following: AFSCME 1674, Black Rose Anarchist Federation–Burlington, the Bread & Roses Collective, Brass Balagan, Burlington Progressive Party Steering Committee, Burlington Showing Up for Racial Justice, Burlington Tenants Union, Champlain Valley DSA, Gender Inclusive VT, Kunsi Keya Tomakoce, Migrant Justice/Justicia Migrante, Peace & Justice Center, Rights & Democracy, Socialist Resurgence–Burlington, Vermont Coalition for Ethnic and Social Equity in the Schools, Vermonters for Justice in Palestine, Vermont State Labor Council, and AFL-CIO.

28   Vermont's social safety net was and remains better than that of most states, but it is still woefully inadequate in guaranteeing the meeting of basic needs of all of its residents.

29   In Vermont, unemployment insurance eligibility was greatly extended, an eviction moratorium was enacted, free childcare and free meals for children were maintained during the darkest hours of the pandemic, many thousands of workers received hazard pay, paid sick days were afforded to most, personal protective

equipment for essential workers did become a priority, and many thousands of union workers who were at high risk were able to stay home with pay. All told, while far from perfect, Vermont did a better job than most in meeting the needs of its people during the hardest times prevaccine.

30 Internally, with the arrival of COVID-19, in order to better protect the health of our executive board, we switched to remote meetings as opposed to our traditional in-person meetings. Further, we conducted our 2020 annual convention remotely (although postvaccine, we would return to in-person conventions in 2021).

31 Smaller but still significant satellite caravans were also held in Vermont at Brattleboro and the Upper Connecticut River Valley.

32 It should be noted that throughout the pandemic United! was supportive of any and all reasonable steps to reduce the infection rate and keep people alive. From the early lockdowns to mask mandates and social distancing guidelines, we sought to be generally supportive and reasonable. Our United! leaders also applauded the development of COVID-19 vaccines. Doing our part, we also decided to hold our 2020 convention remotely, and at our in-person 2021 convention we required indoor masking. The one exception among the United! leadership was Omar Fernandez of APWU. Brother Fernandez, from the start, viscerally opposed any and all mask mandates and was utterly against the vaccine and any workplace requirements, even if negotiated by a union, to mandate vaccinations. Fernandez further refused to accept the democratic decisions of the executive board when it came to COVID-19 measures, like the masking requirement for our 2021 convention, when they came into contradiction with his personally held non-science-based beliefs. Thus, he refused to attend the 2021 convention (instead getting a COVID-related exception from the board). Even so, recognizing that he was in line with the other objectives of United! he was still allowed to run for his executive board seat in 2021 as part of the United! slate. But in March 2022, after the national AFL-CIO sent out information about the 2022 national AFL-CIO convention, and when that material included a notice that proof of vaccine would be required in order to attend, Fernandez offered his resignation as a Vermont AFL-CIO officer. Given that Brother Fernandez was increasingly becoming fixated on his disdain for masks and the vaccine, to the detriment of all else, I accepted his resignation.

33 The economic free fall was effectively stemmed through effective intervention by the federal government, which injected a significant amount of stimulus money into the economy under the Biden administration. However, a systematic and progressive alteration of the social safety net never materialized, as the Republican Party and enough members of the Democratic Party combined to block passage of Build Back Better legislation and the PRO Act. Thus, without comprehensive reform undertaken, as I write these words in May 2022, our country is again facing a new economic crisis, this one of inflation (presently at 8.5 percent).

34 The picket was endorsed by: Vermont AFL-CIO, Green Mountain Central Labor Council, AFSCME Local 1343 (Burlington City/Chittenden County), AFSCME Local 490 (Bennington County), AFSCME Local 1201 (Rutland/Addison County), AFSCME Local 1369 (Washington County), AFSCME Local 1674 (Howard Center), AFSCME Local 2413 (Northeast Kingdom), AFSCME Local 3797 (Windsor County), AFSCME Local 3977 (Lamoille County Mental Health), AFSCME Local 4802

(Home Healthcare Providers), American Federation of Teachers–Vermont, United Academics/AFT at UVM, VSCFF/AFT Local 3180, Vermont Federation of Nurses & Health Professionals, IATSE Local 919, UFCW Local 1459, UAW Local 2322, NWU/UAW-VT Local 1891, APWU-VT, APWU Local 520, Teamsters Local 597, Vermont NEA, Orange Southwest Education Association, VT NEA Staff Union (VT-NSO), UNAP Local 5086, UNAP Local 5087, SEIU Local 200United, Vermont State Employees' Association, UE Local 203, Migrant Justice, VSCS Thrive, the Vermont Workers Center, Rights & Democracy, UVM Union of Students, 350 Burlington, Bread & Roses Collective, Champlain Valley DSA, Central Vermont DSA, Upper Valley DSA, Burlington Progressives, Vermont Progressive Party, Vermont House Progressive Party Caucus, Vermont General Assembly Workers Caucus, and Vermont lieutenant governor David Zuckerman (Progressive).

35   I wrote this statement and then explained to Gilbert and Greeno why issuing it seemed the only right thing to do. They took me at my word and signed.

36   Personally, I don't dislike Vermont NEA executive director Jeff Fannon. Further, while Fannon and the NEA are not as progressive as the Vermont AFL-CIO, they are a competent union that represents their members well with a quality staff. They are also, at times, unafraid of going out on strike or organizing informational picket lines in order to defend the interests of their members. And even while AFSCME and the Vermont AFL-CIO had a serious conflict with them in 2018 regarding collective bargaining rights concerning health care, in general, or at least *outwardly*, they have not attacked the Vermont AFL-CIO or United!, at least not publicly. Further, since the passage of statewide bargaining legislation concerning school health care, AFSCME and the NEA have worked together on a joint union bargaining team. And here I have witnessed firsthand the responsible and effective job they have done in advocating for their members in this format.

37   Unbeknownst to VSEA, them pulling Aimee Towne (who would go on to become a reactionary VSEA president) from the speaking spot was a gift. Originally 1343 and the Vermont AFL-CIO offered a spot to a more progressive VSEA leader, John Davy, who represented a wing of the union that supported the changes United! was seeking to make in the labor movement. Later, after VSEA proper endorsed the picket, we offered up an additional spot to a person of VSEA's choosing. When they appointed their first vice president, behind the scenes the rank-and-file progressives from this union lodged a complaint with the Vermont AFL-CIO and asked that this officer not be allowed to address the picketers, as it was felt that her politics embraced business unionism and not the more forward-looking views of United! and our allies within the VSEA. Here I expressed that I did not feel it to be right for me, or 1343, to define who the speaker would be from any one major union willing to stand in solidarity with us. Thus, by my count we would simply have to tolerate two divergent speakers from the same union. But with VSEA pulling Towne, our friends from the inside of their union were elated.

38   The president of United Academics AFT Local 3203, Julie Roberts, also called me to express concern. But my discussion with her was very much of a reasonable nature. She pointed out that the same mass email with the statement also included something on Vermont AFL-CIO support for Progressive Party candidates, thus giving her the impression that the picket could also be in support of this party concerning the next election. I assured Roberts that that was not the intent and that the picket would still have a focus on preserving city jobs as

originally intended. She was satisfied with this response, and that was the end of it.

39   Those on motorcycles included myself (with Dr. Rhiannon Maton of UUP NY on the back), Steve Groelinger (steward, AFSCME 1343), Dana Wilkinson (AFSCME 1674), and Dan Cornell (president, AFSCME Local 490).

40   Local 1343, with encouragement from the Vermont AFL-CIO, also invited Black Lives Matter of Greater Burlington to endorse the picket and have a speaker at the event. Given the mass protests happening in the wake of the George Floyd murder, and given that in recent days big protests against the murder had also been taking place in Burlington, seeking to include them was the right thing to do. However, they never got back to the local, nor were they responsive to Migrant Justice's outreach (which they conducted at our request). Thus, they were not present. Six months later, the Vermont AFL-CIO was able open a dialogue with another key Burlington organization engaged in the fight against racial discrimination. This group, the Black Perspective, would go on to partner with the Vermont AFL-CIO on a panel discussion concerning "race at work" and would come to share podiums with us at events like the 2021 May Day demonstration in Montpelier.

41   It was good that Gilbert spoke these words in public. It was the right thing to do. Just days before, he had come close to explicitly not inviting the local Black Lives Matter group to the picket, or at least he had contemplated telling them who of them could speak and what subjects they could speak on. This came out of Gilbert being very troubled by a speech that had been given recently by BLM leader Harmony Edosomwan in Burlington that seemed to say that they would burn the local police station down if the cops killed another citizen. Of course, for a white man to tell Black community leaders what they can or cannot say is not the type of intervention Gilbert would have been well advised to make. But here, Local 1343 and Vermont AFL-CIO leader Dwight Brown, a Black man, a friend and confidant of Damion's, set him straight and got Gilbert back on the right path. Thus, Damion's choice to highlight the fight against racial injustice while on our union picket, and his prior decision to extend an official invitation to BLM to take part in the picket, was a welcome act of solidarity, but one that could have veered toward disaster within the left if not for Brown's intervention.

42   During the earlier stages of the pandemic, we did negotiate many furlough agreements with cities, towns, and employers, but generally speaking the great majority of these took place when the feds had in place the extra $600 a week benefit (which resulted in most of our members making more money while on furlough then they did while working), and we generally were able to secure a continuation of our other benefits, like health care, during the furlough period. Thus, this was a very different thing than mass layoffs.

CHAPTER VI Concerning Elections: Rejecting the Premise of the Democrats and Building a More Direct Democracy

1   That is, Democratic Party chair Terje Anderson, State Representative Joanne Donovan, former state representative and present VSEA executive director Steve Howard, and Vermont Democratic Party staff organized into USW Local 4.

2   Voter turnout in Vermont for the 2020 presidential election was 73.27 percent. That said, I recognize that some on the far left, especially those with anarchist leanings, desire a complete rejection of any and all electoral engagement from

a more militant labor movement. The reality within the Vermont AFL-CIO was and remains that the lion's share of members are not agreeable to their unions vacating electoral activity but do not want such activity to benefit candidates or parties that do not support them and their needs. And even if a union leader was inclined to shepherd the state labor council toward a no-endorsement policy, such a desire would be out of sync with the membership. And here a good leader should aim to be one pace to the left of the general will, but not leaps and bounds, as too much distance rapidly lends itself to the leadership and membership becoming asunder, with the membership inevitably stagnating and the leftward shift becoming largely impossible through willful action. Thus, the Vermont AFL-CIO was ripe for a realignment with candidates and parties to the left, but not a total break from electoralism in the name of a leftist mythology grounded in ideology over actual history and reality. Further, one would be blind to not see that our endorsements for Progressive candidates in the Burlington City Council elections in 2020 (elections we were active in and won) had a direct bearing on the ability to pass the responsible contractor ordinance thereafter. The same could be said about the Barre City Council endorsements and the passage of another responsible contractor ordinance in 2023.

3   Representative Brian Cina, in addition to being a member of DSA, is also a member of the Vermont Progressive Party.

4   Here it was consistently the Progressives such as Lieutenant Governor Zuckerman, State Senator Pollina, State Representative Cina, and Senator Bernie Sanders who time and again walked the line with us and showed themselves to be a friend of the unions.

5   The executive board had to take a vote on the new election and endorsement policy and the legislative priorities. Although we had members vote on the matter, that vote was only indicative in nature (and members were made aware of that). Being a political summit and not an official convention meant that floor votes lacked official authority to bind us to such decisions. By way of the national AFL-CIO constitution and the Vermont AFL-CIO constitution, only official conventions have the authority to allow members to make binding decisions based on floor votes.

6   Also passing in 2020 was a general union-related bill that provided for more rapid Vermont Labor Board certification elections, mandated union orientations in organized shops, and required employers to provide more and better bargaining-unit contact information to unions. While the Vermont AFL-CIO supported the bill, the effort to pass it was led by the Working Vermont coalition (which we were not a member of). It was a good bill, but it did little to alter the balance of power between workers and bosses.

7   Another bill we supported, which would have established paid maternity and paternity leave for all workers, also was vetoed by Republican governor Phil Scott. The override effort, despite support from the Vermont AFL-CIO, failed by one vote in the House (that one vote being Democrat Randall Szott, who felt the bill did not go far enough). Universal paid family leave was a secondary priority for the Vermont AFL-CIO in 2020.

8   In 2023, year one of the 2023–24 biennium, the Vermont AFL-CIO was successful in seeing card check passed in the Vermont Senate (with a two-thirds majority) as part of the larger Vermont PRO Act. This act, in addition to establishing card

check for the public sector, bans captive audience meetings during organizing campaigns and legalizes unions on farms and for domestic workers. State Senator Kesha Ram Hinsdale (Democrat/Progressive) was our champion on this legislation. In 2024, we will continue the effort to see it pass in the Vermont House.

9   Burlington city elections for city council and mayor are staggered, so all city council races do not happen in the same year.

10   While Gilbert's support for the Progressives in Burlington was both admirable and impactful, his motivation may have been more pragmatic than ideological. In 2023, he himself ran for city council in his home city of Plattsburg, New York, in the Democratic primary. After losing to his Working Families Party–backed opponent, he told the *Press-Republican* newspaper that he was still looking at possibly running a write-in campaign in the general election by appealing to Republicans. To quote Gilbert: "The Republican votes are still out there.... Maybe my conservative values align with them." Joe LoTemplio, "Jacob Avery Apparent Winner in City of Plattsburgh Ward 2 Democratic Party Primary," *Press-Republican*, June 27, 2023.

11   All of these candidates were running as Progressives except Dieng. Dieng was running as an independent, but he pledged to caucus with the Progressives. Dieng, shortly after the election, would choose not to caucus with them and would claim that he had never made such a pledge. However, I have personally seen the written communications Dieng conducted with the Progressive Party executive director, Josh Wronski, and there is no question that Dieng broke his word.

12   In many state labor councils, local endorsements fall to regional central labor councils (which are bodies of the state labor council). However, in Vermont we do not have CLCs organized in the great majorities of our counties. Thus, local endorsements fall to the executive board unless the timing of an election coincides with a statewide convention, in which case endorsements go to the membership as is represented by convention delegates.

13   We also endorsed the Progressive mayor of Montpelier, Anne Watson (an incumbent), and Democratic candidate for Montpelier City Council Conor Casey (also an incumbent). Both these candidates won their race. Note that our moratorium on endorsing Democrats would not go into effect until later spring 2020 and only applied to statehouse races. Casey, for his part, was and remains a reliable union ally and was key to passing the responsible contractor ordinance in Montpelier.

14   Our only defeat was Nate Lantieri. In a close race, Lantieri lost to the Democratic incumbent.

15   However, that majority would rapidly turn into a plurality when independent city councilor Ali Dieng broke his campaign agreement and chose not to caucus with the Progressives. Even so, with the 2020 win, the Progressives became the party with the largest voting bloc on the Burlington City Council and Progressive Max Tracy would thus serve as city council president. Concerning Progressives Freeman and Hanson, their city council seats were not up for election in 2020.

16   In the 2020 Vermont general election, even with the moratorium in place, the Vermont AFL-CIO Executive Board did grant endorsements for a total of nine state legislators who were Democrats and members of the Legislative Workers Caucus. These nine (Mari Cordes, Addison-4; Chip Troiano, Caledonia-2; Bob Hooper, Chittenden-6-1; Mary Howard, Rutland-5-3; Peter Anthony, Washington-3; Kari

Dolan, Washington-7; Emilie Kornheiser, Windham-2-1; Kevin "Coach" Christie, Windsor-4-2; and Andrew Perchik, Washington Senate) had all previously signed a letter supporting the Local 1343 picket after the mayor of Burlington threatened layoffs if concessions were not forthcoming. These nine Democrats were labor champions and were supported by more than two-thirds of our executive board (as our new endorsement policy required). But issuing a total of nine endorsements for pro-union Democrats is a far cry from the fifty to a hundred endorsements for unreliable Democrats issued by the Vermont AFL-CIO prior to United! coming into office.

17 Zuckerman would lose his race for governor to incumbent Phil Scott (Zuckerman, a true friend to labor, received 27.5 percent of the vote). Hoffer would win his race for auditor.

18 The Progressives who won are as follows: Senator Anthony Pollina (Washington County), Senator Chris Pearson (Chittenden County), Representative Mollie Burke (Windham 2-2), Representative Selene Colburn (Chittenden 6-4), Representative Brian Cina (Chittenden 6-4), Representative Emma Mulvaney-Stanak (Chittenden 6-2), Representative Tanya Vyhovsky (Chittenden 8-2), Representative Taylor Small (Chittenden 6-7), and Representative Heather Surprenant (Windsor 4-1). There are a total of 30 state senators and 150 state representatives from all the parties (and independents) in the Vermont General Assembly.

19 Tracy would lose this race to incumbent Miro Weinberger (a Democrat) by a mere 129 votes. Tracy, at the time, was working as a union organizer for AFT-Vermont. This was a three-way race, with city council member Ali Dieng finishing a distant third. Recall that Dieng, an independent, broke his word to the Progressive Party following his last city council election win and failed to caucus with them. Here, running against Tracy, he very well may have handed the election to the incumbent Democrat.

20 The Progressive slate in 2022 was Zoraya Hightower for Ward 1, Gene Bergman for Ward 2, Joe Magee for Ward 3, Faried Munarsyah for Ward 5, Olivia Taylor for Ward 7, and Ali House for Ward 8. Other Progressive incumbents, Perri Freeman and Jack Hanson, were not up for election in 2022. Of our 2022 candidates, Hightower, Bergman, Magee, and House all won.

21 After this chapter was written, in Town Meeting Day elections in Barre and Burlington, we also issued endorsements for Progressive candidates. In Burlington, Melo Grant (Progressive) won for city council. In Barre (in which party affiliations do not appear on the ballot), all three of the candidates we backed won: Teddy Waszazak, Emel Cambel, and Samn Stockwell.

22 Katie Harris was also elected to a seat on the Vermont AFL-CIO Executive Board as part of the United! slate in 2021. Later in 2021, she was additionally elected as president of AFSCME Local 1674. In September 2023, she would be elected president of the Vermont AFL-CIO.

23 Omar Fernandez, an elected member of the Vermont AFL-CIO from United! in 2019 and 2021, served on the national leadership of the Movement for a People's Party. Also of note, in early 2021 the Vermont AFL-CIO arranged for a meeting between leaders of Movement for a People's Party and leaders of the Vermont Progressive Party. The People's Party had recently organized in Vermont, and the Vermont AFL-CIO wanted to arrange for an agreement, if possible, for these parties to not compete against each other but rather to find a way to be in

partnership. Through this meeting, which I facilitated, it was agreed by the two that the People's Party would not run against Progressive candidates in Vermont, and in turn the Progressives would invite representatives of the People's Party to attend their fall convention. Building such trust by taking these small steps made sense to me if, in the long run, discussions about the Progressive Party (while retaining its name and autonomy) becoming the Vermont affiliate of a broader left national party were to ever become possible (something I saw value in). However, playing into Progressive concerns expressed during this meeting, soon after a person or persons from the Vermont People's Party began posting disparaging statements against elected Progressives. While I flagged this to the People's Party after Progressive Party executive director Josh Wronski brought it to my attention, and although the posts were eventually taken down, this breach of trust set back the goodwill we at the Vermont AFL-CIO had sought to build between the parties.

24   Sometime around fifteen years ago, I recall having a drink with Progressive Peter Sterling. (At the time, he was a highly effective farmer organizer working with Anthony Pollina.) Sterling, a few years later, would go on to be the chief of staff for the Vermont Senate pro tem Tim Ashe (a Progressive). Good-naturedly I told Sterling that I would be a firm supporter of the Vermont Progressive Party until they came into power as the majority party, but from that point on, I would expect that they too would become a stifling agent in the movement toward social trans-formation. We had a bit of a laugh over that, but truth be told I would still argue that that is true.

25   While constitutional amendments can be hard to advance, the Vermont AFL-CIO did actively support one such amendment in 2022: one that would guarantee unfettered abortion access for all women. With Katie Harris (who by that time was serving as our executive vice president) serving as our point person on the issue, in fall 2023 it was adopted overwhelmingly by the voters and now is a right entrenched in our Vermont Constitution.

CHAPTER VII Black Lives Matter, the Police, and the Politics of Reality

1   Brown, in 2021, would become my United! running mate and would be elected to the position of executive vice president. He would retain that position and serve with honor until stepping back in late June 2022. In his place, after an indicative vote of the membership at our August 2022 convention, Katie Harris would be appointed to this position.

2   As of 2024, Vermont AFL-CIO unions now represent only one small municipal police department (Morrisville, organized with IBEW Local 300). The only other sworn law enforcement represented by AFL-CIO unions is a tiny minority within the VSEA (state police lieutenants, DMV police, Liquor Control police, and deputy sheriffs), which brought them with them when they affiliated with the AFL-CIO in 2023. Previously, Brattleboro PD was represented by IUPA, but they chose to pay no dues to the Vermont State Labor Council and have since affiliated with the NEPBA (which is not part of the AFL-CIO). Since 2020, St. Johnsbury PD, Newport PD, and Manchester PD (all formerly with AFSCME) chose to leave to be repre-sented by the right-wing pro-Trump NEPBA.

3   Further, even among people I considered confidants, divisions were appar-ent. In early June, as Local 1343's efforts to organize an informational picket in

support of city workers ran concurrently with protests against racial discrimination and police brutality in Burlington, Local 1343 president Damion Gilbert
initially refused to extend an open invitation to Black Lives Matter of Greater
Burlington to take part in and speak at the union action (even though other
community groups were being given such invitations without conditions). On
a private phone call with me, he said he had already been getting pushback from
a (very small) minority of his members for attending the demonstration against
the Floyd murder. Gilbert also expressed that he had serious concerns about
a speech previously given by Black Lives Matter leader Harmony Edosomwan,
which stated that if police killed another person (Black, Brown, or white), the
police station would be burned to the ground. Over and over he said he would
not and could not allow for a situation to arise where there was any possibility of
such militant statements to be made on his picket line. By his thinking, he would
only offer an invitation to BLM if they would agree to *not* have Edosomwan be
their speaker and if he could preapprove whatever speech they gave. For my part,
I argued that since the local was inviting what amounted to all the other leading
community organizations and offering them a speaking spot with no conditions
attached, morally and politically, as a white union leader, he could not seek to
dictate to a Black organization who they send and what they say. To me, that
would be fucked up on many levels and would serve as yet another example of
how racism and racial censorship manifests itself in our own movement. But, in
conversation with me, Gilbert was steadfast, and my reasoning did not move him.
He would *not* invite BLM unless they agreed to conditions. While I was deeply
troubled by this development, less than twenty-four hours later Gilbert called me
back to say he had changed his mind. Black Lives Matter would be invited with no
conditions. He informed me that he had talked in-depth with fellow 1343 leader
Dwight Brown about his thinking, and Dwight, like myself, rejected Damion's
positions and apparently made a forceful argument that the *only* right thing to do
was to seek to include them and for the local to afford them the same autonomy
and solidarity being offered to all the other organizations we sought to form an
alliance with. Gilbert also told me that Dwight had reminded him that the right
thing to do is not always easy, and regardless of what happened on the picket line,
he (and other principled union members) would have Damion's back. Personally,
I was pleased that this moral crisis was averted, by Dwight, before it grew legs.
But the incident did give me concern regarding the core political principles of
Gilbert in relation to the broad popular front I knew we had to build among leftist
organizations. In short, despite Gilbert being a friend and effective ally leading
up to that point, I suspected this was not the last time United! or the progressive
wing of the labor movement would suffer a difficult situation due to Damion's
decisions. So in the end 1343 did invite BLM to take part in the picket and offered
to provide a speaker slot. While BLM ultimately did not take part, the fact that
the offer was made, with no conditions, was good and the right thing to do.

4   As of September 2023, our AFL-CIO union membership in Vermont now stands
     at twenty thousand.

5   These major developments are discussed in detail in a later chapter.

6   Note that Morris, in 2022, would rise to the position of executive director of
     Rights & Democracy (a position she would hold into 2023). I also floated a draft
     to my friend Netdahe Stoddard. Stoddard (who is white), the son of deceased

political prisoner Richard Williams, was raised by Black Panthers in Vermont after his father's incarceration. I asked Stoddard if he could float the draft to former Black Panther contacts he had. While the turnaround window ultimately did not allow for that kind of old New Left vetting, Stoddard did express his support for the draft statement and encouraged me to move ahead. Also of unofficial assistance in the draft language was SUNY Courtland professor Dr. Rhiannon Maton, who, at the time, I was in a relationship with. Dr. Maton, whose area of research focused on teacher unions along with issues of race and class, provided me with much positive feedback and recommendations that found voice in the resolution.

7   This point was included as a direct response to the recent actions of VSEA executive director Steve Howard (a Democrat). Days before our resolution was adopted, Howard arranged for a police academy trainer, on behalf of VSEA, to provide testimony to the Vermont House of Representatives *in support* of police use of chokeholds and against any change in the law that would prevent cops from choking citizens. Howard, in the shadow of the murder of George Floyd, was actively opposing meaningful changes to use-of-force regulations concerning law enforcement. I, like most of the Vermont left, found this decision by Howard to be sickening and a clear example of the moral and strategic failures he brought to the Vermont State Employees' Association.

8   After the statement was made public, I received a message from former Weather Underground leader Jeff Jones. Jones in part said the resolution was "probably the most radical and principled statement to come out of organized labor in decades. A great accomplishment."

9   Council 93 was not the only player in the labor movement to push back. But where Council 93 expressed their concerns and disagreements directly to me and the Vermont AFL-CIO, others were not so principled. One attempt to undermine United!'s leadership on the issues relating to Black Lives Matter came in the form of an email from former VSEA executive director Annie Noonan that was circulated among those she (wrongly) believed to be reliable old guard leaders within labor. Noonan, it should be noted, was also a Democrat, and the partner of Vermont secretary of state Jim Condos (a Democrat). The email that she circulated read as follows:

> Dear Friends:
> I am sending this information to you because I am so concerned (actually horrified) about the Vermont AFL-CIO under the leadership of President David Van Deusen, and I hope you will be concerned too.
> I have attached (below) the statement that was sent out to all Vermont AFL-CIO members by President Dave Van Deusen. Please take a minute to read it all the way through, and note that as the President of the VT AFL-CIO he is saying, "no more organizing of police unions," "cut the budgets of VSP and Burlington Police" (all of whom are UNIONIZED Vermont employees), etc. In addition, AFSCME Local 409 is the police union for the Bennington PD and one of Van Deusen's own union locals. [Author's note: It is actually Local 490, and they do not represent the Bennington Police, but rather Bennington DPW and Manchester PD, and their local president, Dan Cornell, is presently on the Vermont AFL-CIO Executive Board as part of United! Cornell was also part of the internal

discussions leading to the adoption of this position on BLM and police reform.]

Unbelievable … my head is exploding.

If you forward any of this don't forward my email to you. Just clip the AFL-CIO message and write your own comments.

Please see the sections in his statement that I have highlighted in yellow.

Van Deusen wrote a book in 2017 called: *On Anarchism: Dispatches from the People's Republic of Vermont*…

Ironically, Noonan, unbeknownst to her, had me to thank for her appointment as commissioner of the Vermont Department of Labor under former Democratic governor Peter Shumlin. In Shumlin's first run for governor, 2010, there was an attempt by the Building Trades to have the Vermont AFL-CIO endorse his Republican challenger (over the issue of the possibility of the Vermont Yankee nuclear power plant being shut down and IBEW losing a number of good union jobs). For my part, I supported Shumlin (who supported closing down Vermont Yankee) as he pledged to pass single-payer health care reform (something that turned out to be a lie). As such, I personally coordinated with Shumlin prior to him meeting with the Vermont AFL-CIO Executive Board. To Shumlin I suggested that he come out of the gate promising to appoint a labor leader to head the Department of Labor if elected. He did just that when he met with us, and that was a contributing factor in his securing of union backing in this election. After he became governor, with the support of the Vermont AFL-CIO, he appointed Noonan (the former VSEA executive director) as commissioner.

10   As the AFSCME union rep for Vermont, I also was aware that my job could be at stake. But to Council 93's credit, never once during this time did anyone from 93 ever say a word or make a threat concerning my employment.

11   The following year, Katie Harris was elected president of this local, with Peyser being elected to vice president. In 2022, Harris did not seek reelection, instead focusing on her work within the state labor council. In her place, Andy Blanchet was elected president, and Nolan Rampy VP.

12   Through good internal organizing, in fall 2022 they surpassed the 45 percent membership mark, thus triggering the reopener on fair share dues. As of 2023, bargaining efforts have been difficult and have been marked by the filing of an unfair labor practice charge by the union, and a grievance. While efforts are ongoing, the question of fair share, at the time of this writing, has yet to be resolved, although I do have confidence that the union shall prevail.

CHAPTER VIII Aftermath: Residual Challenges, New Elections, and Structure Building

1   The loss of the firefighter local was unfortunate but minor in impact. In Vermont this international, leading up to fall 2019, was only paying per caps for one local (St. Johnsbury) with nine members.

2   One major structural problem with the AFL-CIO is that the monthly dues paid to state labor councils per member, called per caps, are essentially optional. If a local chooses not to pony up, the only ramification is that that local no longer is afforded delegates to the next convention, and their members cannot serve the state labor council in any officer role. Thus, a local can opt out for any reason,

thereby breaking solidarity with their fellow workers, at will. In this way, the AFL-CIO becomes a diminished organization with reduced resources.

3   Jason Winston is an old friend of mine who I have much respect for. We first met in 1997 when he was a member of the #10 Collective, which was affiliated with the Love and Rage Revolutionary Anarchist Federation. At the time, I was a student at Marlboro College in southern Vermont and a member of a leftist student group called the Liberation Movement. We organized a presentation, to be given by Winston and another from the #10 Collective, on the Zapatista struggle in Chiapas, Mexico. After the event, I spent some hours drinking with Jason and talking politics. We have been friends ever since. Winston and the #10 Collective would go on to found the Vermont Workers' Center.

4   While in some ways it is true that Pickering represented the old guard of organized labor, I will always have respect for him because of the simple act of returning my call back before he knew me, or I him. In 1998, when I was twenty-four, I was working at the bottom of a ski lift at Mount Snow in West Dover, Vermont. I and most other workers at the resort were making minimum wage or close to it. One day I decided to see what it would take to form a union. I placed two calls asking for help: one to the area IWW and another to the United Steelworkers. The IWW never so much as returned my call. The USWs, on the other hand, called back inside forty-eight hours. And here it was Pickering himself who called and offered any support I needed. While we never did unionize Mount Snow, I always respected the fact that Pickering called back and offered to stand with me and my coworkers. Even so, Pickering would go on to oppose and seek to undermine the efforts of the reform-minded president that would come after him, Dan Brush (of the Teamsters). Brush and I are good friends to this day, and the truth is that Pickering was wrong to not embrace Brush's reform efforts.

5   Labounty would eventually win an election for state representative in fall 2022.

6   Out of respect for Labounty's many years of service to the labor movement, before terminating him, I afforded him the opportunity to voluntarily resign (an offer he then declined). While myself and the executive board understood that he had to be held accountable for his grave errors and that he had to be let go, it was never our intent to needlessly diminish his dignity in a way that a termination would. Even so, the termination, through a settlement agreement reached during the arbitration process in fall 2020, was eventually changed to a resignation. These developments are discussed later. Also of note, the most vocal (internal) union opponent of our decision to terminate Labounty was LIUNA business agent Larry Moquin, who very strongly felt we should retain Labounty. Perhaps unsurprisingly, Moquin would run against United! for president of the Vermont AFL-CIO in 2023. And he, like all our past opponents, would also lose.

7   Key to gaining support from Local 6 was AFSCME Council 93 executive director Mark Bernard. Bernard lived in the same town as their business agent, George Noel (who sadly passed away in 2023), and the same local represented AFSCME office staff in Boston. Bernard talked with Noel to encourage his local's support for United! I also talked with Noel and reached out to some of his members in Rutland. In this case, it was the inside game that secured their support. I say this to highlight that while rank-and-file organizing and member-to-member engagement is by far the superior way to build a movement for change, sometimes pragmatism necessitates less ideological approaches. After all, the object is to win.

8   United! supporters voted against Labounty's motion to go to weighted voting out
     of principle, as we assert that democracy should be participatory in nature and
     should encourage locals sending all their delegates to conventions and elections.
     However, ironically, Labounty's only chance of beating our candidate was by
     not having weighted voting. With the support of OPEIU Local 6 and their three-
     hundred-plus members, there was no conceivable way he could have prevailed if
     the vote had been weighted. But apparently Labounty either did not realize Local
     6 was with United! or he failed to think things through. Either way, we beat him
     by the delegate vote alone.

9   Belcher and I had been friends and shared a mutual respect since we served
     together in VSEA.

10   Belcher, an excellent labor attorney and committed progressive within the labor
     movement, would later be fired by then VSEA president Aimee Towne and her
     conservative-majority board of trustees in August 2023. While other dubious
     reasons were given, I have zero doubt that his sympathy with United! was the
     primary motivation.

11   On the morning of the arbitration, VSEA executive director Steve Howard would
     go so far as to personally call Labounty and leave a voicemail wishing him luck at
     the hearing. I know this because the call went to the Vermont AFL-CIO cell phone
     that we had taken back from Labounty after he was terminated. Clearly, Howard
     did not realize this.

12   Likewise, former VSEA executive director Annie Noonan, also very much from
     the old guard, privately offered to help Labounty find an attorney to fight the
     termination.

13   Among others, Labounty's witness list included a leader from the firefighters
     and the executive director of the Vermont NEA, as well as former VSEA executive
     director (Democrat, former commissioner of the Vermont Department of Labor
     and partner to Vermont secretary of state Jim Condos) Annie Noonan.

14   Kornheiser was running against a liberal incumbent who the Vermont AFL-CIO
     (prior to the United! era) was more inclined to back. Kornheiser, on the other
     hand, was the much more progressive candidate. She was also an old friend of
     mine whose floor, in my twenties, I had often slept on after nights of whiskey and
     conversation. In the end, she won the primary and went on to win her election
     to the statehouse (where she served on the Legislative Workers Caucus) and has
     since also received the endorsement of the Vermont Progressive Party.

15   We had the summary of the national AFL-CIO investigation report, but despite
     multiple requests, the national refused to provide us with the full report (which
     would have been incredibly helpful in this arbitration). So once again the national
     AFL-CIO proved itself unreliable when solidarity was requested.

16   The agreement was later ratified by a vote of the full Vermont AFL-CIO Executive
     Board.

17   When we brought Medina on board, we also agreed to her having union
     representation through a contract between us and the UAW. Unlike Medina,
     Labounty had a personal employment contract, not a union contract. Also of note,
     in Medina's contract we agreed that a primary focus of her work would be organ-
     izing and that, in order to allow her time to focus on organizing, she could not be
     compelled by the president or executive board to be in the statehouse any more
     than two days a week when it was in session. Further, in 2023 our membership

and resources grew enough to allow us to also bring on an organizer, Trey Cook (a member of DSA), and to expand our on-call organizer program, as well as to bring on interns to take part in a new salting program.

18   Soteria House is a residential facility of about twenty workers in Burlington. The dairy-processing facility includes about seventy-five workers but will go unnamed as the effort is ongoing as of May 2022. Suffice to say that we are presently working with the UFCW to seek to not only provide support to the workers in their efforts, but also to salt the facility with our on-call organizers and a number of workers who attended one of Medina's trainings.

19   Vermont AFL-CIO support for new organizing has not been just limited to our own affiliates. In 2022, we also provided advice and support to South Burlington workers who were actively seeking to organize the first Starbucks in Vermont with SEIU. And on May 1, 2022, these workers achieved a supermajority, signing union cards and filing for an NLRB election. Postrecognition it is our expectation that this SEIU local will sign a solidarity charter with the Vermont AFL-CIO. And further of note, the lead worker-organizer in this campaign, Gaz Romp, has since become an on-call organizer with us. Further, in 2023 the Vermont AFL-CIO played an important early role in helping Burlington Ben & Jerry's workers organize (SEIU) and win recognition. This win marked the first unionized Ben & Jerry's shop in the nation.

20   In 2023, the Vermont AFL-CIO was happy to provide this training opportunity with McAlevey again.

21   The event was facilitated by labor journalist and former CWA organizer Steve Early.

22   From late 2022 through the present (summer 2023), Medina further organized a number of other trainings for union members, including an in-person steward training in Burlington, facilitated by Labor Notes, that drew over fifty Vermont AFL-CIO stewards from a multitude of internationals and locals.

23   Prior to becoming an AFSCME rep and member, I had firsthand experience building such a system within the Vermont Agency of Transportation as part of VSEA. It was my experience that having such a system in place resulted in a massive increase in shop-floor activism, participation in demonstrations, and contract victories. For detailed reports on this progress within AOT, see my *Building Rank & File Union Power During Hard Times: The Story of Vermont's Agency of Transportation 2015–2016*, the Anarchist Library, https://theanarchistlibrary.org/library/david-van-deusen-co-founder-of-the-green-mountain-anarchist-collective-building-rank-file-union.

24   In 2023, to help our efforts to develop a network on rank-and-file union contacts and to encourage peer-to-peer education and mutual support, we began to organize workers' circles in Burlington, Montpelier, and Rutland. These workers' circles are designed as geographically based informal monthly meetings of rank-and-file union members (and shop-floor leaders) from different unions. At the meetings, workers are encouraged to share and discuss various challenges they are facing in the workplace and to seek ideas on new approaches. In some ways, these groupings fill some of the role envisioned by central labor councils, but they are more accessible due to their lack of formality, and they are overtly open to non-AFL-CIO unions. If successful, we will seek opportunities to build them out to other Vermont cities and towns.

25   The full 2021 United! slate was as follows: president, David Van Deusen, AFSCME Local 2413; executive vice president, Dwight Brown, AFSCME Local 1343; secretary-treasurer, Danielle Bombardier, IBEW Local 300; vice-president-at-large, Ron Schneiderman, UFCW Local 1459; vice president for AFT, Helen Scott, AFT Local 3203; vice president for AFT, David Feurzeig, AFT Local 3203; vice president for AFSCME, Katie Harris, AFSCME Local 1674; vice president for IBEW, Brian Ritz, IBEW Local 300; vice president for postal workers, Omar Fernandez, APWU-VT; vice president for federal government workers, Tristin Adie, AFGE 2604 (later Adie, after changing employment to a job outside the federal government, would be replaced by Liz Harkins); vice president for Bennington County, Dan Cornell, AFSCME Local 490; vice president for Chittenden County, Marty Gil, IATSE Local 919; vice president for Franklin and Grand Isle Counties, Alex Potvin, UA Local 693; vice president for Lamoille County, Brittany Rhodes, AFSCME Local 3977 (later replaced by Sarah Williams); vice president for Northeast Kingdom, Rubin Serrano, AFSCME Local 2413; vice president for Washington and Orange Counties, Traven Leyshon, OPEIU 153; vice president for Windham and Windsor Counties, Ali Brokenshire, AFSCME 1343 (later replaced by Renee Nied of UFCW Local 1459). Also, not running on the United! ticket, Danielle Grey of OPEIU Local 6 would later be appointed vice president for Addison and Rutland Counties.

26   See David Van Deusen, "Vermont AFL-CIO Is the Most Progressive State Labor Council," *VTDigger*, September 2, 2021, https://vtdigger.org/2021/09/02/david-van-deusen-vt-afl-cio-is-the-most-progressive-state-labor-council.

27   The fact that the 2021 convention was again one of our largest in decades, even with these locals not participating, makes the mobilization that much more remarkable. Further, unlike in 2019, we also had participation from USW Local 340 and OPEIU Local 6, thus again widening our connection to the base.

28   Also elected to the executive board was Larry Moquin of the Laborers. Larry was elected as the vice president for the Building Trades. He chose not to run with United! because of our critical position concerning the Democratic Party. United! did not run a candidate against him, as he was vice president of the Vermont Building & Construction Trades Council, and here we already had three other persons from the Trades running on our slate for executive board. Further, the Trades were a key aspect of United!, and given that this one seat was not crucial to maintaining power, we chose to not run against him but instead welcomed his point of view into the leadership. Moquin would later, in 2023, run against the United! candidate for president (Harris, my successor); Moquin would lose this democratic contest. It should also be noted that we did not field a candidate for the VP position for Rutland and Addison Counties. Initially, Eric Steel (AFSCME Local 1201) was our United! candidate, but Steel later dropped out for family reasons. After the election we appointed Danielle Gray (a nurse from OPEIU Local 6) to serve in this role.

CHAPTER IX Exporting the Revolution within Labor: United! in VSEA and NEA

1   From the moment I ran for Vermont AFL-CIO president, I intended to only serve two terms (if my members would have me). Thus, I will hand off the baton of leadership to someone else in fall 2023. While I would not begrudge an effective progressive president if they chose to run for top office more than twice, for me, two terms were enough for Washington and they are enough for me. And while

I do not believe I would ever be corrupted through proximity to establishment power, I do know that choosing to serve for a limited and defined set of time certainly lessens the exposure to such risk. And finally, for United! to have a life beyond me, I feel very strongly that it is important for me to allow for a transition to a new leftist leadership while the movement is still vibrant.

2 Jerold and I had been good friends for some years. A fellow Harley rider, he and I rode together on a number of occasions, and more than a few times shared a bottle of whiskey. We first met some years earlier when I was the union rep (within VSEA) for AOT and he was a steward. Jerold, a true brother, always had my back, and I always had his. Thus, I was happy to support him during his run for VSEA president.

3 The Vermont State Workers United! caucus essentially adopted our platform during the campaign, but added provisions that called for VSEA to support AOT seeking to become their own bargaining unit, allowing the seventy-plus police in their state contracts to leave the union (as they had previously sought to do) and for the removal of the reactionary Steve Howard from the executive director position.

4 Kelman, a history teacher and longtime member of the Vermont Workers Center, was a leftist through and through and understood what transforming the Vermont NEA into a more progressive and unrestrained force would mean to the Vermont labor movement.

5 United!-like campaigns for union office were not limited to VSEA and NEA. In 2020, a United! ally ran for and won the presidency of UFCW Local 1459. And in 2023, Vermont AFL-CIO Executive Board member (and United! member) Liz Harkins likewise ran for and won the office of president of AFGE Local 2604. Both prevailed in contested elections against old-guard incumbents.

6 Vermont's third public pension, the municipal pension, was well funded and was never the target of these attacks. It was this third pension that was the most relevant to the many AFL-CIO members who worked in the public sector. Thus, in a direct way it was NEA (teachers) and VSEA (state workers) who were suffering these pension assaults, and it was through them that the main thrust of the resistance would have to be launched. But here the Vermont AFL-CIO was ready and able to provide solidarity as the battle played out.

7 In 2022, the Democratic-led general assembly did once again turn its sights on the teacher and state worker pensions. But this time their objectives were massively less ambitious, and here modest legislation was passed that did include minor increases to worker contributions along with a huge one-time allocation of federal money received as part of the COVID recovery effort. Thus, the victory in 2021 did in fact carry over into 2022. But none of this would have ever happened without union members picketing, taking action, and making clear they would not accept the gutting of their pensions.

8 It is of note that after VSEA leadership cancelled their competing event, a number of VSEA leaders did turn up at the rally (one they had previously worked to diminish). In one of the stranger moments of the day, the VSEA president, Aimee Towne, asked event organizers from the caucuses if she could briefly speak. They agreed, being put on the spot and not having anticipated this request. But after the fact, one told me that that was unfortunate, and in hindsight that request should have been declined.

9   In 2022, attempts by Republican governor Phil Scott to again attack public
     pensions was defeated, and nothing more than minor reforms were carried out,
     along with increased pension funding. Thus, the 2021 victory was made complete.

CHAPTER X Building International Solidarity: Rojava, Palestine, and Cuba

1   The revolutionary aims in Rojava are guided by the social and political writings
     of Vermonter and anarchist Murray Bookchin.
2   I wrote this resolution, and the Green Mountain Labor Council president, Traven
     Leyshon, brought it to a vote, where it was passed.
3   Other signers of this statement were as follows: American Kurdish Association,
     Kurdish Alliance of North America, Democratic Kurdish Federation of Canada,
     Sara Free Women Collective, Toronto Kurdish Community Center, Kurdish
     People's Democratic Assembly of Britain (NADEK), Solidarity Economy
     Association, Cooperation Mesopotamia, Rojava and Kurdish Solidarity Seattle,
     Cooperative Assembly of Cascadia, Portland Rising Tide, and Kurdish Human
     Rights Action Group South Africa.
4   In fall 2022, at the request of Rojava trade unionists (which was relayed through
     the Emergency Committee for Rojava's Debbie Bookchin and Anya Briy), we were
     happy to host a joint leadership meeting, remotely, with our executive board and
     Rojavan union leaders. Then, in May 2023, we jointly sponsored a public panel
     discussion that included Syrian Democratic Council representative to the US
     Sinam Mohamad, speaking from DC, and TEV-DEM Trade Union representative
     Eid Brahim, speaking from Rojava, Syria. The intent of this event was to educate
     US labor leaders on the revolution and help the Rojavan trade union build connec-
     tions with US unions. I and our executive vice president, Katie Harris, also served
     on this panel. The event was attended by a number of union leaders from across
     the country.
5   The Vermont AFL-CIO is a member of Labor against Racism and War, and since
     2021 I have served on its National Representatives Assembly.
6   The solidarity we showed the Cuban people by signing on to this anti-embargo
     statement led us to engage in a longer discussion with Zahra, Labor against
     War and Racism, and US-based Cuban solidarity groups about what we could
     do to further highlight the need for the embargo to be brought to an end and
     to lend support to the Cuban people. Initially, we discussed the possibility of
     the Vermont AFL-CIO raising $100,000 to charter and fill a plane full of food
     and medicine and to deliver it to Cuban trade unionists. In fact, our executive
     board voted to approve of this action. Unfortunately, other financial pressures
     and various rising political matters compelled us to drop this effort in order to
     prioritize other activities. Even so, by way of these discussions, Zahra brought
     to our attention an opportunity to send one of our members to Havana for the
     2022 May Day celebrations as part of a youth delegation. This would be following
     a course on Cuban history, conducted remotely in the weeks prior to May 1. Here,
     as state labor council president, I was happy to recommend the youngest member
     of our executive board, Katie Harris (VP for AFSCME and president of Local 1674).
     Harris took part in the course and was honored to be in the Cuban capital for May
     Day 2022.
7   Vermont AFL-CIO executive vice president Katie Harris, by invitation, met with
     Cuban deputy foreign minister Carlos Fernandez de Cossio and Venezuelan

vice minister for North America Carlos Ron in New York City to hear how the US embargo and economic policies are having painful effects on the working class and poor within these two socialist-led nations.

8   Azov Battalion founder and leader Andriy Biletsky has unapologetically stated that the mission of Ukraine is to "lead the white races of the world in a final crusade ... against Semite-led [Jewish] *Untermenschen*."

9   Although now, in 2023, I do feel that should the issue be considered by the executive board, a majority would remain critical of actively supporting the right-wing Ukrainian government.

10   My friend Ariel Zevon, a former/sometimes member of SAG (and ardent anti-fascist whose ancestors came from what is now Ukraine), helped me craft and tighten up this first op-ed on the war in Ukraine.

11   See David Van Deusen, "Concerning the War in Ukraine: No Love for Putin, No Guns for Nazis," *CounterPunch*, March 24, 2022, https://www.counterpunch.org/2022/03/24/concerning-the-war-in-ukraine-no-love-for-putin-no-guns-for-nazis.

12   On October 21, 2021, in response to the national AFL-CIO interfering in the deliberations of the San Francisco CLC concerning the issue of Palestine, I, as president of the Vermont AFL-CIO, issued the following statement through social media:

> Not only will the national AFL-CIO not take the correct progressive stance on international issues, but it also has shown that it will dedicate time, money, and resources toward repressing rank-and-file democracy among the base when the base dares to take a progressive stand!
>
> The San Francisco Central Labor Council of the AFL-CIO is their latest target. This principled CLC was set to have a vote on the issue when the national AFL-CIO stepped in to seek to crush the effort, asserting that those workers have no right to take such a democratic vote. And to be clear, the San Francisco CLC is right to seek a vote in solidarity with the Palestinian people. And they are right to seek to lead where the national AFL-CIO will not.
>
> While I am committed to the AFL-CIO to my core and know that we can and must become the vehicle for foundational change in the US, this latest attack on union democracy once again shows me that we all must fight tooth and nail to transform the AFL-CIO from within and make it a truly democratic organization of workers, and not the vehicle of Democratic Party apologists that it is now (who would not know working-class power if it kicked them in the teeth)!

CHAPTER XI Preparing for the Trump Coup: The General Strike Vote and Antifascism

1   Early in 2020, at the request of Bernie Sanders campaign staffer Sheila Healy, a friend of mine, the Vermont AFL-CIO publicly "recommended" that the national AFL-CIO endorse Bernie Sanders in the Democratic primary. At the time, we knew that the national AFL-CIO would demand that we pull down any and all social media concerning our backing for Bernie (as the national AFL-CIO has the exclusive authority to make national political endorsements), but the campaign wanted the endorsement to counterbalance a number of union endorsements for Elizabeth Warren in Massachusetts that were slated to become public within

a matter of days. Thus, us getting our endorsement up in public, if even for a few hours, could be seized on by Bernie's people and surrogates, thereby taking on a life of its own. Bernie has long been a reliable friend of the Vermont AFL-CIO, so we were happy to do it. Our public statement stayed up for maybe twelve hours (before the national AFL-CIO got on our ass) and was picked up by Bernie's people. So, mission accomplished.

2   I now have a third child, Niamh Crawford Maton, born in November 2021.

3   Rights & Democracy appointed former SEIU organizer and former AFT-Vermont executive director Andrew Tripp as their point person on the Defend Democracy effort. With decades of impactful union organizing experience, and as a proven outstanding labor leader with many wins under his belt (and a steadfast antifascist), he was a good choice for this role. I appreciated his analysis and perspective throughout this challenging period.

4   Vermont AFL-CIO executive director Liz Medina spoke on our behalf at this action.

5   The text of my full speech can be found in Appendix C.

6   In 2022, the Vermont AFL-CIO Executive Board passed a resolution supporting one-member-one-vote for national AFL-CIO officers and forwarded the resolution to the national AFL-CIO for consideration at their June convention in Philadelphia. Ironically (but not surprisingly), the national AFL-CIO Executive Council undemocratically refused to allow the resolution to be debated and voted on by the members. However, as delegates, myself and Vermont AFL-CIO executive director Liz Medina on multiple occasions spoke from the floor about this resolution and the need to transform the AFL-CIO into a truly democratic worker organization.

7   This preamble was written by Vermont AFL-CIO executive director Liz Medina of the UAW.

8   See Vermont State Labor Council AFL-CIO, "Historic Vermont AFL-CIO General Strike Authorization Vote," Facebook, March 14, 2021, video, 55:50, https://www. facebook.com/vtworkers/videos/3127791327447958.

9   Noel and his local (representing nurses at Rutland Regional Medical Center) supported the United! slate in the 2020 and 2021 elections.

10   To read the full general strike resolution as it was adopted, see Appendix D.

11   The publisher of the now-defunct *Vermont Guardian* newspaper was the excellent left-leaning journalist Shay Totten.

12   Unlike most other state national guards, in Vermont the adjutant general is elected by members of the general assembly. This is a holdover from over two centuries ago, when the Green Mountain Boys elected their own officers. Thus, the Vermont National Guard is subject to at least some degree of political pressure.

13   At the same time, the United! leadership within the Vermont AFL-CIO clearly understood that if and when we successfully navigated through the looming crisis, with the Democrats in charge of the White House and Congress, given that they were unlikely to live up to even a modest portion of their more progressive campaign promises, we would have to rapidly pivot to an adversarial stance against this capitalist party machine. But first we had to see Trump removed from power.

14   There were many dangers layered into January 6. First, Vice President Pence faced pressure from Trump to refuse to certify the election (a demand he seriously

considered). And oddly, it was advice given by former Republican vice president Dan Quayle that impacted Pence in ultimately making the correct decision that it was his duty to do so. Further, it has also been revealed that far-right groups were organizing rapid reaction forces and what amounted to arms depots in Washington, DC, should it come to organized shooting in the streets. And Trump, for his part, contemplated use of the National Guard to give protection and support to his insurrectionists should an excuse to do so avail itself (and also appointed loyalists to key government positions after the election loss in case he chose to utilize their full resources in a civil conflict). The dangers were many, these just being a few that rose to the top.

15   Following January 6, even our Republican governor, Phil Scott, called for Trump to resign from office.

16   Taking the lead in forming the Green Mountain Riders Motorcycle Club was Local 490 president Dan Cornell and Local 2413 president Rubin Serrano. As of May 1, 2022, retired Teamster Dan Brush (a former Vermont AFL-CIO president) is president of the MC. At the 2021 Vermont AFL-CIO Convention, the MC took on the role of security/sergeant-at-arms. All these mentioned union leaders who helped form the MC are supporters of United! I too, as a rider of a 1995 Harley Wide Glide, am a member of the MC.

17   For the 2021 convention, I personally drafted the antifascist/anti–gun control resolution as well as another resolution that rejected any notion of labor support for regressive carbon taxes while stating our support for a progressively funded union-led Green New Deal. Part of my thought was to allow our members, should they so choose, to give expression to an anti–gun control position and an anti-regressive carbon tax position through a leftist framework. Here I recognized that both issues were often used by the right as a wedge to turn workers against the liberal politics of the Democratic Party. And here the right was able to effectively use these issues to attract working-class people into their more reactionary camp. And where the Democrats, for the most part, built a pro–gun control, pro-carbon tax position into their platform as a kind of upper-middle-class gospel, there remained the impression that the Republicans were the party that got guns and the carbon tax right. Further, I full well knew that many of our rank-and-file members were far from liberal and held very different positions from the Democratic mainstream, and I knew that over the last two years the Vermont AFL-CIO had taken many positions that sometimes lined up with liberals even while we were certainly not liberal (rather we were and remain working-class left). Thus, with the anti–gun control and anti–carbon tax resolutions I wanted to signal to our base that we, as a labor movement, represented a leftist alternative that was capable of articulating policy positions that ran counter to the Democrats. And allowing for us, through a democratic process, to come out against gun control and against the regressive carbon tax would serve the purpose of holding our diverse membership together while remaining a leftist pole within the political spectrum. In the end, both these resolutions overwhelmingly passed. As an interesting side note, the only one who anticipated these underlying reasons for charting this course was Chris Lagrange from UCOM Live. When interviewed by him soon after the convention, he point-blank asked me if United! brought the anti–gun control resolution forward as an olive branch to the often more conservative Building Trades members.

18   Executive Director Medina flew down to Philly for the convention (as she had
      to immediately fly to Chicago afterward to represent us at the Labor Notes
      Conference). I, on the other hand, rode my 1995 Harley Wide Glide down. All told,
      I clocked more than eight hundred miles round trip. Great excuse for a ride.

19   As it turned out, in the upside-down world that was the chaos and reaction of the
      Trump administration, it was the chairman of the Joint Chiefs of Staff, General
      Mark Milley, and CIA director Gina Haspel who quietly sought to undermine
      Trump's coup attempt from the inside. Together it is reported that they recog-
      nized the real danger of a coup and actively sought to keep the armed forces and
      the CIA out of any of Trump's machinations leading up to January 20, 2021. But it
      did not have to be that way. If persons with less honor had been in those seats in
      2020 and 2021, it is very possible that the US military and CIA could have taken
      an active role in ending democracy in the United States. And this alone shows
      how precarious US democracy has become in recent years.

20   In 2022, recognizing that the threat of fascism had not sufficiently abated in the
      US, the Vermont AFL-CIO Executive Board voted to pass a resolution calling for
      the national AFL-CIO to take steps to prepare for the calling of a national general
      strike if a new right-wing coup attempt were to materialize in the aftermath of
      the 2024 presidential election, and to create an antifascism committee tasked
      with making recommendations to the AFL-CIO by May 1, 2023, as to how the labor
      movement could more effectively combat the rise of fascism on the community
      level throughout the United States. This resolution was provided to the national
      AFL-CIO for consideration at their 2022 convention in Philadelphia. The national
      AFL-CIO Executive Council, for their part, refused to allow the resolution to be
      debated and voted on by the delegates.

CHAPTER XII **War against the Old Guard**

1   See Vermont State Labor Council AFL-CIO, "Historic Vermont AFL-CIO General
     Strike Authorization Vote," Facebook, March 14, 2021, video, 55:50, https://www.
     facebook.com/vtworkers/videos/3127791327447958.

2   In the 2022 national AFL-CIO elections, progressive labor leader Sara Nelson
     chose not to run when it became clear she did not have the institutional support
     from a critical mass of the internationals (although she certainly would have
     had our support). And given the undemocratic and rigged method of national
     AFL-CIO elections (whereby five hundred, plus or minus, delegates, largely hand-
     picked by the leadership within the internationals, choose the national officers),
     a winning insurgency campaign was not realistic. This moderate IBEW staffer/
     officer, Liz Shuler, was elected president. She ran unopposed. At the conven-
     tion, myself and Vermont AFL-CIO executive director Liz Medina (as delegates)
     abstained from the vote and coronation. This undemocratic system again high-
     lights why a movement from below to establish one-member-one-vote within
     the national AFL-CIO needs to be a major progressive priority.

3   No relation to the Patrick Brown previously mentioned in this book as a member
     of United Academics.

4   Again, as of September 2023, AFL-CIO union membership in Vermont stands at
     twenty thousand.

5   The Obama presidency, and especially those first two years when once again the
     Democrats were in the majority in Congress, was unsurprisingly another period

of disappointment for labor. Like what had happened before and has since, a labor agenda failed to move. Campaign promises such as passing card check (i.e., the Employee Free Choice Act) went exactly nowhere.

6   The signers of the New Left letter were as follows: Paul Atwood, retired faculty, University of Massachusetts Boston, Veterans for Peace; Sharon Black, Peoples Power Assembly, former UFCW Local 27 and meatcutter shop steward; Peter Bohmer, Economics for Everyone, faculty emeritus, the Evergreen State College; Keith Brooks, UFT, National Writers Union, director of New York Unemployed Committee (1990–96); Paul Buhle, historian of the Left and US labor movement; Roxanne Dunbar-Ortiz, professor emeritus, California State University (AFT); Max Elbaum, activist and author; Robert Ferraro, University of Maryland SDS, retired shop steward, UFCW Local 400; Jon Flanders, past president, IAM 1145 (retired); Henry Harris, Center for Grassroots Organizing, Marshfield, Vermont; Jeff Jones, former director of the New York State Apollo Alliance, climate and environmental justice activist; George Katsiaficas, author and president, Eros Effect Foundation; Kira Kelly, National Lawyers Guild; Fred Klonsky, local president, IEA/NEA (retired); Nancy Kurshan, LCSW, Chicago school social worker and member of Chicago Teachers Union (retired); Fred Magdoff, professor emeritus and former member of the faculty union at UVM; Claude Marks, codirector, Freedom Archives; Patrick McCann, lifetime NEA/AFT member, former IAM (AW) member, national president of Veterans for Peace; Joseph Moore, former UAW member and UVM United Academics organizer; Richard Ochs, University of Maryland SDS, retired shop steward, IUMSWA, Local 24, pensioned GCIU; Jonah Raskin, professor emeritus, Sonoma State University; Russell Shoatz III, Ankh Restorative Justice diversity content creator; Craig Simpson, former executive director, Washington Metropolitan Council AFL-CIO, retired member Amalgamated Transit Union 689, UFCW 400 (retired); Tom O. Smith, shop steward UE Local 120, building rep, AFT-Baltimore, Vermont state representative, Vermont General Assembly (two terms); Netdahe Stoddard, codirector of Building Fearless Futures, Cabot, Vermont; Bob Tomashevsky, SDS, NYC Taxi Drivers Organizing Committee, Local 100 TWU; and Ron Jacobs, president, AFSCME Local 1343.

7   Individual union members, leaders, and allies signing were as follows: Charles Dineen (AFSCME), Johnathon Cooper, Lori Drohan, Steve Early (News Guild/CWA member and former international representative, Communications Workers of America), Cassandra Edson (VSEA), Michael Eisenscher (Alameda Labor Council Climate and Environmental Justice Caucus), Mike Gimbel (retired executive board member, Local 375, AFSCME), Andres Gonzales (United Steelworkers of America), Daniel Guza (admin for Facebook group Labor and Politics), Davey Heller (classconscious.org and Australian Services Union), Heather Harman (IWW and Socialist Party USA), Mahanama Heller, Owen Hseish, Leslie Hight (VSEA), Klaus Helms (Industrial Workers of the World, Germany), James Marc Leas, Traven Leyshon (president of Green Mountain Labor Council), Dave Levi (Jews against Fascism, Australia), Brandon Marsden (member of Reform and Revolution Caucus of the DSA), Gareth Martin, Bob Montgomery (AFSCME DC), George Montgomery (IBEW 2222), Barbara McGrew, Mary Morton, John O'Conner (AFM Local 442 and 1000), Robert Oeser, Jamie Partridge (NALC 82), Charles Rachlis (Communist Workers Group), Gabriel Rivera, Carla Ringler, Arlene Treacy, Marcus Vickers (Workers Power USA), Brian Walsh, and Daniel Waterman.

8   See Vermont State Labor Council AFL-CIO, "The Video Trumka Will Not Allow
       You to See," Facebook, June 10, 2021, video, 2:17, https://www.facebook.com/
       vtworkers/videos/1394003327635621.
9   The PRO Act, as of 2022, of course did not pass. Nor did the human infrastructure
       aspect of Build Back Better, nor any meaningful piece of legislation aimed at
       defending the voting rights of Americans. These efforts, in conjunction with the
       American Rescue Plan and the physical infrastructure bill (which did pass), taken
       together, is what I would see as a very modest start down the road of a meaningful
       Green New Deal. But again, due to the betrayals of the Democratic Party (and the
       utter lack of support from the corporate Republican Party) progress was once
       again stifled by the machines that are the American political system.
10   The letter was immediately leaked to the press, and that very day we received it
       was published by *In These Times*. I asked our United! leadership if any of them did
       so, and the answer was no. Having no reason to disbelieve my comrades, I suspect
       it was the Trumka administration who fed it to the press. And here, giving it to a
       leftist media outlet like *In These Times* has some internal logic to it. The thinking
       could have been that they did not want to spark wider attention from mainstream
       media but would welcome a kind of rebuttal by way of justification on their left
       flank (a flank that was already very aware of the conflict). Regardless, the *In These
       Times* article was generally favorable to us, so it had no negative impact.
11   By September 2023, AFL-CIO membership in Vermont stands at twenty thousand.
12   All through United!'s time in office, we consistently continued to offer solidar-
       ity to those AFT locals that withheld their membership, and at no time have we
       spoken publicly against them or their leadership to the media. Thus, our efforts
       at building a new solidarity are ongoing.
13   On August 5, 2021, less than six weeks after this victory, Richard Trumka was
       dead of a heart attack.

AFTERWORD

1   This membership number includes all AFL-CIO affiliates, including those not
       paying per caps. Concerning VSEA, in July 2023, the national AFL-CIO approved
       a direct affiliation application submitted by the six-thousand-member (inde-
       pendent) union. Previously, as president, I expressed my full support for such
       a possibility to the national AFL-CIO. Bringing this significant aspect of the
       Vermont labor movement into the AFL-CIO, long-term, will be a great thing for
       labor unity and union power. However, former VSEA general counsel Tim Belcher
       told me that he clearly sees that VSEA's leadership is motivated not by a sense of
       solidarity but by "fear and loathing," a notion that I agree with. To be candid, VSEA
       fears a raid by AFSCME. And aspects of their leadership despise the Vermont
       AFL-CIO's leftist politics. So for those reactionaries in their ranks, affiliation
       takes the raid threat away while giving them influence (through voting seats
       at the table) regarding our politics. But what such reactionaries may not calcu-
       late is the fact that with closer ties political influence can travel two ways. And
       already, United! has been able to provide moral support for the left opposition
       in one of their previous elections, resulting in nearly 30 percent of the vote for
       president being captured by (United! ally) Jerold Kinney. Thus, by my estimate,
       a direct affiliation could lead to further (positive) transformation within VSEA
       as it will be harder for a conservative VSEA leadership to act as gatekeepers in

relation to their rank and file. And meanwhile, as the price of diminishing their fear of a raid by AFSCME or another international, they are compelled to pay the AFL-CIO a hefty monthly tribute of about $18,000 a month (a significant portion going to Vermont) in the form of per cap dues—resources the Vermont AFL-CIO can and does use to advance its progressive platform. Also needing mention on this subject, VSEA president Aimee Towne and the reactionary VSEA Board of Trustees, channeling the absolute worst in antidemocratic unionism, unilaterally implemented this affiliation with zero feedback from their members and zero vote taking place to ratify this major realignment. In fact, they despicably only informed their members after the affiliation was complete. Immediately on learning of the national AFL-CIO approval for affiliation, I reached out to Towne. The following was the core of the brief text exchange:

Me: Aimee Towne, I would like to welcome VSEA into the AFL-CIO. I am thrilled about this opportunity for all our unions to build a new solidarity and together to create the most powerful rank-and-file-driven labor council in the country. Even though I shall only be your Vermont AFL-CIO president until September (as I am not running for reelection), while I am in this position, please do not hesitate in reaching out if I can be of assistance in any way shape or form. Solidarity! —David Van Deusen, President of the VT AFL-CIO

Aimee: I'm elated; I've worked for three years to make this moment happen. It's not final; we are a democratic union and our members will have an opportunity to weigh in. VSEA has made strides, working in solidarity with other unions, in the statehouse, picket lines and offering help/resources to others whenever requested over the course of my tenure as president. You have worked, purposefully trying to thwart any forward VSEA progress our activists have taken. Things you have said about our organization, and things you have said about me personally, are totally unbecoming and not at all the solidarity you seemingly profess. Ironically all of it has made us a stronger and more transparent union so I guess I should say thank you. While I can't speak for anyone other than myself, I look forward to working to build and strengthen the Vermont labor movement. Good luck to you on your future endeavors.

Me: You're welcome. I was and am genuinely happy and pleased that two of the three biggest union groups are coming under the same roof. It will be good for VT organized labor for many generations to come. And I was happy to make the recommendation to allow this to happen to the national AFL-CIO some time ago. And I know that the future is bright for rank-and-file unionism. It is my understanding the letter to VSEA from the national AFL-CIO will be signed by President Shuler and will be forthcoming. So again, welcome to the House of Labor. United We Are Union Strong.

And on September 11, 2023, VSEA executive director Steve Howard went on record with *VTDigger* concerning his reasons for affiliating with the AFL-CIO, citing access to discounts as the major factor. To quote from *VTDigger*: "Finally, he said, VSEA's 6,000 members now have access to AFL-CIO discounts on mortgages and auto insurance." Howard's choice of a talking point and messaging to the members he is supposed to represent tells me all I need to know about his character.

2   We also supported additional rallies and pickets in support of newly unionized UA/AFT support staff at UVM and nurses at UVMMC.

3   On a personal note, in 2023, I received a message from Vermont Progressive Party executive director Josh Wronski asking if I would have an interest in sitting down with the party to have a discussion about running for governor in 2024. With my second term as Vermont AFL-CIO president reaching an end, and having not sought reelection, the prospect of running for governor was a real possibility. Josh and I did in fact talk. I also talked with Lieutenant Governor David Zuckerman (Progressive), who was supportive of the possibility. However, after consulting with dozens of trusted union leaders and allies, I decided to not seek the governorship as I felt my candidacy would compel or tempt the labor movement to refocus attention and resources on this campaign (at the expense of the organizing of workers), and prioritizing of internal and external organizing over electoral politics needs to remain the mission of United!

4   Understanding that culture (and more specifically building a progressive working-class culture) plays an important role in the struggle against the anticulture of capitalism, and over this time the Vermont AFL-CIO also engaged on that front, forming a partnership with the Burlington-based Vermont Green Football Club in 2022 in which this semipro club worked with us to organize "union" games in 2022 and 2023 during which ticket prices were reduced for union members, unions tabled the game, and labor leaders spoke from the field on our issues to crowds of 1,500. In 2022, we also organized a traditional Vermont contra dance for union members at the central Vermont Grange Hall in December.

5   It should be noted before this book concludes that in July 2023 Vermont also suffered massive flooding that caused major damage to many communities, including the cities of Montpelier and Barre. Within days of the devastation, the Vermont AFL-CIO raised money through various labor organizations and the national AFL-CIO (with President Liz Shuler in full support). These funds were rapidly used to provide resources to flood-impacted union members. We also organized volunteer labor, which was deployed to the recovery efforts in Barre, and sent a team of workers to Montpelier to help Rabble-Rouser (a union shop devastated by the floods) with their recovery efforts.

6   Katie Harris won her contested election over LIUNA business agent Larry Moquin (who ran on the more conservative New Wave slate) by a margin of 53 percent to 47 percent of the weighted delegate vote.

7   Kaye won the office of executive vice president in a landslide. Her opponent, VSEA president Aimee Towne, was humiliated, losing to Kaye by 12 percent of the weighted delegate vote (56 percent to 44 percent).
       A more troubling aspect of the race for executive vice president was that 1343's Damion Gilbert, once a close ally, announced in July 2023 (long before the reactionary Aimee Towne entered the contest) that he would be switching teams and would seek to be the Trades/New Wave–backed candidate for executive vice president and then, within his own local, red-baited United!, criticizing our sympathy for Cuba, claimed that United! had caused undue conflict with the internationals, strangely asserted that he wanted to return democracy to the AFL-CIO (an odd claim, given what we did to achieve just that), proclaimed that he would make universal paid FMLA a legislative priority (even though it is already part of our United! platform), and alleged that United! had driven the

state labor council into the ground, leaving it in a poor financial state (which we did not, as by 2023 we not only had money in the bank, but we also had more resources coming in than in previous years, along with a growing staff). Damion's motivation seemed to be personal. He had previously asked Katie and me if we would support him as the United! candidate for executive VP. We declined this request (although I did tell him that even without my support he could attend the United! caucus meeting we would have for slate nominations and seek to get an endorsement democratically through that means—an offer he chose not to pursue). Katie and I were not inclined to back Gilbert, as we both felt it hugely important (in an open election) to have a VP candidate from AFT (our largest international) and, if possible, to field a slate of executive committee candidates who were all women (as that would be a historic first). But we did support him running for election to the position of VP for AFSCME on the United! slate. But this, apparently, was not acceptable to Gilbert. Here my and Katie's rejection of Damion's request was political, not personal (Gilbert was my friend). But once feeling rejected, even after giving me his personal word that he would not run and would back Katie, he was quick to break his word, run, and offer his full support to the Trades/New Wave (in public opposition to United!) after Larry Moquin offered him a spot as his running mate. And even in the eleventh hour, wanting to preserve unity among AFSCME locals, I offered to propose to United! that they not run against him for executive VP, or even to consider an endorsement, if he would *not* publicly or privately back the Trades ticket or campaign against United! However, this offer was made before Gilbert took positions against us, before he sought to negatively campaign against us, and before we held our caucus and officially nominated Ellen Kaye (AFT), and regardless, Damion rejected it all and thus ultimately sealed his own fate. It's my view that for Damion, running for higher office was not political. It was a personal ambition, a desire to receive affirmation and power. But his campaign was doomed from the start. While he showed himself to be a very good local president, by aligning with the Trades he demonstrated his politics to be transactional. And like Karl Labounty in 2019, he failed to peel off other AFSCME locals into his camp. Finally, even within 1343, a significant portion of the membership, organized by members Graham Lebel (St. Mike's College custodians) and Tom Proctor (Rights & Democracy), continued to support United!, thus not only complicating his path to becoming a viable candidate but ultimately resulting in his local deciding to send *no* delegates to the convention (due to the divided nature of the membership and the reality that they had waited too long to run an internal contested delegate election), thus making Damion ineligible as a candidate (as Vermont AFL-CIO bylaws require all candidates to be delegates). So instead, we beat the reactionary Aimee Towne for executive vice president. Damion lost *hard*, and so did Towne. The only lesson here is again the reality, the reminder, that there will always be those union leaders who, when decision time comes, will be apt to put their personal ambitions above those of building a progressive labor movement. On a personal note, I was saddened by Damion's defection and betrayal. He was an ally and a comrade. He played a key role in the rise of United!, and it is tragic that in the end he rejected a legacy that he helped to build (and should rightly take pride in). It is my hope that one day he sees that and comes back to the fold. No one, myself included, is above mistakes.

Along with Harris and Kaye, Danielle Bombardier was again elected to secretary-treasurer. However, being a member of IBEW Local 300 (i.e., the Trades), she decided not to run with United!

8   Like in 2019, 2023 was again a hotly contested election once I announced I would not seek a third term. This time the Building Trades (with VSEA) ran a ticket of their own (called New Wave), with LIUNA's Larry Moquin as their candidate for president. While I was disappointed that the Trades chose to go their own way in this election, they and Moquin ran a principled campaign (Larry not showing ill will until after he lost), which put an emphasis on statehouse lobbying over organizing and leftist politics. Their break with United! did not shock me, as from the start I viewed their support for United! as motivated by a recognition that it was time for a change and a rebuilding rather than a total ideological shift to the left. And further, Moquin, even while serving on our executive board, never identified himself as being part of United! However, their shift away from United! does serve as a reminder that political change in labor, winning elections, is the easy part. The harder task will always be creating a lasting cultural change at the base, one that will more permanently solidify the left turn of the unions regardless of the personalities in office. While I am confident that such a cultural change can and will be achieved, that task will inevitably take time to realize. Even so, it is significant that prior to the election Moquin, should one be inclined to believe him (which I do not), personally told me that should he win the presidency, he would seek to retain our Ten-Point Program for Union Power as the platform of the Vermont State Labor Council. But even so, Moquin, in defeat, was not gracious. In October 2023, he filed a challenge to the election results with our elections committee. Like Riemer in 2019, unable to win a free and fair election, he put his hope into an appeal with no meaningful merit, largely citing my public endorsement of United! as the basis for his loss. The Vermont AFL-CIO Executive Board rejected all his challenges by an overwhelming vote on December 10, 2023. That appeal process may end with a ruling of the national AFL-CIO (and being baseless, the only way the national AFL-CIO could rule in favor of the Moquin charges is if they chose to use this challenge as an excuse to justify unprincipled political action against United!, thus making apparent their naked hostility toward a member-driven leftist movement within their ranks).

9   Along with Harris and Kaye, Danielle Bombardier was again elected to secretary-treasurer. However, being a member of IBEW Local 300 (i.e., the Trades), she decided not to run with United!

10 That said, the fact that a progressive leadership, as of June 2023, has been elected into office in APWU (Dimondstein), AFA (Nelson), the Teamsters (O'Brien), and UAW (Fain) shows that change is afoot.

APPENDIX A Ten-Point Program for Union Power: The Little Green Book

1   As of September 2023, we now have twenty thousand AFL-CIO union members in Vermont, thus making us one of the few state labor councils in the US who are growing (and not in decline).

2   While Trump was defeated by Democrat Joe Biden in the 2020 US general election, much of the damage Trump and his billionaire anti-union backers did to labor remain in place. And President Biden and his Democrats in Congress, as of July

2021, have failed or refused to pass prolabor legislation such as the PRO Act (just as President Obama and his Democrat majorities failed to pass the Employee Free Choice Act). Thus, our struggle continues.

3   At the 2020 Vermont AFL-CIO Convention, members further democratized the Vermont AFL-CIO by increasing the minimum delegate allotment from two per local to five per local, increased allotted delegates based on local size, and increased the threshold to move from participatory elections/votes to weighted votes from a delegate vote of 20 percent to 30 percent. These reforms went into effect in 2021. In 2022, the Vermont AFL-CIO Executive Board also voted to advance a resolution to the national AFL-CIO convention calling on the national constitution to be changed in order to allow rank-and-file members to elect national officers under the principle of one member, one vote. This resolution was undemocratically killed by the national AFL-CIO Executive Council.

4   Since 2019, executive board meeting agendas and minutes have been made available to all union members through our social media.

5   From 2019 forward, the executive board has opened up their meetings to any and all Vermont AFL-CIO members to attend and participate in as they may desire. A presidential advisory committee, composed of rank-and-file members, was also created to increase the members' voice in the leadership.

6   From 2023, led by the efforts of new Vermont AFL-CIO executive director Liz Medina, staff organizer Trey Cook, and on-call organizer Tom Proctor, regular meetings of rank-and-file union members, called "workers' circles," have been conducted in Burlington, Montpelier, and Rutland. While not currently organized into a CLC, these meetings are serving a similar function.

7   At the 2020 Vermont AFL-CIO Convention, members voted to change the Vermont AFL-CIO constitution whereby fascists and racists, should they come into a position of leadership by whatever means within the state labor council, can now be removed. Further, Cold War–era language regarding communists not being allowed in the organization was removed and replaced with antifascist and antiracist language. These changes went into effect in 2021.

8   In 2020, with support from the Vermont AFL-CIO, progress was made toward a livable wage for all, with $12.55 an hour set to be the minimum wage in 2022 (and increasing for inflation thereafter). As of May 2023, the Vermont minimum wage is $13.18 an hour.

9   During the COVID-19 pandemic, with support of the Vermont AFL-CIO, an eviction moratorium was enacted. Now we must fight to secure affordable housing for all as the new standard.

10   During the COVID-19 pandemic, with support of the Vermont AFL-CIO, essential workers had access to free childcare. Now we must fight to make free childcare available to all as the new standard.

11   In 2021, the Vermont AFL-CIO stood side by side with our union brothers and sisters from Vermont State Workers United! (VSEA) and Vermont School Workers Action Committee (NEA) as they successfully fought back against attacks on their public pensions from Democrats and Republicans in Montpelier. But here we must not only defend what we have, but we must also fight to extend this social benefit to *all* working Vermonters.

12   Through the leadership of the Vermont AFL-CIO, and with unprecedented support from Vermont state senator Kesha Hinsdale Ram (a Democrat/Progressive), in

2023 the Vermont Senate, by a two-thirds majority, passed the Vermont PRO Act, which not only establishes card check for all public sector workers but also bans captive audience meetings during union drives (for the public and private sector) and gives the legal right to form a union for domestic workers and farmworkers. It is the top legislative goal for the Vermont AFL-CIO to see this bill pass the Vermont House and become law in 2024.

13 Internationally, in addition to the Green Mountain Central Labor Council passing a resolution in support of the YPG and YPJ in northeast Syria, the Vermont AFL-CIO has also added our name to other labor leaders and organization who have called for solidarity with the Palestinian people and for an end to the occupation of their lands by the right-wing Israeli government. Domestically, in 2020, we proudly stated our unequivocal support for Black Lives Matter and the historic struggle against racism in the United States.

14 Since 2019, the Vermont AFL-CIO has sought to meet with, partner with, and work as closely as possible with allied organizations (on our issues and theirs) such as Migrant Justice (supporting the Milk with Dignity Campaign), the Nulhegan Abenaki Tribe and Rights & Democracy (Renew), 350Vermont (Climate Strike and Renew), the Vermont Workers Center (toward health care as a human right), the Black Perspective (the Race at Work panel discussion), and DSA and the Vermont Progressive Party on a multitude of issues of common concern.

15 At the Vermont AFL-CIO 2020 Convention, we were pleased to have as nonvoting participant guests a number of allies, including those from DSA and the Vermont Progressive Party, in attendance.

16 In 2020, the Vermont Building and Construction Trades Council, with support from the Vermont AFL-CIO, led the successful effort to pass a responsible contractor ordinance in our capital city of Montpelier. Similar ordinances have now also been passed by the Burlington City Council and the Barre City Council. These ordinances will guarantee that prevailing wages be paid to construction workers for all major projects done with public dollars. Furthermore, in 2021, the Vermont AFL-CIO and Vermont Building and Construction Trades Council won the guarantee of prevailing wages on the Burlington CityPlace project (should that project get off the ground).

17 In 2020, the Vermont AFL-CIO successfully fought against Vermont joining the Transportation Climate Initiative because the cornerstone of this effort would amount to the implementation of a regressive gas tax disproportionally having an adverse impact on working people. The Vermont AFL-CIO will continue to oppose any new regressive carbon tax. We need action on climate change, but it's time the rich were made to pay their fair share!

18 To further advance the priority of implementation of a Green New Deal, the Vermont AFL-CIO is now an active member of the Renew coalition.

19 This committee reported its findings back to the Vermont AFL-CIO at the December 2019 political summit. Here, after much discussion, a new endorsement policy was adopted by the executive board whereby political parties will face endorsement moratoriums for statehouse races if they fail to adequately support our union agenda. This endorsement policy is included later in this book. As a result of this new direction in our electoral efforts, the Vermont AFL-CIO has now backed the Vermont Progressive Party slate in four elections for the City of Burlington, and we endorsed the full Vermont Progressive Party slate for

statehouse (and candidate for governor David Zuckerman) in the 2020 general election (conversely, we only backed nine Democrats, all from the Legislative Workers Caucus, in statehouse races). In the 2022 general election, we again backed the full Progressive Party slate (and Zuckerman again, in a winning bid to again become lieutenant governor) while only endorsing a total of eight Democrats for statehouse. We have also endorsed the national effort to build the People's Party. Finally, we recommended that the AFL-CIO endorse democratic socialist Bernie Sanders for president of the United States in 2020.

20   It was the expectation that such a constitutional amendment would be introduced by our allies in the Vermont Senate in 2023. However, this effort got delayed and now we are looking to see it introduced in 2024.

21   Since 2019, the Vermont AFL-CIO has been growing. CWA, the LIUNA, IBEW, UFCW, SEIU, AFSCME, and AFT have all organized new shops. AFSCME 1343, 1369, 1674, and 4802 among them have added 250-plus new members. AFT, doing *great* work on their own, has added well over 2,000 new members (largely through organizing two new large units at UVM and at UVMMC). The Vermont AFL-CIO, as of June 2023, now has over 13,500 members.

22   The political director position was eliminated in 2020 and was replaced with an organizing-focused executive director position.

23   In 2019, line-item money traditionally directed at an external paid lobbyist was switched to instead fund a stable of on-call organizers. In turn, since 2019, on-call organizers have been assigned to assist United Academics at UVM with their campaign to combat program and job cuts. Such on-call organizers were also assigned to AFSCME Local 1674 and 4802 to help them grow their internal membership. As a result, 1674's membership is presently double what it was just a few years ago. On-call organizers were also deployed to help build local community support for card check in 2020 and have been recently assigned to new organizing efforts for an affiliate. In addition to on-call organizers, we have also created a part-time field organizer position presently (August 2023) staffed by DSA member Trey Cook.

24   In 2018, the Vermont AFL-CIO Facebook page had just over one hundred followers. We are happy to report that as of September 2023 that number has grown to over four thousand, and we are currently the most-followed labor organization in Vermont.

25   At the 2020 Vermont AFL-CIO Convention, by a vote of 87 percent of the delegates, rank-and-file union members authorized the executive board to call for a Vermont general strike in the event of a neofascist Trump coup. We are proud of our members' willingness to stand up for and defend democracy. We are also pleased that the coup did not come to fruition, that there was a transfer of federal power on January 20, 2021, and that we did not have to call for mass work stoppages. The Vermont General Strike Authorization Resolution is included in this book in Appendix D.

26   The Vermont AFL-CIO was proud to support striking machinists in Williston in late 2019 and striking UAW members at Goddard College in 2023. And they both won their strikes!

27   The Vermont AFL-CIO, in 2023, created a model contract taking the best existing language from our forty-five Vermont CBAs. This model contract is slated to be rolled out to affiliates in summer 2023.

28   The Vermont AFL-CIO is happy to have, on occasion, worked in solidarity with UE Local 203 and Local 255 jointly supporting union picket lines.

29   In 2020, SEIU Local 200 affiliated with the Vermont AFL-CIO through the signing of a solidarity charter. In addition, two Vermont carpenter locals also affiliated through the signing of such a charter.

30   The top strategic priority for the Vermont AFL-CIO is to build an internal structure whereby a local union contact is identified, recruited, and utilized in every Vermont AFL-CIO shop, on every shift, everywhere in Vermont. We view the creation of such a structure as key to exponentially growing our ability to directly communicate with rank-and-file members, increase our ability to conduct mass mobilizations, and have a more powerful political voice.

31   The Vermont AFL-CIO is pleased to report that movements for change are unfolding now within VSEA and NEA. Sharing many of the same values articulated in this program, the Vermont State Workers United! caucus candidate for VSEA president, Jerold Kinney, received nearly 30 percent of the vote in 2020. The Vermont School Workers Action Committee caucus candidate for president, Tev Kelman, received 45 percent of the vote in 2021. Further, out of fear of raids and fear of United! playing a more active role in internal VSEA elections, VSEA became a direct affiliate of the AFL-CIO in August 2023. And while VSEA's reactionary leadership believes this will insulate them, I would assert that such an affiliation will only hasten the growth of their internal progressive movement among their rank and file.

Index

Page numbers in *italic* refer to illustrations. "Passim" (literally "scattered") indicates intermittent discussion of a topic over a cluster of pages.

About the Authors

David Van Deusen is a longtime libertarian-socialist thinker, organizer, and militant union leader. He served two terms as president of the Vermont AFL-CIO (2019–21 and 2021–23) and is part of the progressive United! slate. He is also a member of Democratic Socialists of America and a past member of Anti-Racist Action and the Green Mountain Anarchist Collective (NEFAC-VT). His previous books include *The Black Bloc Papers* and *On Anarchism: Dispatches from the People's Republic of Vermont*. Van Deusen resides in northern Vermont.

Kim Kelly is an independent journalist, author, and organizer. She has been a regular labor columnist for *Teen Vogue* since 2018, and her writing on labor, class, politics, and culture has appeared in the *New Republic*, the *Washington Post*, the *New York Times*, the *Baffler*, the *Nation*, the *Columbia Journalism Review*, and *Esquire*, among many others. She is the author of *Fight Like Hell: The Untold History of American Labor* and resides in Philadelphia.

Steve Early was an international union representative for the Communications Workers of America for three decades in New England and worked closely with CWA members in Vermont. He is a longtime supporter of the Vermont Progressive Party, was a cofounder of Labor for Bernie, and has written five books about labor or politics.

ABOUT PM PRESS

PM Press is an independent, radical publisher of critically necessary books for our tumultuous times. Our aim is to deliver bold political ideas and vital stories to all walks of life and arm the dreamers to demand the impossible. Founded in 2007 by a small group of people with decades of publishing, media, and organizing experience, we have sold millions of copies of our books, most often one at a time, face to face. We're old enough to know what we're doing and young enough to know what's at stake. Join us to create a better world.

PM Press
PO Box 23912
Oakland, CA 94623
www.pmpress.org

PM Press in Europe
europe@pmpress.org
www.pmpress.org.uk

FRIENDS OF PM PRESS

These are indisputably momentous times—the financial system is melting down globally and the Empire is stumbling. Now more than ever there is a vital need for radical ideas.

In the many years since its founding—and on a mere shoestring—PM Press has risen to the formidable challenge of publishing and distributing knowledge and entertainment for the struggles ahead. With hundreds of releases to date, we have published an impressive and stimulating array of literature, art, music, politics, and culture. Using every available medium, we've succeeded in connecting those hungry for ideas and information to those putting them into practice.

Friends of PM allows you to directly help impact, amplify, and revitalize the discourse and actions of radical writers, filmmakers, and artists. It provides us with a stable foundation from which we can build upon our early successes and provides a much-needed subsidy for the materials that can't necessarily pay their own way. You can help make that happen—and receive every new title automatically delivered to your door once a month—by joining as a Friend of PM Press. And, we'll throw in a free T-shirt when you sign up.

Here are your options:

• **$30 a month** Get all books and pamphlets plus a 50% discount on all webstore purchases

• **$40 a month** Get all PM Press releases (including CDs and DVDs) plus a 50% discount on all webstore purchases

• **$100 a month** Superstar—Everything plus PM merchandise, free downloads, and a 50% discount on all webstore purchases

For those who can't afford $30 or more a month, we have **Sustainer Rates** at $15, $10, and $5. Sustainers get a free PM Press T-shirt and a 50% discount on all purchases from our website.

Your Visa or Mastercard will be billed once a month, until you tell us to stop. Or until our efforts succeed in bringing the revolution around. Or the financial meltdown of Capital makes plastic redundant. Whichever comes first.

About Us

Working Class History is an international collective of worker-activists focused on the research and promotion of people's history through our podcast, books, and social media channels.

We want to uncover stories of our collective history of fighting for a better world and tell them in a straightforward and engaging way to help educate and inspire new generations of activists.

Through our social media outlets with over one million followers, we reach an audience of over 20 million per month. So if you're on social media, you can connect with us in the following ways:

- Instagram: @workingclasshistory
- Facebook: facebook.com/workingclasshistory
- Twitter: @wrkclasshistory
- YouTube: youtube.com/workingclasshistory
- Mastodon: mastodon.social/@workingclasshistory
- Tumblr: workingclasshistory.tumblr.com

We receive no funding from any political party, academic institution, corporation, or government. All of our work is funded entirely by our readers and listeners on Patreon. So if you appreciate what we do, consider joining us, supporting our work, and getting access to exclusive content and benefits at patreon.com/workingclasshistory.

Labor Power and Strategy

John Womack Jr.

Edited by Peter Olney and Glenn Perusek

ISBN: 978-1-62963-974-1

$16.95   192 pages

What would it take to topple Amazon? To change how health care works in America? To break up the media monopolies that have taken hold of our information and imaginations? How is it possible to organize those without hope working on the margins? In *Labor Power and Strategy*, legendary strategist, historian and labor organizer John Womack speaks directly to a new generation, providing rational, radical, experience-based perspectives that help target and run smart, strategic, effective campaigns in the working class.

In this sleek, practical, pocket inspiration, Womack lays out a timely plan for identifying chokepoints and taking advantage of supply chain issues in order to seize and build labor power and solidarity. Interviewed by Peter Olney of the International Longshore and Warehouse Union, Womack's lively, illuminating thoughts are built upon by ten young labor organizers and educators, whose responses create a rich dialogue and open a space for joyful, achievable change. With stories of triumph that will bring readers to tears this back-pocket primer is an instant classic.

"In Our Revolution we shout, 'When we Organize, We Win,' but organize who and win what? Labor Power and Strategy is a great collection of Womack and 10 organizers debating strategic workplace organizing vs associational or more general organizing at workplaces or in communities. Womack, in a long initial interview and in the conclusion, argues that without organizing workplace chokepoints, we are left with the spontaneous movements that come and go. Several of the 10 organizers essentially argue that the spontaneous can become conscious and long lasting. Grab the book and take up the debate."
—Larry Cohen, board chair of Our Revolution, past president of Communications Workers of America

"In this fascinating and insightful dialogue, the distinguished historian John Womack and a set of veteran labor activists probe the most fundamental of questions: How do we organize the 21 century working-class and give it the power to transform world capitalism? Are workers with vital skills and strategic leverage the key to a labor resurgence, or should organizers wager upon a mobilization of working people whose relationship to the economy's commanding heights is more diffuse? Or can we arrive at some dialectical symbiosis? Whatever the answer, this is the kind of constructively radical conversation essential to the rebirth of working-class power in our time."
—Nelson Lichtenstein, historian and author of *Capitalism Contested: The New Deal and Its Legacies*

Labor Law for the Rank and Filer: Building Solidarity While Staying Clear of the Law (2nd Edition)

Staughton Lynd and Daniel Gross

ISBN: 978-1-60486-419-9
$12.00   120 pages

Have you ever felt your blood boil at work but lacked the tools to fight back and win? Or have you acted together with your co-workers, made progress, but wondered what to do next? If you are in a union, do you find that the union operates top-down just like the boss and ignores the will of its members?

Labor Law for the Rank and Filer: Building Solidarity While Staying Clear of the Law is a guerrilla legal handbook for workers in a precarious global economy. Blending cutting-edge legal strategies for winning justice at work with a theory of dramatic social change from below, Staughton Lynd and Daniel Gross deliver a practical guide for making work better while re-invigorating the labor movement.

Labor Law for the Rank and Filer demonstrates how a powerful model of organizing called "Solidarity Unionism" can help workers avoid the pitfalls of the legal system and utilize direct action to win. This new revised and expanded edition includes new cases governing fundamental labor rights as well as an added section on Practicing Solidarity Unionism. This new section includes chapters discussing the hard-hitting tactic of working to rule; organizing under the principle that no one is illegal; and building grassroots solidarity across borders to challenge neoliberalism, among several other new topics. Illustrative stories of workers' struggles make the legal principles come alive.

"Workers' rights are under attack on every front. Bosses break the law every day. For 30 years Labor Law for the Rank and Filer *has been arming workers with an introduction to their legal rights (and the limited means to enforce them) while reminding everyone that real power comes from workers' solidarity."*
—Alexis Buss, former General Secretary-Treasurer of the IWW

"As valuable to working persons as any hammer, drill, stapler, or copy machine, Labor Law for the Rank and Filer *is a damn fine tool empowering workers who struggle to realize their basic dignity in the workplace while living through an era of unchecked corporate greed. Smart, tough, and optimistic, Staughton Lynd and Daniel Gross provide nuts and bolts information to realize on-the-job rights while showing us that another world is not only possible but inevitable."*
—John Philo, Legal Director, Maurice and Jane Sugar Law Center for Economic and Social Justice